# Language Culture

# 语 言 与 文 化

## ——英汉语言文化对比

邓炎昌　刘润清　著

外语教学与研究出版社
**FOREIGN LANGUAGE TEACHING AND RESEARCH PRESS**
北京　BEIJING

## 图书在版编目(CIP)数据

语言与文化：英汉语言文化对比 / 邓炎昌，刘润清著 . — 北京：外语教学与研究出版社，1989.3 (2009.7 重印)

ISBN 978 - 7 - 5600 - 0430 - 3

Ⅰ. 语… Ⅱ. ①邓… ②刘… Ⅲ. 英语—对比研究—汉语 Ⅳ. H31

中国版本图书馆 CIP 数据核字 (2009) 第 124477 号

悠游网—外语学习 一网打尽
www . 2u4u . com . cn
阅读、视听、测试、交流、共享

封底刮刮卡，获积分！在线阅读、学习、交流、换礼包！

出 版 人：于春迟
责任编辑：夏　天
出版发行：外语教学与研究出版社
社　　址：北京市西三环北路 19 号 (100089)
网　　址：http://www.fltrp.com
印　　刷：北京京科印刷有限公司
开　　本：850×1168　1/32
印　　张：8.5
版　　次：1989 年 3 月第 1 版　2010 年 8 月第 20 次印刷
书　　号：ISBN 978 - 7 - 5600 - 0430 - 3
定　　价：19.90 元

＊　　＊　　＊

购书咨询：(010)88819929　电子邮箱：club@fltrp.com
如有印刷、装订质量问题，请与出版社联系
联系电话：(010)61207896　电子邮箱：zhijian@fltrp.com
制售盗版必究 举报查实奖励
版权保护办公室举报电话：(010)88817519
物料号：104300101

# 前　言

　　语言是文化的重要载体。语言与文化的关系是当今公认的一门值得研究的学科。

　　人们对语言的研究已有悠久历史。但长期以来,语言学家关心的是语言的形式和结构,研究的是语言的内在系统;对语言的社会功能和其他外在因素的探讨则是最近 20 年才开始的。现在人们认识到,语言至少有两套规则:一是结构规则,即语音、词汇、语法等,二是使用规则,即决定使用语言是否得体的诸因素。一句完全合乎语法的话,用于不恰当的场合,说得不合说话人的身份,或者违反当时当地的社会风俗习惯,就达不到交际的目的,有时甚至造成意想不到的后果。语言的使用规则实际上就是这种语言所属文化的各种因素。

　　因此,学习和运用外语必须了解与这种外语有密切关系的文化。如果掌握语法知识有助于保证所造的外语句子结构正确,那么熟悉有关文化知识则有助于保证使用外语得当。

　　英语当然也不例外。熟练掌握英语句子的结构固然重要,了解英语的使用规则也是掌握好英语不可缺少的环节。例如,初学英语的人能正确地说出 How old are you? 这个句子。不过,这句话何时用,对谁说,却有很多讲究。西方人不喜欢别人打听自己的私事,不论话语本身的发音、语调、语法多么正确,问一个成年人的年龄是不礼貌的。又如,对亲密朋友说话过于拘谨,可能意味着有意疏远对方;对有身份的人说话过于随便,可能意味着对他不够尊敬。如不了解这些社会习惯,就不可能用英语进行有效的交际。偶尔违反了语言的结构规则(如忘记复数名词加 s),对方可以谅解,至少不会影响彼此的感情。如果违反了语言的使用规则,就可能引起不良后果,甚至破坏双方的关系。从这个意义上讲,使用规则比结构规则更为重要。目前,不少外国学者在研究语言与社会、语言与文化、语言与人种、语言与人类的关系,提出许多重要见解。这些科学研究活动值得重视,对英语教学也有现实意义。

我国出版的英语语法专著已有多种,关于英语与文化的关系的论著却寥寥无几,不能适应外语教学与研究的需要。笔者参考当代普通语言学、社会语言学、文体学以及同语言、文化有关的著作,根据自己多年英语教学经验,通过比较中国文化与西方文化的差异,讨论一下在使用英语时所涉及的最基本、最重要的文化因素。

为适应阅读英语材料尚有困难的读者的需要,并把问题讲得更透彻一些,本书采用英汉两种语言撰写。我们认为有关西方文化的问题,用英语表达比较自然,有关中国文化的问题,用汉语讨论更为方便;而且,英语有英语的行文规范,汉语有汉语的写作准则。因此,本书汉语部分只是英语部分的译述,在语言上和内容上,有时并不完全对应,望读者注意。

在编写此书的过程中,我们得到了许多中外人士的支持和帮助。特别要提出的是 Timothy Wong, Carolyn Wakeman, Marilyn Young 三位美国教授和北京外国语学院的林易、吴岫光、俞涓同志,他们分别审阅了全部英文稿或汉语稿,并提出宝贵的修改意见和建议。在此,我们致以衷心的感谢。

作者

1988 年 1 月

于北京外国语学院

# Key to Symbols

AHD　　*American Heritage Dictionary of the English Language*, Paperback edition, Dell Publishing Co., N. Y., 1976.

COD　　*Concise Oxford Dictionary of Current English*, 6th edition, Oxford University Press, London, 1976.

LCE　　*Longman Dictionary of Contemporary English*, Longman, London, 1978.

LME　　*Longman Modern English Dictionary*, 1976 edition, Longman, London.

OAL　　*Oxford Advanced Learner's Dictionary of Current English*, 3rd edition, 1974.

OED　　*Oxford English Dictionary*, Compact edition, Oxford University Press, 1971.

WNC　　*Webster's New Collegiate Dictionary*, G. & C. Merriam Co., Springfield, Mass., 1981.

WTI　　*Webster's Third New International Dictionary*, G. & C. Merriam Co., Springfield, Mass., 1976.

CEI　　《汉英成语词典》*A Chinese-English Dictionary of Idioms*, 商务印书馆, 1982.

CED　　《汉英词典》*A Chinese English Dictionary*, 北京外国语学院英语系《汉英词典》编写组, 商务印书馆, 1980.

XYH　　《新英汉词典》, 上海译文出版社, 1978.

YHD　　《英华大词典》修订第二版, 郑易里等, 商务印书馆, 1984.

HYC　　《汉语成语大词典》, 湖北大学语言研究室, 河南人民出版社, 1985.

# 目　录

# CONTENTS

# Chapter 1

## Introduction

*"But words are things, and a small drop of ink. Falling
like dew upon a thought, produces
That which makes thousands, perhaps millions, think."*

—George Gordon Byron, *Don Juan*

*"Words are what hold society together."*

—Stuart Chase, *Power of Words*

Once a group of Chinese was visiting the home of a fairly well-to-do American. As they were shown around the house, they commented, "You have a very nice home. It's so beautiful." The hostess smiled with obvious pleasure and replied in good American fashion "Thank you"—which caused surprise among some of her Chinese guests. Later, while conversing at the dinner table, the host remarked to the Chinese interpreter, a young lady who had graduated not long ago from a Chinese university, "Your English is excellent. Really quite fluent." To this she demurred, "No, no. My English is quite poor"—an answer that he had not expected and found a bit puzzling.

Was the American hostess' reply immodest, as it seemed to

some of the Chinese?

Was the young Chinese interpreter's remark insincere, as it sounded to the Americans?

In both cases the answer is *no*. To English-speaking people, praise is to be accepted, generally with a remark like "Thank you." It is assumed that the compliment is sincere, that the praise is for some not unworthy achievement or thing. Therefore, there should be no show of false humility, no pretended modesty. To Chinese, however, the customary reply to a compliment would be to claim that one is not worthy of the praise, that what one has done is hardly enough, or that success was more a matter of luck or some other circumstances. Acceptance of a compliment would imply conceit or lack of manners. So, in the two cases above, the reason for such different reactions was differences in customs and habits. Each was interpreting what the other said according to his or her own culture.

Events like these are fairly common when people of different languages and cultures communicate. Because of cultural differences, misunderstandings may arise, although the language used in communication may be faultless. The same words or expressions may not mean the same thing to different peoples. Because of cultural differences, a serious question may cause amusement or laughter; a harmless statement may cause displeasure or anger. Because of cultural differences, jokes by a foreign speaker may be received with blank faces and stony silence. Yet the same stories in the speaker's own country would leave audiences holding their sides with laughter.

The reader is probably aware by now that the term *culture* here is being used in a sense different from the ordinary. What do we mean by *culture*?

2

Obviously the Chinese term 文化 in the expressions 他没有文化 or 文化班 does not apply. Nor do we mean *culture* in the sense of sophisticated tastes in literature, music, art, etc. Here we have a much broader meaning. Following the definitions of sociologists and anthropologists, our term *culture* refers to the total pattern of beliefs, customs, institutions, objects, and techniques that characterize the life of a human community.

"Culture consists of all the shared products of human society" (Robertson, 1981). This means not only such material things as cities, organizations and schools, but also non-material things such as ideas, customs, family patterns, languages. Putting it simply, culture refers to the entire way of life of a society, "the ways of a people."

Language is a part of culture and plays a very important role in it. Some social scientists consider it the keystone of culture. Without language, they maintain, culture would not be possible. On the other hand, language is influenced and shaped by culture; it reflects culture. In the broadest sense, language is the symbolic representation of a people, and it comprises their historical and cultural backgrounds as well as their approach to life and their ways of living and thinking.

We shall not go further into the relationship between language and culture. What needs to be stressed here is that the two interact, and that understanding of one requires understanding of the other.

Social scientists tell us that cultures differ from one another, that each culture is unique. As cultures are diverse, so languages are diverse. It is only natural then that with difference in cultures and differences in languages, difficulties often arise in communicating between cultures and across cultures. Understanding is not always easy.

Learning a foreign language well means more than merely mastering the pronunciation, grammar, words and idioms. It means learning also to see the world as native speakers of that language see it, learning the ways in which their language reflects the ideas, customs, and behavior of their society, learning to understand their "language of the mind". Learning a language, in fact, is inseparable from learning its culture.

In this book, we shall attempt a brief study of certain cultural differences between Chinese and native speakers of English. There are many such differences and we shall take up only those involving language, omitting those that do not—such as manners of dress, conduct in public, eating habits. Even so, we shall be able to deal with only a small number of the more common ones.

The term *native English speakers* includes people of many countries—Americans, Englishmen, Australians, Canadians, New Zealanders and others. Each of these belongs to a culture that is somewhat different from the others, in spite of their common language. Actually, even the language differs somewhat from country to country, although such differences may not be noticeable at first. For example, *lorries* in England are called *trucks* in the U.S.; Americans say *You're welcome* in reply to *Thank you*, whereas Englishmen would say *Not at all* or *Don't mention it* or *It's a pleasure*. Since we cannot possibly cover all of the English-speaking peoples, we shall restrict ourselves to American culture and American English. This is partly because of the political, economic and cultural position of the U.S. in the English-speaking world, partly because of the author's greater familiarity with the language and culture of the Americans than with that of the others.

It is difficult, of course, to generalize about a whole nation, especially one that is as large and complex as the U.S. There are differences of national origin, class, geographical region, occupation, age and sex. However, there are certain attitudes and ideas, certain culturally prescribed rules of behavior that seem to be accepted by most Americans, certain ways of social interaction that are generally observed. It is these attitudes, ideas and ways that we shall be referring to throughout this book.

Turning to China, the problem is similar. When referring to Chinese language and culture, we have in mind present day *Han* language and *Han* culture. With the different cultures that exist among China's many ethnic groups, and with the diversity in languages and dialects, it would be impossible to study and compare all. Even the *Han* language and culture have local variations, therefore we shall limit our study mainly to the Beijing area.

This study is intended for students and teachers of English, for interpreters and translators; that is, for people who have frequent contact with native English speakers, or who must use English frequently. It is not intended as a scholarly work. The research that was done, while intensive, was far from exhaustive. We hope that in the following chapters, most readers will find items of interest and of possible use; that a few readers will be stimulated enough to go on, to explore and produce studies of their own, that this and further studies will in a very modest way contribute to international understanding.

# Chapter 2

## Words—Same, Similar, Different?

*"'Careful with fire,' is good advice, we know:*
*'Careful with words,' is ten times doubly so."*
— Will Carleton, *The First Settler's Story*

*"'When I use a word,' Humpty-Dumpty said, 'it means*
*just what I choose it to mean —neither more nor less.'"*
—Lewis Carroll, *Through the Looking Glass*

Do words or terms in one language have the same meaning when translated into another language? Can we rely on our dictionaries to give us the proper English for a Chinese term, or the proper Chinese for an English word?

These questions themselves might be surprising to some people; after all, *a book* is 一本书 and *tiger* is 虎, 总司令 is *commander-in-chief* and 哲学 is *philosophy*.

But are the answers to these questions always *yes*? Are the meanings of equivalent words exactly the same in both languages? Consider the following:

Does *weekend* mean the same to an American or a European as 周末 means to a Chinese? Does 知识分子 have the same meaning as *intellectual*?

The answer to these two questions would seem to be yes. The Chinese for *weekend* is 周末 in all English-Chinese dictionaries; the same with 知识分子 for *intellectual*. Yet there are differences.

In China, where the work week is six days, 周末 would mean Saturday evening and Sunday. But in industrialized countries of the West, where the work week is five days, the *weekend* would begin Friday evening and last through Saturday and Sunday. If this difference is not understood, it may lead to the kind of reaction that a visiting Chinese had shortly after he arrived in the United States. After seeing signs with *T. G. I. F.* and hearing people talking about *T. G. I. F. parties*, he raised the question: "What does T. G. I. F. mean?" He was told that the letters stood for *Thank God it's Friday*. He was surprised at first and asked: "But why Friday? Why not Monday, Wednesday, or any other week-day?" The answer suddenly came to him just as his American friend started explaining: Because Friday is the last day of the work week and people are looking forward to two days of fun and leisure. They're glad to get away from their jobs.

Likewise, there are important differences in what 知识分子 and *intellectual* mean in their respective cultures. In China, the term 知识分子 generally includes college teachers, college students, and such people as medical doctors, engineers, interpreters—people who have had a college education—and middle school teachers. In many Chinese rural areas, even middle school students are considered 知识分子. In the U. S. and Europe, however, *intellectuals* would include only people of high academic status such as college professors, but not ordinary college students. So the term covers a much smaller range of people. There are other differences as well, including the fact that *intellectual* is not always a complimentary term in the U. S. It is sometimes used in a derogatory sense, with a meaning somewhat like 臭老九 that was in common use during the Chinese Cultural Revolution. However, these other differences will not be taken up here.

These two examples illustrate that one must be careful in assuming that bilingual dictionary definitions give exact equivalents in meaning or that different languages always have words to express the same thing.

In this and the following chapter, we shall look into semantic differences between selected English and Chinese terms. These differences might be grouped according to the following:

1. A term in one language that does not have a counterpart in another language.

2. Words or terms in both languages that appear to refer to the same object or concept on the surface, but which actually refer to quite different things.

3. Things or concepts that are represented by one or perhaps two terms in one language, but by many more terms in the other language; that is, finer distinctions exist in the other language.

4. Terms that have more or less the same primary meaning, but which have secondary or additional meanings that may differ considerably from each other.

## A

Chinese have a saying: 夏炼三伏;冬炼三九, urging people to exercise and keep fit. What is the English for 三伏 and 三九? A young interpreter was heard to use *three fu* and *three nine* to a

8

group of Canadians. Naturally, they were puzzled. He could have just said: *In summer keep exercising during the hottest days; in winter do the same thing during the coldest weather*.

A young Chinese went for a swim in a nearby public pool. To the surprise of his roommates and a foreign friend, he returned very shortly. "The pool was too crowded," he explained. "And the water should have been changed a long time ago. It was so dirty. It was like 芝麻酱煮饺子(dumplings being cooked in sesame paste). His Chinese friends chuckled at the unusual but vivid comparison. But to the foreigner, who had never tasted sesame paste and had never seen *jiaozi* (dumplings) being cooked, the humor was lost. To describe a very crowded gathering, Westerners often say *It was packed like sardines*. Such a comparison might be understood by some Chinese, but the vividness would be lost, for very few Chinese have ever seen a newly-opened can of sardines, with neat rows of finger-sized fish packed tightly in a small flat container.

There are numerous other examples that we could cite of an object or concept that exists in one culture but not in another.

Among terms referring to people, there is the Chinese 干部, which is most commonly rendered in English as *cadre*. But a *cadre* is not the same as a 干部. Furthermore, *cadre* is not a common word. Many English-speaking people do not know what it means; those who do know pronounce it in different ways —it has three or four common pronunciations. No wonder various other terms have been suggested as substitutes: *official*, *functionary*, *administrator*, etc. But none of these is exactly the same as 干部.

Similarly, there is no Chinese equivalent for *cowboy* or *hippie*—two well-known products of American society. There is much legend and romance associated with the cowboy of the early American west, but 牧童 or 牛仔 carry none of this. Nor does 希比士 or 希比派 convey anything about the young people of the 1960's whose behavior seems so strange to Chinese. 嬉皮士 might be a better term, although the words that make up the term might be a bit misleading. Many hippies were serious-minded people, even though their lifestyle appeared unusual to most people.

From language for political or social activities we could pick a number of examples; for instance, a 斗争会 might be called a *struggle meeting*, but such a term does not give much information about what happens at such gatherings. On the other hand, what does a *revival meeting* mean to a Chinese? Nothing, unless the person has actually been to or seen one of those highly emotional religious gathorings in the U.S. The same is true of a *bingo party* or *bingo game*.

In day-to-day activities, most English-speaking people have never slept on a 炕(*kang*, a heatable brick bed), eaten a stick of 冰糖葫芦(candied haws on a stick), nor used a 秤(steelyard). Most Chinese have never been to a *motel*, tasted a *hamburger*, nor had to punch a *time clock*. There are no equivalents in the other culture, often nothing even similar. The number of such examples is far too great to mention more here.

Turning to language that deals with natural phenomena and related concepts, many of the Chinese 节气 do not have equivalents in English. (It might be mentioned that the phrase *solar terms* is not understood by most westerners). 雨水,惊蛰,清明 for example, are translated as *Rain Water* (*2nd Solar Term*), *Waking of Insects* (*3rd Solar Term*), *Pure and Brightness* (*5th Solar Term*) in a widely used contemporary Chinese-English Dictionary ( CED, 1979). But such names mean little or nothing without some sort of

10

additional explanation. A few, however, do have equivalents in English, as 春分 = *Spring Equinox*; 夏至 = *Summer Solstice*; 秋分 = *Autumnal Equinox*; 冬至 = *Winter Solstice*.

Among old traditional Chinese terms regarding cosmic forces and the universe, we find 阴 and 阳, which have no counterparts in English and are explained as "two forces through whose essences, according to Taoist cosmology, the universe was produced and cosmic harmony is maintained. *Yin* is dark, female and negative, and *yang* is light, male and positive" (LME).

It is concepts like *yin* and *yang*, which for centuries were part of the underlying principles in traditional medical treatment that make Chinese medicine so difficult to explain to westerners; likewise, the concepts of 寒 and 上火. One probably cannot do much more than explain that a person suffering from 上火 has "excessive internal heat", and then describe the symptoms.

The examples mentioned reflect the diversity that exists. Such diversity may be the result of differences in environment or tradition; or they may reflect disparity in level of industrial and technological development, or dissimilar political and social systems, etc.

What are the usual ways of dealing with these problems?

1. Explaining the term—for example, *brunch* is explained in one English-Chinese dictionary as 晚吃的早餐, 早吃的午餐; 早餐和午餐并作一顿吃的一餐。(XYH)

2. Giving a name that sounds the same as the original term—for example, 雷达 for *radar*; 咖啡 for *coffee*; *dazibao* for 大字报; *qigong* (*chigong*) for 气功. Lu Xun (Lu Hsun) did likewise by using 费厄泼赖 for *fairplay*.

3. Creating a name—such as *martial arts* for 武术; 软件, 硬件 for computer *software*, *hardware*. However, such names are often

not well-known or commonly accepted, at least at the beginning of their use, so that some explanation is often needed, as in the Chinese term(宇宙飞船在水面上)溅落 for *splashdown*.

4. Using two or more methods—such as this explanation from a dictionary for 磕头, 叩头 "kowtow;... to kneel, touching the ground with the forehead, as a token of homage or deep respect among the Chinese" (LME). And for 锅, "wok... a bowl-shaped cooking utensil used esp. in the preparation of Chinese food" (WNC, 1981). The English spelling does not sound like 锅 in *putonghua*, one might remark. Actually, it is based on the sound of the word in Cantonese, or the Guangdong dialect.

The English word *engine* is explained thus: 引擎, 蒸气机, 发动机(YHD).

# B

The story is told of a shoe store in Rome which had a sign in front of the shop to attract English-speaking customers: *Shoes for street walking. Come in and have a fit*. The sign caught the attention of many English-speaking tourists, who gathered in front of the shop—not to look at the shoes displayed in the windows, but to read the sign and then break out into laughter. The Italian shop owner, who could speak some English, did not realize that a *street walker* means a prostitute, while *to have a fit* does not mean to have a try, but to become suddenly and violently angry or upset. No wonder the amusement and laughter!

Chinese who know only a smattering of English have been known to introduce a companion as my *lover*, which causes foreigners to stare in surprise. How could Chinese, who are known to be so circumspect in such matters, be so open about having a *lover*? Actually, the companion is not a lover, but the person's spouse, not 情妇 or 情夫, but 爱人(丈夫或妻子). The term 爱人, literally meaning *the person I love*, obviously needs a different rendering in English: simply *husband*, *wife*, *fiance or fiancee*.

The title *First Lady* for the wife of the U. S. President or of an American state governor likewise may cause misunderstanding when some Chinese read about 第一夫人. There have been cases with such reaction: "So the President has several wives, eh?" The assumption is that if there is a *first lady*, there must be a *second lady*, and maybe even a *third*, *fourth*, or even more. Polygamy in the White House!

When Chinese ask a person about his 籍贯, they may mean the *place of birth* or *where a person is from*; or they may mean, more often, *where a person's parents or ancestors came from originally*. Sometimes the two places may actually be the same, but often they are not. In English, *place of birth* means just that, and does not involve information about one's ancestors. This difference occasionally causes confusion in filling out identification cards, personal data forms, passports, etc.

Below are other examples of some common terms with surface similarity but actual semantic differences.

Places, establishments:

*high school* ≠ 高等学校

This is the American term (not British) for *secondary school*.

*service station* ≠ 服务站

This is a place where people go to get gasoline or other services for their cars.

*rest room* ≠ 休息室

In American usage, a *rest room* is a room in a theater, department store or other large building equipped with toilets, and washbasins, etc., for the use of customers, employees, etc.; *rest room* is a polite term for bathroom or toilet; the English equivalent for the Chinese 休息室 might be *lounge*, or sometimes *lobby*.

## People：

### *busboy*≠公共汽车上的青年售票员或司机

A *busboy* is not a young bus conductor or driver, nor is he a person who does some kind of work on a bus. Actually, a *busboy* does not have anything to do with a bus; rather, he is one whose job is to remove the dirty dishes and set the tables in a restaurant. (American English)

### *goldbrick*≠金锭

The term *goldbrick* is an American slang term for a person who shirks assigned duties, especially a soldier who does so; a shirker, a loafer.

### 大忙人≠*busybody*

A *busybody* is one who pries into the affairs of others. The Chinese equivalent to *busybody* is 爱管闲事的人.

For the Chinese 大忙人, people usually use the phrase *a very busy person*, or just say *He/She is always busy*, or *He/She is always busy with something*.

Both *goldbrick* and *busybody* are pejoratives, although one would not think so from the way the terms are formed.

## Political and social activities：

### *political campaign*≠政治运动

The English term in America refers to the organized activities by a candidate for public office, such as a candidate for the U. S. Presidency, to build up the person's image in order to attract the votes in an election.

### 改善生活≠*improve one's standard of living*

This short term in the *People's Daily* (February 26, 1984) is an example of its present day meaning:"我的邻居是一位六十多岁的老太太,隔三差五,到街头饭馆改善一次生活。但每次都是去一家私人饭馆。她说,原因不是别的,就是这家小饭馆服务态度好,总听到一声'里边请'。"("One of my neigh-

14

bors is a woman over sixty. Every now and then, she goes out for a meal for a change. But she always goes to one particular eating place—one owned and run privately. When asked why she stuck to that place, she explained that it was because of the friendliness of the people there—They always greet you with a smile and a word of 'welcome'.") In current Chinese usage, 改善生活 means simply to have an occasional good meal or feast.

Idioms, expressions, sayings:

## 令人发指≠to make one's hair stand on end

The Chinese expression is used to show anger, whereas the English is for fear. Example: *The sight made his hair stand on end—he thought it was his dead brother's ghost*. In English, *to bristle with anger* does mean that anger makes one's hair stand up, but it is used for animals and not human beings, except in a metaphorical sense; e. g. *His hair bristles on his scalp with anger*. (YHD) *The hog bristled up*. (YHD)

## 自食其言≠to eat one's own words

The Chinese means to go back on one's word; i. e., to break one's promise. The latter, the English, means to be forced to take back one's words, usually accompanied by a sense of humiliation. Example: *He told everyone he was absolutely certain that his article would be published by the "Times", but when the letter of rejection came, he had to eat his own words*.

## to get a kick out of something≠被踢出去

This informal and very idiomatic expression means to get enjoyment or pleasure out of something; e. g., *I got a kick out of watching those kids perform; their play made me realize how strange and funny we grown-ups must seem to them*. It has nothing to do with actually being kicked.

## to blow one's own horn (or trumpet)≠各吹各的号

The expression means to praise oneself; to call attention to one's own successes, skill, intelligence, etc.; e. g., *If he's so successful, why does he have to keep blowing his own trumpet?* The meaning of the expression is similar to the Chinese 老王卖瓜,自卖自夸. The Chinese 各吹各的号,各唱各的调 is closer in meaning to the English *each doing his own thing*.

15

# Chapter 3

## More on Words—
## Cultural Distinctions and Connotations

*"Dictionaries are like watches; the worse is better than none, and the best cannot be expected to go quite true."*
—Samuel Johnson, *Johnsoniana*

*"'The questions is,' said Alice, 'whether you can make words mean so many different things.'"*
—Lewis Carroll, *Through the Looking Glass*

### A

In some languages, there may be only a single word for a certain object, creature or concept, whereas in another language, there may be several words, even quite a large number. Generally, the greater number would be to show finer distinctions. In Chinese there is only the single term 骆驼; in English there is *camel* (or *dromedary* for the one-humped camel, and *Bactrian camel* for the two-humped animal). But in Arabic, it is said that there are more than 400 words for the animal. The camel is of far greater importance as a means of travel with most Arabic-speaking people. The

16

greater number of words relating to the camel are an obvious reflection of this. The 400 or so words may show differences in the camel's age, sex, breed, size, etc.; they may indicate whether the animal is used for carrying heavy loads or not. It is said that there is at least one term which indicates that the camel is pregnant.

In Chinese-English intercultural communication, kinship terms often present problems because satisfactory equivalents are not always available. The statement *Linda's brother married Michael's sister* is not easy to render into Chinese without further information about whether the *brother* is older or younger than Linda and whether the *sister* is Michael's elder or younger sister. The reason

| Chinese term | English term | English explanation if needed | | |
|---|---|---|---|---|
| 祖父(母) | grandfather (grandmother) | paternal grandfather (grandmother) | | |
| 外祖父(母) | | maternal grandfather (grandmother) | | |
| 父 | father | | | |
| 母 | mother | | | |
| 兄,弟 | brother | elder brother, younger (kid) brother | | |
| 姐,妹 | sister | elder sister, younger (kid) sister | | |
| 伯父 | uncle | paternal uncle | father's brother | elder brother |
| 叔父 | | | | younger brother |
| 姑父 | | husband of father's sister | | |
| 舅父 | | maternal uncle | mother's brother | |
| 姨父 | | | husband of mother's sister | |
| 姐夫 | brother-in law | husband of elder sister | | |
| 妹夫 | | husband of younger sister | | |

is that in Chinese there are many more terms to designate specific relationships. The chart on the previous page only begins to indicate some of the complexities involved.

We need not go further into such distinctions as 姨公(婆), 堂 (表)兄弟(姐妹), 嫂子, 弟妹, 小舅子, 侄, 外甥等. These often cause Westerners to throw up their hands in despair. The term *relative* is so much simpler!

It might be pointed out that in English, if a term of kinship is used instead of the person's name, the "generation" to which that person belongs is often disregarded. A *greatuncle* might simply be called *Uncle* or *Uncle Jim*, *Uncle Henry*, etc. In fact, addressing the person as *Greatuncle Liu*, *Greatuncle Chen* would sound quite out of the ordinary. Furthermore, many Westerners would not be particularly pleased to have their old age stressed.

In referring to animals and birds, the Chinese practice is generally, but not always, to use simply 公 or 母 to show whether a creature is male or female. In English, more specific terms are often used, including terms for the young.

| Generic term | Name for male | Name for female | Name for young |
|---|---|---|---|
| chicken | cock, rooster | hen | chick |
| duck | drake | duck | duckling |
| goose | gander | goose | gosling |
| horse | stallion | mare | foal |
| (cattle) (cow) | bull | cow | calf |
| pig | boar | sow | shoat |
| dog | dog | bitch | puppy |
| sheep | ram | ewe | lamb |
| deer | stag | doe | fawn |

Not all animals or birds have specific names to denote different sex. Some have specific names that are not well known. With cer-

18

tain less common animals and birds, *bull or cow* and *cock or hen* are frequently used to distinguish sex; e.g., *bull seal*, *cow seal*, *bull elephant*, *cow elephant*; *cock pheasant*, *hen pheasant*, *cock sparrow*, *hen sparrow*. Also, using the terms *male* or *female*, or sometimes *she* with the generic name, is acceptable, as in *male leopard*, *female panda*, *she wolf*.

Examples of other such differences:

Names for legislative institutions:

| Chinese | Name in English |
|---|---|
| 国　会 | Parliament (United Kingdom and others) |
| | Congress (U.S. and others) |
| | Diet (Japan and others) |

Terms to show position just below the highest rank:

| Chinese | Terms in English | Examples of titles in English |
|---|---|---|
| 副 | vice | vice-chairman, vice-president |
| | associate | associate professor, associate director |
| | ①assistant | assistant manager, assistant secretary |
| | deputy | deputy director, deputy chief-of-staff |
| | lieutenant | lieutenant governor, lieutenant general |
| | under | undersecretary (of State, U.S.) |

---

① **assistant** is often rendered as 助理 in Chinese. However, in English, the position and title are often equivalent to 副.

What is *connotation*?

The *Longman Modern English Dictionary* gives this definition: "the implication of a word, apart from its primary meaning."

*Webster's New Collegiate Dictionary* defines the word as: "the suggesting of a meaning by a word apart from the thing it explicitly names or describes."

These two definitions show that the connotation of a word is different from its denotation—its explicit meaning. For students of a foreign language, it is essential that they know not only the denotation of words, but also the connotations. Serious blunders have been committed because of ignorance of a connotation: sometimes misinterpreting an innocent or well-meaning remark, causing harm or ill-feeling; sometimes mistaking deliberate jibes and sneers as compliments, leading people to laugh up their sleeves.

When talking about the Chinese countryside, English-speaking people in China have occasionally asked: "Why do you call rural people *peasants*? I thought their status had changed and that they are now respected."

To many Chinese, the question itself might be puzzling. Why not call them *peasants*? Why should the term imply lack of respect?

An alert Chinese would probably realize from the foreigner's question that the English word *peasant* does not have exactly the same meaning as the Chinese 农民. He would sense that there must be some difference in connotation, that the English term quite likely has a derogatory meaning. In order to make certain, he/she might turn to a dictionary. Among the definitions for *peasant* would be found the following:

> "a usually uneducated person of low social status" (WNC)
>
> "a countryman; rustic"; "an ill-bred person" (AHD)

No wonder an American or Englishman would think: In a country that stresses equality, why use a term that implies the rural masses are of low status and ill-bred? Or that they are "rascals and villains" (OED).

The Chinese term 农民 does not, of course, have such derogatory coloration. In China today, the English term *peasant* is used in its primary sense:

> "A member of the agricultural class, including farmers, laborers, etc." (AHD)
>
> "... a hired farm labourer or the owner or tenant of a farm or holding, in a country where the mass of farm workers and small farmers are very poor" (LME)

In connection with the term *peasant*, it might be worthwhile to consider how most English-speaking people would react to this sentence: *The poor peasants talked about their happy life today*.

The statement would be readily understood by people who know about the changes in China's countryside after 1949. But most English-speaking people do not realize that *poor peasant* has a special meaning, as does *rich peasant*. They do not know that the term is one of class status before liberation. To them, poor simply means having little money, few goods and no luxuries. So how could peasants who are poor have a happy life? Obviously, they would be puzzled.

A further note: *poor peasant* and *laborer*, are words with positive connotations in China, but often carry somewhat negative meanings to some people in Western countries. Conversely, *land-*

lord, *capitalist*, *boss* are often pejoratives to Chinese, but are not so to many people in countries with capitalist systems. Such connotations, in a way, reflect different attitudes towards the different social classes. Whether one approves of such or not, the facts must be recognized in order to have proper understanding.

In the remainder of this chapter we shall deal with other examples of different connotations, words with different cultural loads, or associations that go with certain terms.

*Idealist*, *materialist*—these two words are often misunderstood by Chinese. If the context in which these words appear is neglected, the former is usually translated as 唯心主义者 and the latter as 唯物主义者. In a strictly philosophical piece of writing, such translations might be acceptable. But more often than not, the words are used in a totally different sense, as in this passage from an actual conversation:

> "She has always been an *idealist*. So you can understand why she turned down a good job offer to work among refugee immigrants and low-income groups after she got her degree in social studies."

It is obvious that "she" is one who wants to work for the realization of her ideals, and not one who is mainly interested in a well-paid job or in accumulating money or material things. She might be called a 理想主义者 or 追求理想的人, but not 唯心主义者. Depending on the circumstances, she might also be considered as one whose ideas are not always down to earth, who is impractical, which is one of the connotations of the English word *idealistic*.

Now this passage, also from a conversation in which one of the authors took part:

> "Quite frankly, I'm a *materialist*. I've got a good-paying job and I want to keep it. I've bought a home near Westlake, and me and my wife

22

want to enjoy the comforts of life. I had a hard time when I was a kid and I don't want to go through all that again."

No further explanation is needed for this. The words are typical of the way a number of American males feel and it shows fully what they mean by *materialist*. Would it then be proper to say in Chinese that he is a 唯物主义者? After all, 唯物主义 in the Marxist sense commonly used in China today, denotes something quite different from what is implied in the passage above.

It is doubtful whether 唯物主义者 should be used in describing such a person as the one quoted above.

*Politician*, *statesman*—Is a *politician* a 政治家? Or conversely, how should 政治家 be translated into English? Not as *politician*, which is often done by students who know some English but are not aware of some of its connotations. In American English, *politician* can be a very derogatory term, one that arouses contempt. It implies a person who is in public life merely for personal gain, one who schemes for self-interest. It can also mean a *smooth-operator*—one who acts or speaks with assurance and easy competence, often in an excessively suave manner. *Statesman* would be appropriate in both British and American English, for it means a person with wisdom and skill in managing the affairs of state. It is often used when referring to a respected person in high government office. *Politicians* can be found everywhere, *statesmen* are comparatively rare.

It might be mentioned that the Chinese term 政治 is often hard to render into proper English. In most cases, *politics* would not convey the proper meaning, for one of its English connotations is "... political activities characterized by artful and often dishonest practices" (WNC); "... scheming and maneuvering within a group" (LME). To choose a more appropriate English term, one should consider the Chinese meaning and context, then decide whether to use *political activities*, *political work*, *political study* or some other term.

*Liberal*, *liberalism*—The Chinese for Liberal Party is 自由党, a rendering which is quite acceptable. But what does such a party stand for? One might say that a Liberal Party is for *liberalism*. But what is *liberalism*? The Chinese term 自由主义 in its most widely used sense does not throw much light on this question.

When we say in Chinese 他犯了自由主义, do we mean that the person has become liberal, has taken on liberal ideas, or is "guilty" of liberalism? No. To Chinese, it merely means he has done something that is frowned on, perhaps a minor breaking of the rules, or perhaps stayed away from a meeting that he should have attended. This is quite different from the term *liberalism* or *liberal* as understood in the West. Consider these definitions of *liberal* given in different dictionaries.

As an adjective:

—(politics in Great Britain) of the party... favouring moderate democratic reforms (OAL)

—1. willing to understand and respect the ideas and feelings of others

2. favouring some change, as in political or religious affairs (LCE)

—1. Favoring individual freedom and nonrevolutionary reform

2. Broad-minded or tolerant (AHD)

As a noun:

—person in favour of progress and reform and opposed to privilege (OAL)

—a person with wide understanding, who is in favour of change (LCE);

—one holding liberal political or cultural views (AHD)

24

*Intellectual*—In the previous chapter, mention was made of the fact that the Chinese term 知识分子 and the English word *intellectual* are not exact equivalents. The English term has a narrower scope and is used mainly for college professors and people of similar high scholastic or intellectual achievement. However, besides this difference, the English term sometimes carries a connotation which might be described as "a person claiming to belong to an intellectual elite, often engaged in empty thinking or the orizing, and often weak in solving practical problems". Two quotes from *Webster's Third International Dictionary* will illustrate:

1. "Don't go for the *intellectual* who knows nothing but $2 words." (Two-dollar word = long words not commonly known)

2. "*Intellectual* is an ugly word... it implies consummate snobbery."

Obviously, the word should be used with care. The context or situation, and the people being referred to must be given due consideration.

Here are other examples of words that are generally considered pejorative in one language, but not generally in the other:

| Pejorative in Chinese but positive or neutral to most Americans | ambitious 野心勃勃的<br>equalitarian 平均主义的 |
| --- | --- |
| Pejorative to most Americans, but positive or neutral in Chinese | propaganda 宣传<br>do-gooder 做好事的人 |

Dr. Annette T. Rubinstein, author of the book *From Shakespeare to Shaw*—well-known to many Chinese students of English literature, tells about her experience with the word *ambitious* when she was teaching in China in 1982 – 1983 at the Beijing Foreign Languages Institute:

"I have taught *Julius Caesar* some 89 or 90 times in high schools and colleges, but never once in the United States without having to explain why Antony can so easily use the term *ambitious* as a pejorative, as when he says about Caesar, 'He was my friend, faithful and just to me, yet Brutus says *he was ambitious*. If this were so it were a grievous fault.' This time I was all prepared to explain that for the 91st time but I didn't get a single question on it. They took for granted that *ambition* was a pejorative; I was really quite puzzled. What did *ambition* mean to them? They put *ambitious and greedy* or *ambitious and ruthless* together. I asked, 'You wouldn't say *poor but ambitious* or *ambitious and hardworking*?' 'Oh, no'—that was not the context in which they would think of *ambition*."

(Rubinstein, 1984)

It may surprise many Chinese that *do-gooder* is considered derogatory in English. How could one who does things for the common good, or for others, be regarded in such a manner? The definition in *Webster's Third International Dictionary* may help to clear up the matter:

"an earnest usually impractical-minded humanitarian bent on promoting welfare work or reform—commonly used with a derogatory implication of naivete or blundering ineffectualness."

What a terrible mistake it would be to call an unselfish, helpful person a *do-gooder*!

The reader may have noticed that most of the terms mentioned in this section have been taken from the social sciences. This is natural and is a reflection of not only cultural, but political differences.

Actually, the term *social sciences* itself deserves some attention. The Chinese is 社会科学. But are they really the same? Do both terms cover the same fields? If we go by contemporary Chinese usage, 社会科学 covers all the fields not in the natural sciences and applied sciences. This would include what are called *the humanities* in English: language, literature, philosophy, etc.; that is, the branches of learning dealing mainly with the cultural aspects of civilization. The English term *social sciences*, however, covers a smaller area of learning—political science, economics, history (which is often classified under the humanities), sociology, etc., branches of learning that study human society, especially its organization and the relationship of individual members to it.

# Chapter 4

## Cultural Differences in Everyday Conversation

*"When in Rome, do as the Romans do."*

—English proverb

### A. Greetings and Farewells

An American studying in China had an appointment at noon. As he was getting on his bicycle a Chinese friend passed by.

吃了吗? the young Chinese asked. This, of course, is a common Chinese greeting around meal time and the American merely nodded with a smile, waved goodbye and went off. He realized that his friend's remark was nothing more than a Chinese way of saying *Hello* or *Hi*. If the greeting had been put literally into English *Have you eaten yet?* or *Have you had your lunch?* It would have sounded rather unusual.

To Americans, the greeting might mean this: "I haven't either. Come on, let's go together and get something to eat," or "If you haven't, I was just going to invite you to my place." In other words, it could indicate an invitation to a meal.

Actually, another foreign student who had not been long in China once complained in broken Chinese 你们为什么老问我吃饭

了没有? 我有钱。To his way of thinking, people were concerned that he was not getting his meals properly because of lack of money. Clearly, he was offended.

There is a similar Chinese greetings, such as 上哪儿去啊? 到哪儿去啦? which if translated literally, would be *Where are you going*? or *Where have you been*? The natural reaction of most English-speaking people to this greeting would most likely be *It's none of your business*!

Fortunately, not all greetings sound strange or arouse displeasure. Many are similar, some are merely different. While greetings in many languages often indicate the time of day, there may be inconsistencies within a language. English has *Good morning*, *Good afternoon* and *Good evening* but not *Good noon*. And *Good night* is not a greeting at all (to most English-speaking people), but an expression of farewell.

When Chinese meet for the first time, there is no special expression for the occasion, but when most English-speaking people meet for the first time, they often say something like *I'm pleased to meet you*. And when they part, they are expected to remark *It's nice meeting you* or *It's nice to have met you* or something similar.

When people part, they usually say *Good-bye*, *Bye-bye*, *Au revoir*, *Hasta la vista*. Similar expressions are found in almost all languages. But in the more or less fixed conversational formulas that precede Good-bye, there may be interesting differences, as in Chinese when a distinguished guest drops in for a visit, or if the visitor is one with whom the hosts are not very familiar. The Chinese custom when such a guest leaves is for the hosts to see the visitor to the door or gateway. It is customary for the guest to say to his hosts 请留步. The final words of the hosts are usually 慢走, 走好, 慢点儿

骑. None of these should be translated directly. *Stay here* would sound strange; *Go slowly*, *Walk slowly* or *Ride slowly* would be equally so. A smile and a gesture of farewell would be enough.

## B. Ways of Address

In recent years, the trend of many English-speaking people has been to address others by using the first name—*Tom*, *Michael*, *Linda*, *Jane*, etc.—rather than calling the person *Mr. Summers*, *Mrs. Howard* or *Miss Jones*. This is especially common among Americans, even when people meet for the first time. This applies not only to people of roughly the same age, but also of different ages. It is not a sign of disrespect. It is not at all uncommon to hear a child calling a much older person—*Joe*, *Ben*, *May*, *Helen*. etc. This may even include the child's parents or grandparents. People of different social status do the same. For example, many college students call their professors by their first names. The professors do not regard this as a sign of disrespect or familiarity, but rather, as an indication that the professor is considered affable and has a sense of equality. This, of course, is quite counter to Chinese custom. One can imagine the reactions of adults if a child were to call a grandparent by his or her first name, or a student to do the same in calling a teacher. A quick reprimand, and possibly even a spanking for the child, would be sure to follow.

One can infer from the preceding that the Chinese custom of addressing members of one's family, relatives or close neighbors as 二哥,三姐,四婶,周大伯, should not be carried over into English. In English, the name alone, whether it be for man or woman, would ordinarily be enough. The main exceptions are addressing

30

one's parents (*Dad*, *Mom*, *Mum* or *Mother*), one's grandparents (*Grandpa*, *Grandma*) and sometimes an older relative (*Aunt Mary* or *Uncle Jim*). Notice that the given name, and not the family name, is used. And even with relatives, Americans tend to use just the first name and leave out the term of relationship. It should be mentioned that in English *Brother Joseph* or *Sister Mary* would commonly be understood as referring to persons belonging to a Catholic group or some religious or professional society.

Another common Chinese form of address is the use of a person's title, office, or occupation, such as 黄局长, 林经理, 马校长. But one seldom hears English speakers addressing others as *Bureau Director Smith*, *Manager Jackson*, *Principal Morris*. In English, only a few occupations or titles would be used: *Doctor __* is common for those who have qualified in the medical profession, and *Judge __* for those authorized to try cases in law courts; *Governor __* and *Mayor __* may be used for those who hold such offices, although often without the name. The same with Professor __. However, there are very few others.

It should be noted that in addressing military officers in Chinese, 陈司令, 郝团长, 梁排长 are common. English-speaking people, however, tend to use the rank of the person, and not the command or duties that he has been assigned; for example, *Captain Johnson*, rather than *Company Commander Johnson*, *Admiral Benjamin*, rather than *Fleet Commander Benjamin*.

English translations of Chinese works usually keep such forms as *Grandpa*, *Auntie*, *Sister-in-law*, but they sound strange to the English ear. In English-language writings about China, such terms are used in order to keep or give a Chinese flavor to the story. Certain of these terms, though, are especially troublesome. How to address a teacher has long been a problem. Should it be *Teacher* or *Teacher Zhang*? Neither of these is in keeping with English custom. Should we say *Comrade* or *Comrade Li*? These involve using the term *comrade*, which is not widely accepted in non-socialist countries. Or should we simply follow the English custom and call the teacher *Mr. Zhang*, *Mrs. Yang*, *Miss Fei*? All of these would sound terrible to Chinese if school-age youngsters were to do so.

Other difficult terms are 师傅, 警察叔叔, 解放军叔叔. To translate the former as *master* carries the idea of a masterservant relationship, or a relationship that 师傅 does not have in present-day usage. The problem is further complicated by the fact that the term is now widely used as a general form of address for people in various occupations, for both men and women, and not just for veteran craftsmen or workmen, chefs or automobile drivers, as in earlier times. *Uncle policeman* for 警察叔叔 sounds very odd—perhaps one reason is that *uncle* connotes endearment, whereas *policeman* does not have the same connotation to English ears. *P.L.A. Uncle* for 解放军叔叔 not only sounds strange, but often leaves people wondering what is meant, for very few people outside of China know what the letters P.L.A. stand for.

Interestingly, there is no general term in English for getting the attention of a stranger, or of a person whose name we may not know. In Chinese we have 同志 and the now fashionable 师傅. Then what do peope do in English if such a need arises? Depending on the situation, English custom might suggest using some such expression as *Excuse me*, *Pardon me*, or in England, *I say there*. Expressions like *Hey*, or *Hey*, *you* or *You*, *there* are used, but are not considered polite. Often, people resort to a way that needs no language. They simply clear their throat loudly, or make some noise or gesture to attract the person's attention.

### C. Compliments and Praise

In a previous chapter, mention was made of American and Chinese differences in replying to compliments: Americans tend to accep the compliment while Chinese generally murmur some reply about not being worthy of the praise.

Here a few more words might be said about this difference. Consider the following examples:

1. A young Chinese woman in the U.S. was complimented for the lovely dress that she was wearing. "It's exquisite. The colors are so beautiful!" She was pleased but somewhat embarrassed. In typical Chinese fashion, she replied, "Oh, it's just an ordinary dress that I bought in China."

2. At a reception in an American college, a newly-arrived Chinese scholar was chatting with the hostess, who was an old friend. As an acquaintance of hers came up she said, "Ron, let me introduce Mr. Chen, an outstanding physicist and one of the nicest people I know." Mr. Chen offered his hand to the newcomer but looked at his hostess and said with a smile, "Should I blush, or should I tell him you don't really mean it?"

In both cases, the words of the Chinese conveyed a message quite different from that which was intended. In the case of the Chinese woman, the reply could have meant that the one paying the compliment did not know what a really good dress is; otherwise, how could she get so excited about an ordinary dress? The implication was that the American woman's taste in clothing was questionable. In the second case, if Chen had not been smiling, his words could have been interpreted as meaning "You're just saying that to be polite; you don't really mean that." So in one case, the person had poor judgment. In the other, the latter case, the hostess was not sincere. Quite a gap between intention and message!

Certain remarks that might be fitting and proper in Chinese could lead to similar negative results.

1. A foreign visitor was looking at the host's potted flowers with obvious admiration. The plants were growing well and some were blooming profuselyl. The host remarked diffidently, "Growing flowers is my hobby, but I'm not much good at it."

2. A Canadian woman acquaintance of a Chinese art teacher asked him to look over an article that she had written about Chinese painting. He agreed, but added that "I really know so little about the subject."

In both cases the Chinese would be suspected of "fishing for a compliment," even though the remarks might have been quite sincere. In the first case, the foreign visitor was almost forced to say something like "But these flowers are beautiful." or "I wish I could do as well!" And in the second case, the Canadian had to say, "Oh, come on, I know you're an expert on Chinese art."

Or she could have said "Well, I certainly don't know anybody who knows more than you do!" Forced compliments like these can leave a bad taste in the mouth. Besides, what could be the value of such praise?

Cultural differences also exist in *who* can be complimented. It would not be unusual to hear an American woman talking about how hard her husband works and how well he has done, about all the promotions and honors that he has received. She might do the same

34

about a son or daughter of hers—how bright he/she is, what good marks he/she makes in school, how active the child is in his/her stamp-collecting group, when and where he/she performed in a concert, etc. In Chinese, this would be considered bad taste; one simply does not praise members of one's own family in front of others.

Another example of a Chinese taboo is complimenting a man on his wife's looks. The remark "You have a lovely wife" would be regarded as almost indecent by many Chinese, especially those beyond their youth. Yet the some compliment would be considered perfectly natural and even highly appreciated by Westerners.

## D. Miscellaneous Social Amenities

Both Chinese and English have expressions for gratitude, apologies, remarks preceding a request; for example, there are 谢谢, 对不起, 请…… *Thank you*, *I'm sorry*, *Excuse me*. On the whole, they are quite similar and present no problem. However, even among these there are certain differences.

*Thank you*, and *Please*—Both of these are used more widely than the Chinese 谢谢, 请……. For minor favors like borrowing a pencil, asking directions, requesting someone to pass on a message, calling a person to the telephone, etc., such polite expressions are often omitted by Chinese, especially among close friends and members of the family. The more frequent use of *Thank you* and *Please* by Westerners is often regarded as unnecessary and even tiresome by many Chinese. On the other hand, the Chinese attitude—that appreciation is understood and need not be expressed—is sometimes taken for rudeness or lack of consideration by Westerners.

Replies to *Thank you* are similar. The most common are *Not*

35

*at all*, *Don't mention it*, *You're welcome*, 没什么, 不用谢. But what reply should be given by guides and service people when a foreign person says *Thank you* for a job well done? This is a situation often met by hotel attendants, museum or exhibition guides and tour guides. To translate the Chinese expression 这是我应该做的 as *It's my duty* conveys the idea that the Chinese attendant or guide didn't really want to do it, that he/she did it only because it was his/her duty. Quite a different message is conveyed! A proper reply might be *I'm glad to be of help* or *It's a pleasure*.

The Chinese term 请 is usually regarded as equivalent to *Please*. However, in certain situations the English *Please* would not be used. When offering or urging another person to be first in going through a door or getting in a car, the expression is generally *After you* (not *You go first*, as some people not well-acquainted with English are apt to say). At the meal table, *Help yourself* is customary when urging someone to start eating, or to take more of the food.

*Excuse me*—This is a general term preceding a request or interruption. In Chinese, however, there are different terms: 劳驾 when asking a favor or requesting a person do something; 借光, 请让一让 when asking a person to step aside or make room; 请问 when asking for information or making a query. Foreigners not knowing this distinction tend to use 对不起 for all such situations when hey speak Chinese.

The Chinese 辛苦了 is a good warm expression showing concern. Or it may be used in recognition of the fact that a person has put in considerable effort or gone through some hardship to achieve something. To put 辛苦了 into proper English, however, demands care; there is no equivalent that can fit all situations. To translate it

36

simply as *You've had a hard time* or *You've gone through a lot of hardships* is hardly enough; in some circumstances it might even give the wrong impression. If used as a greeting to a person who has just completed a long trip, 辛苦了 could be expressed as *You must have had a tiring journey* or *You must be tired from such a long trip* or *Did you have a good trip?* When commending people who have finished a difficult task or are still working on it, one might say *Well done; That was (You've got) a hard job*. None of these English expressions, however, carries as much meaning or warm feeling as the Chinese.

When a person sneezes, people nearby often make a remark. Some Chinese say something like 有人想你了,有人说你了 or humorously 谁在骂你了. An American or Englishman would probably say *God bless you*.

# Chapter 5

## Idioms, Proverbs and Sayings

### A

Idioms, proverbs, and sayings are an important part of the language and culture of a society. They are often hard to understand, especially idioms, and harder to use correctly. However, their proper use in a language is often a mark of a person's command of the language. Speech or writing without them lacks color and is uninteresting, but overuse or improper use makes the language sound affected and unnatural. It is often said that nothing marks a foreigner more than his unnecessary use of idioms.

The story is told of a foreign student in the U.S. sitting by a window reading a book. She heard someone yelling *Look out!*, so she stuck her head out the window. Just then a board hurtled down from above, narrowly missing her. She looked up, half in anger, half in fright. There was a man on the roof doing repairs. *Didn't you hear me call "look out"?* he demanded. *Yes, and that's what I did*, she replied.

Whether true or not, the story illustrates the problem with idioms. They are almost impossible to understand from the meanings

38

of the individual words. And with English idioms, even the same words may have different meanings, as in the example above, or in such phrases as *make up*, *set off*, *turn out*. *Turn out*, for example has a different meaning in each of the following situations: *Turn out the light*. *Turn out the guard*. *The whole town turned out for the event*. *This machine can turn out 300 copies a minute*. *It turned out to be a mistake*.

Of all the different kinds of English idioms, perhaps the hardest to learn are those comprising the forty or so most common verbs in various combinations with about a dozen prepositions or adverbs like *up*, *down*, *in*, *out*, *on*, *off*. The different meanings of such combinations amount to several hundred, and the confusion that they cause for the learner is immense.

So, first of all, a student should learn not to *look down on* such idioms just because they're *made up of* such simple and easy words. He should *look out for* identical phrases with different meanings and *look them up* in a dictionary if he's not sure. He's bound to *run into* a lot of trouble when he first uses them, but he shouldn't *give in*, much less *give up*. If he keeps trying and *keeps at* it long enough he'll *make out* and things will *turn out* well in the end.

Besides the verb phrases mentioned above, there are other idioms just as hard for the student to understand, but perhaps not so hard to remember.

Before he *gets the hang of* how to use them he'll make a lot of mistakes. Some mistakes will cause people *to hold their sides with laughter*, but that shouldn't *put him in a stew*. He should learn to *put up with* such things. You might say that's *part of the game*.

A few words about Chinese idioms. As with idioms in any language, the meanings of Chinese idioms cannot be derived from the meanings of the individual words alone. The problems they present

39

to foreigners who are learning Chinese are as great as those that English presents to its learners. The mistakes that are made can be just as amusing, or embarrassing.

At the beginning of a program in spoken Chinese in an American university, the two teachers (non-native speakers of Chinese) were using actual objects to demonstrate certain expressions. After practising 这是什么? (What's this?)——这是书桌(椅子等)(It's a desk, chair...) with various objects, the teachers took up 这是东西吗? (Is this a thing?)——是, 这是东西。 (Yes. It is a thing.) They then turned to negative answers. Pointing to himself, one of the teachers asked: 我是东西吗? (Am I a thing?) The other teacher shook her head, saying: 不, 你不是东西。 (No. You are not a thing.) The male teacher then pointed at her and asked: 你是东西吗? (Are you a thing?) Again she shook her head, answering: 不, 我不是东西。 (No. I'm not a thing.)

A native Chinese speaker was sitting in on the class at the time. He could hardly control himself from bursting out in laughter. One can imagine the teachers' red faces when they found out later what it means to say that a person 不是东西 (is not a thing—a demeaning cursing expression).

The problems of rendering idioms of one language into another are always complex, much more so if the two languages involved are of backgrounds and cultures so unlike each other. The complexities of this were well brought out during the compilation of *A Chinese-English Dictionary*, considered by many as the best of its kind produced to date. One of the chief editors, Professor Wang Zuoliang, writes thus in an article *Reflections on a Dictionary* (Wang, 1980):

"A translator's first job is to grasp the meaning of the original. If he doesn't understand the original, he won't get an equivalent. When Lin Yutang translates 吃软不吃硬 as *bully the weak but yield to one who fights back*, he not only writes clumsy English but shows a characteristic ignorance of the real meaning of that colloquial phrase. ... Where the understanding of the Chinese is adequate, the question becomes whether the translator's grasp of English, the target language, is really firm or his knowledge of English conditions up-to-date. To translate 布衣蔬食 literally as *wear cotton clothes and eat vegetable food*, for instance, may be misleading nowadays. Cotton clothes and vegetable food may be symbols of plain living in China, but are they also in Britain and America? Certainly a vegetarian diet, so far from being the poor men's monopoly, is nowadays every Western doctor's prescription for their [his] overfed millionaire patients."

The final version chosen for the dictionary was *coarse clothes and simple fare* which "catches the real sense and, what with the sightly archaic, old-world flavour of the word *fare*, matches the original in style as well."

Professor Wang explains how the dictionary went through three major revisions, "each one a long and painful process," but ending in "somewhat more adequate English translation". Examples are given to show the improvements made in successive versions. A few of those he cited are given below.

害人虫：an evil person/an evil *creature*

　　The change is small, but significant; gives more of the original Chinese flavour and enhances the English.

自投罗网：throw oneself into the trap/*walk right* into the trap

　　The first version is a more literal rendering, the later version is more in keeping with the English way of saying this.

奇花异木：rare flowers and trees/*exotic* flowers and *rare* trees

　　The changes are a stylistic improvement and more in harmony with

# B

Now we shall look at proverbs and sayings. Proverbs are short sayings of folk wisdom—of well-known facts or truths—expressed succinctly and in a way that makes them easy to remember. Because the sayings are so pithy, they have universal appeal. Students love to pick up proverbs, and the use of one or two in the original language is often a minor triumph for beginning foreign language learners.

Proverbs may provide interesting little glimpses or clues to a people's geography, history, social organization, social views, attitudes. People who live along sea coasts and whose livelihood is dependent on the sea will have proverbs about sailing, about braving the weather, about fish and fishing. Nomadic people, such as the Arabs, will have sayings about the desert or pasture-land, about sheep and horses or camels, about wolves and jackals. In cultures where old age is revered, there will be proverbs about the wisdom of the elders. And in societies where women's status is low, there will be a number of sayings demeaning them.

Human experiences and observations of the world are in many respects similar. So, in spite of the dissimilar cultural backgrounds of the Chinese and the English-speaking peoples, the number of proverbs or sayings in the two languages that are equivalent or close approximates is rather surprising. Consider the following:

Strike while the iron is hot 趁热打铁

Many hands make light work 人多好办事

Haste makes waste 欲速则不达

Out of sight, out of mind 眼不见, 心不烦

Birds of a feather flock together 物以类聚, 人以群分

Look before you leap 三思而后行

Where there's smoke there's fire 无风不起浪

Where there's a will there's a way 有志者事竟成

Give a person a dose of his own medicine 以其人之道还治其人之身

All good things must come to an end 天下没有不散的宴席

Since culture is important in giving a language its characteristics, the dissimilarities are naturally more apparent. Compared with English proverbs, the Chinese show certain distinctive features. First of all, the immense number. Chinese seem to have a proverb or saying for almost all conceivable situations—whether they be human-nature situations, or human-human relations. Secondly, the distinctive Chinese quality of many of the sayings. 小卒过河, 意在吃帅 and 挂羊头, 卖狗肉 are typical—the first having its origin in Chinese chess, the second referring to a Chinese butcher's shop with items that would be shocking to the West. Thirdly, the number that reflect social inequalities and the feelings of those deprived and oppressed, such as 卖花姑娘插竹叶, 卖线姑娘裙脚裂 or 只许州官放火, 不许百姓点灯. Fourthly, the influence of Buddhism on Chinese customs and thinking, as in 远看菩萨, 近看泥巴 and 平时不烧香, 临时抱佛脚 whereas English proverbs reflect the influence of Christianity. Another feature is what might be called social harmony, or brotherhood, or "doing good"; Chinese seem to have more of such proverbs, as 前人栽树, 后人乘凉; 一人掘井, 众人吃水; 一个篱巴三个桩, 一个好汉三个帮.

The points of difference mentioned above are not exhaustive, but will help to give the reader some idea.

Chinese proverbs without commonly-known equivalents in English are too numerous to be listed here. A sampling of such sayings is given below. Some have been chosen because their pithy wisdom may particularly interest English speakers. Several show insights that are different from English views. A few may be similar in their message, but difficult to understand because their literal meaning is foreign to the English mind. The English versions are our own.

良药苦口利于病, 忠言逆耳利于行: Frank advice is like good herbal medicine; hard to take, but ultimately beneficial.

No further explanation is needed for this, although it is likely that many people in the West have never taken herbal medicine and can only imagine how bitter the taste can be.

爪田不纳履, 李下不整冠: Neither adjust your shoe in a melon patch; nor your hat under a plum tree.

Or, for the sake of rhythm, *nor straighten your hat 'neath an apple tree*. This is sure to cause English-speaking people to chuckle, although they might not catch the implication immediately.

要知朝中事, 乡间问老农: Ask the common folk if you want to know how the country is faring.

This is not a very catchy proverb, but it contains a bit of universal folk wisdom.

衙门自古朝南开, 有理无钱莫进来: Court doors may open, but not to the poor.

This English version of ours takes only the most essential elements of the Chinese and leaves out the rest. Why the gates face the south, in the Chinese original, and what this signifies would require considerable explanation.

一人得道, 鸡犬升天: Even the dog swaggers when its master wins favor.

This will bring a nod of grim amusement from many. Leaving out *chickens* in our English version in no way detracts from the meaning; if anything, it makes the English more concise.

There are also some fairly common English proverbs that do not seem to have common Chinese equivalents. The sampling below includes some that reflect different everyday life habits, some that show a different perception of things, and some that indicate a different philosophy or attitude. Consider:

Absence makes the heart grow fonder. 越是不见越想念。

An apple a day keeps the doctor away. 常吃苹果少得病。

You can't have your cake and eat it too. 两者不可兼得。

Let sleeping dogs lie. 莫惹是非。

You can't teach an old dog new tricks. 年逾花甲不堪教。

The four proverbs below deserve special mention because they illustrate differences, although the sayings have surface similarities:

*It takes two to make a quarrel* could be regarded as similar to 一个巴掌拍不响. The Chinese saying has roughly the same connotation as the English—meaning both people may be at fault. However, the Chinese also has another meaning: that it often takes more than one person to achieve anything significant.

*A miss is as good as a mile* might be considered as equivalent to the Chinese 差之毫厘, 失之千里. However, the moral often associated with the Chinese is: a small fault or deviation if not corrected will end up in a major error or catastrophe. The Chinese is thus a warning, whereas the English merely states a fact, or a philosophic attitude, that to miss one's mark even very slightly is as bad as missing it by a mile.

*Gilding the lily* would seem to be a close approximate to the Chinese 锦上添花. Such is not the case, for the English implies spoiling something already fine, good or beautiful by adding something in an attempt to make it better. It express an attitude of disapproval, whereas the Chinese means adding somehing to make a good thing even better: Add flowers to the brocade—turning excellence into perfection.

*Life begins at forty* can be compared with two Chinese proverbs. The

45

first one, 人到四十五, 正如出山虎 has roughly the same moral, but the age shows a 5-year difference. The second one, 潮怕二十, 人怕四十, has the same age, but takes a dim view about reaching that stage: tides ebb after the twentieth (lunar calendar), people decline after forty.

The problems of rendering Chinese proverbs and sayings into English are more or less the same as those for finding acceptable English versions for Chinese idioms, but with the cultural component being more important and making the task more difficult. A study of several examples will illustrate this:

盲人瞎马: A blind man on a blind horse—rushing headlong to disaster. (CED)

The first part is a literal translation, which could mean several things to Englishmen. The second part is the one that supplies the "punch line", the moral of the saying.

黄鼠狼给鸡拜年, 没安好心: The weasel goes to pay his respects to the hen—not with the best of intentions. (CED)

Here again, the phrase after the literal translation adds meaning and vividness, and brings out more the flavor and style of the original.

挂羊头, 卖狗肉: Hang up a sheep's head and sell dogmeat— try to palm off sth. inferior to what it purports to be. (CED)

Another version might be *The sign says mutton, but the meat is dogmeat—try to peddle something under false claims*. Both *sheep's head* and *dogmeat* would cause revulsion among Westerners, so the English version must take this into consideration.

芝麻开花节节高: A sesame stalk puts forth blossoms notch by notch, higher and higher. (CED)

This is a literal rendering of the Chinese; what it actually means is that with each successive development, things get better and better. Because the sesame plant is comparatively unknown in the West, the picturesque charm of the saying is lost in ran lation.

46

一个和尚挑水吃, 两个和尚抬水吃, 三个和尚没水吃: There's a Chinese saying about monks fetching water: One monk, two buckets; two monks, one bucket; three monks, no bucket, no water—more hands, less work done.

One might add: "This is somewhat like the English *Too many cooks spoil the broth* ." The difficulty of rendering this into English is that there are no special English words that show the distinction between 挑 and 担; in English there would be only the single word *carry* (by shoulder pole). There might also be questions about why *monks* are singled out for the saying.

Seemingly, the best method is to give a literal translation—with due attention to tone and style, then add a tag phrase or comment that brings out the wit or humor. The tag phrase is often most effective if there is one ready made in English.

# Chapter 6

## Metaphor and Association

> *"Rise like lions after slumber*
> *In unvanquishable number—*
> *Shake your chains to earth like dew*
> *Which in sleep had fallen on you—*
> *You are many—they are few."*

This poem by Percy Bysshe Shelley has thrilled millions of working people, arousing them to shake off their chains, to take up arms, to fight against their oppressors.

"Rise like lions"—an apt metaphor.

Metaphors are found in all languages. They make images vivid; they bring so much life to language. English is rich in metaphors and one often finds expressions such as the following:

She's like a *rose*—fresh, delicate, beautiful.

He went about the job like a *bull* in a china shop.

We shall not be moved—just like a *tree* standing by the water.

What a dull speech! He's merely *parroting* what many others have said.

One look at his face and we realized that a *thunderstorm* was about to break.

In the examples above, we find trees, flowers, animals and

phenomena of nature used to make striking comparisons. One can imagine how dull the statements would be without the metaphors.

But metaphors in a different language may not always be easily understood. Students learning English may have come across sentences like these:

> "You *chicken*!" he cried, looking at Tom with contempt.
> The *stork visited* the Howard Johnstons yesterday.

The students may have been puzzled, unless they knew that *chicken* means a coward, a person without courage; that *a visit by the stork* means the birth of a baby. Similarly, English speakers learning Chinese would probably wonder about the meaning of: 你真熊! or 那家伙简直像个泥鳅!

To English-speaking people, the *bear* does not carry the same associations as it does to Chinese. The animal might be considered fierce or dangerous; a *bear* in a zoo or wildlife park might be regarded as mischievous or playful, but not stupid, incompetent, good-for-nothing, as is implied in the Chinese remark above.

The *loach*, which is not all common in most English-speaking countries, would merely be considered as another kind of fish; people would not think of it as being slippery and untrustworthy. However, there does exist the English saying *slippery as an eel*—which has the same meaning and feeling as the Chinese expression about the loach above.

From what has been said, it is clear that people often associate certain qualities with certain creatures or objects. These qualities often arouse certain reactions or emotions, although there is little or no scientific ground for such association. The qualities that are associated, or the emotions that are aroused, are not always the same with different peoples. In this chapter, we shall discuss such cultural similarities and/or differences relating to certain birds and animals.

First, the similarities.

> He's as sly as a *fox*. He's *foxy*. You've got to watch him.
>
> You *ass*! You stupid *ass*! How could you do a thing like that?!
>
> He doesn't have an idea of his own. He just *parrots* what other people say.
>
> The children were as busy as *bees*, making preparations for the festival.

The qualities that Chinese associate with the creatures above are roughly the same as those that Americans, Canadians, Englishmen would associate. In fact, in Chinese we have similar expressions; for example, 蠢驴, 鹦鹉学舌, 像狐狸一样狡猾.

Other animals that have similar associations in both cultures: deer are meek and gentle; lambs are lovable; pigs are dirty and greedy; monkeys are naughty, playful; jackals are greedy, contemptible; wolves are bloodthirsty and cruel.

Now, the differences. We shall consider two categories:

1. Creatures having certain associated characteristics in one culture, but not in the other; 2. Creatures with certain associated qualities in both cultures, but with different qualities.

Under the first category we shall take as examples the *bull*, the *beaver*, the *crane*, and the *tortoise*.

To Chinese, the first two creatures carry no particular association. They are merely animals that may or may not be common, may or may not be useful. Chinese might be able to guess the meaning of a *bull in a China shop*, but they would not have the image that would be evoked in the minds of English-speaking people: an angry, snorting bull charging into a shop filled with exquisite fragile porcelain. Consequently, Chinese would be less appreciative of the

50

vividness of the expression—meaning a person who is clumsy and bungling and causes a lot of trouble in a situation requiring tact and delicacy.

The *beaver* is chiefly a North American animal, not widely known in China. Its constant activity, its habit of gnawing down trees and building complex "homes" and its skill and ingenuity in doing this have earned for the animal the name *eager beaver*. In metaphor, an *eager beaver* is a person who is anxious to get something done, works hard, and is somewhat impatient. The term sometimes has a slightly derogatory connotation.

The *crane* is a symbol for longevity in Chinese culture. Thus parents giving names like 鹤年 and 鹤龄 show their hope that the child will live to a ripe old age. The crane is often paired with the pine tree, which is a symbol for sturdiness and long life. In paintings and art designs, the two often appear together with the motto 松鹤延年. Gifts with such designs are favorites for older people, especially on birthday occasions. But to Western minds, the crane does not arouse any such association. If there are any associations at all, they probably came from stories about the bird in Aesop's fables.

Chinese symbolism that goes with the *tortoise* or *turtle* is twofold. On the one hand is longevity. Stone tortoises symbolic of venerable old age can be seen in front of ancient halls, temples and palaces. On the other hand, the creature is also the symbol for the cuckold. To call a person a turtle or tortoise(王八)or a turtle egg (王八蛋)is highly insulting, highly profane. In Western culture, there is no such association; the turtle is just a slow-moving and not very attractive creature. The English term *turtleneck sweater* often brings a grimace to Chinese when they learn that such is the English

51

name for the 翻领毛衣 they are wearing.

Under the second category let us consider the *owl*, the *bat*, the *dog*, the *tiger*, and the *petrel*.

*As wise as an owl* indicates that English-speaking people associate wisdom with this bird. In children's books and cartoons, the owl is usually solemn and wise. In disputes among birds and beasts, it is the owl that acts as judge. In moments of crisis, it is the owl that they go to for advice. Sometimes the bird is considered as impractical and foolish, but in the main, the owl stands for wisdom. Among many Chinese, however, there is a superstitious belief that this bird is a sign of bad luck. There is a saying 夜猫子进宅(an owl visiting a home), portending misfortune in that household. The mere sight of an owl or the sound of the creature's hooting is enough to cause people to draw back in fear.

An American woman, ignorant of the Chinese feeling, often wore her favorite owl pin on her dress when she first came to China. She was surprised that people often stopped to stare or point at the pin. A number of times she was asked why she was wearing such a thing. Only when it was explained to her how Chinese feel towards the bird did she realize how inappropriate her habit was.

The bat is usually associated with negative qualities in the West. *As blind as a bat*, *crazy as a bat*, *he's a bit batty*, *have bats in the belfry* are typical expressions of the negative associations. They may be even worse. Mention of the bat often evokes the image of an ugly, sinister, blood-sucking creature. This may possibly be because of the vampire bat. The emotions aroused in English-speaking people are similar to those that the dreaded owl arouses among Chinese: fright and revulsion.

To Chinese, however, the bat is a symbol of good fortune,

well-being, happiness—all positive qualities. The reason for such associations is probably because the name of the creature is pronounced the same as the word 福. Thus the popularity of the traditional design that shows the bat and the deer together, 蝠鹿, pronounced the same as 福禄—good fortune, happiness, wealth and position.

*Man's best friend* is sometimes heard in English conversation or seen in English writing. How many Chinese know what animal is being referred to? Many would be surprised that it is the *dog*. To many Chinese, it would be unthinkable for the dog to be given such honor. Dogs, in China, are generally associated with unpleasantness. Consider name-calling in Chinese: 狗东西,狗娘养的,狗改不了吃屎. Admittedly, the qualities that have endeared the animal to Western people are found in dogs in China as well: loyalty, dependability, courage, intelligence. But in China, dogs are first of all watchdogs, not pets. They are kept because they are useful, not because they make good companions. Generally they are considered a necessary evil, to be tolerated but not loved.

It should be pointed out, however, that English-speaking people do not always speak of dogs endearingly. *You dog*! *That cur*! *Son of a bitch*! are fairly common swear words in English. But such swearing does not change the animal's status. The dog is still "man's best friend" in the U.S. and Great Britain.

To the English, and to most Westerners, "the king of the beasts" is the lion. The lion enjoys high prestige, as can be seen from such expressions *regal as a lion*, *majestic as a lion*. Richard I, king of England in the latter part of the 12th century, was known as *lion-hearted* for his courage and chivalry. And in his poem at the beginning of this chapter, Shelley calls on the oppressed to *rise like lions*. It is no wonder, then, that the English have chosen the lion as their symbol.

In Chinese culture this beast has fewer such associations. He is regarded commonly as being fierce and powerful, but not necessarily majestic or regal. To Chinese, it is the tiger that more likely evokes such associations.

The characteristics associated with the tiger in Chinese culture are two sided: positive and negative, good and bad. On the positive side are courage, vigor, decisiveness. On the negative side are ferocity, cruelty, ruthlessness. Reflecting the positive associations are terms and expressions such as 虎将, 干起活来像小老虎, 虎老雄心在, 虎虎有生气, and masculine names like 大虎, 二虎, 小虎. Reflecting the negative associations are terms and expressions like 拦路虎, 狐假虎威, 苛政猛于虎.

The petrel in present-day Chinese culture is a bird to be emulated. The mental image that the term evokes is a small lonely bird winging over the vast ocean—braving storms and flying with stamina and courage. Many young people in their moments of fantasy compare themselves to the petrel, struggling to get ahead in the vast world of humanity, braving hardships and adversity, advancing with perseverance and courage. The petrel emerges in many juvenile diaries, flits in and out of youthful fictional writings, and appears as the trade mark for a number of products. What a blow it is, then, to discover how little respect Westerners have for the bird. A stormy petrel is "a person regarded as a herald of trouble, strife or violence or someone who delights in such trouble, etc." (LME) What a difference!

Lastly, we shall take up two legendary or mythological creatures. In the dynastic times in China, the traditional symbols of royalty were the *dragon* and the *phoenix*. The dragon stood for the

54

king or emperor, and the phoenix for the queen or empress. There were few negative connotations and even today, these mythological creatures occasionally appear in traditional Chinese designs. As an auspicious creature that supposedly brings good luck, the dragon gave rise to the saying that parents 望子成龙—longing to see one's son become a dragon, that is, be successful. Also, the character for dragon often appears in male names: 龙翔(Dragon-soars), 龙虎 (Dragon-tiger), 一龙(A dragon).

To Westerners, however, the *dragon* is often a symbol of evil, a fierce monster that destroys and therefore must be destroyed. Several stories of saints or heroes deal with struggles against the monsters, which in most cases are slain in the end. The most notable perhaps is the story of Beowulf, an Anglo-Saxon epic around the year of 700 A. D. telling how the hero Beowful defeats a monster called Grendel, but is eventually killed in slaying a dragon. Interestingly, Western drawings of dragons show the monsters with wings, whereas in Chinese design and drawings, the creature has none.

The *phoenix*, in Western mythology, is associated with rebirth and resurrection. According to Greek legend, the phoenix lives a certain number of years—500 by one account. At the end of the period, it makes a nest, sings a death song, then sets fire to its nest by flapping its wings. The phoenix is burned to ashes, but from these ashes emerges a new bird. Thus, when a town, a place, or the headquarters building of an organization is destroyed by fire or other form of disaster, well-wishers may express the hope that it will "... like the legendary phoenix, rise from the ashes in new splendor."

In Chinese mythology, the phoenix was regarded as the king of birds. The male was called *feng*, 凤, the female, *huang*, 凰. Although there is no commonly known legend about the phoenix, as there is in Greek mythology, it is considered by Chinese as a creature of good omen. The character 凤 is often found in female names, as in 凤莲(Phoenix-lotus), 金凤(Golden-phoenix). The phoenix is also used in metaphors, standing for something rare and precious, for exampe, 凤毛麟角(phoenix feathers and unicorn horns—rarity of rarities).

# Chapter 7

## "Colorful" Language

### —More on Metaphor and Association

What does *green with envy* mean? Do people turn green when they have feelings of envy?

If *Paul was in a blue mood*, what kind of mood was he in? Was he joyful, excited, sad, or what?

In the expressions above, *green* and *blue* obviously do not mean just the color. Each has additional meanings—certain cultural associations—that are not evident from the words alone. In this chapter, the cultural associations of certain colors will be discussed, with "colorful" phrases and expressions in both English and Chinese used as illustration.

RED This color is usually associated with celebrations and joyful occasions, This is true in English-speaking countries as well as in China. So in English one finds, for example, *red-letter days*—holidays such as Christmas and other special days. Such days are printed in red on calendars, rather than in black for ordinary days. Another example is *to paint the town red*—meaning to celebrate widy, to go out to drink and have a good time; also, *roll out the red carpet for someone*, meaning to give a lavish welcome, as in: *He was the first*

*European head of state to visit their country*, and they rolled out the red carpet for him.

In Chinese there is the example of 红双喜—double happiness written in red—the traditional symbol for an event of special joy, such as a wedding. Similarly, in 开门红 the color red is symbolic of good fortune. This expression, however, should not be translated literally, but explained as meaning *to begin well*, *to make a good start*.

*Red* is also associated with certain emotions. In English, *to become red-faced* or her *face turned red* shows embarrassment, as it does in Chinese 脸红. But some English expressions involving the color red may not be so easily understood by Chinese. What is the meaning of *to see red* and *waving a red flag*? Both are associated with anger. The former means to be made angry or to become angry suddenly, the latter means doing something that could cause quick anger in other people, e. g., *The mere mention of his hated cousin's name was like waving a red flag in front of him*.

What should the English be for 你红光满面? Obviously, not *Your face is very red*, for that would mean embarrassment. *A ruddy complexion* means having a healthy pink glow, but does not carry the additional Chinese meaning of *energy and vigor*. One might say *You look so healthy and full of pep*, or *You look the very picture of health and energy*. Here, *red* need not be mentioned at all.

*Red* is the color associated with revolution and socialism. Expressions using *red*, such as *red guard* (红卫兵) exist in both English and Chinese. The English word *Red* with a capital "R", is often used as a synonym for a communist, usually in a derogatory sense. With certain Chinese expressions, however, the word *red* does not help convey the meaning in English. For example, *red and*

58

*expert* for 又红又专 is not as helpful as *both socialistminded and professionally qualified*. Likewise, 一颗红心, *a red heart* would not be understood unless explained as *loyal to the Party, having socialist virtues*.

WHITE To most Chinese and Westerners, *white* has certain similar connotations: purity, innocence, 洁白, 清白无辜. But does this apply to the English term *white lie*? Can a lie be innocent? The answer is that *a white lie* is supposed to be a harmless one. For example, an older sister might say to a younger sister and her boy friend: "You two go ahead to the movie. I've got a lot of work tonight. Thanks anyway." She knows that the two want to go out alone and that she was invited just for the sake of politeness. So she makes up the excuse that she has a lot of work to do. This is a *white lie*, one by which no harm or deceit is intended.

The connotation of the color *white* in the Chinese expression 红白喜事 would be confusing to most Westerners. It would probably be best not to translate the colors at all and merely say *weddings and funerals*. This is because *white* is the traditional color for brides at Western weddings. To have *white* at funerals would be offensive; to have *funerals* described as *happy occasions* (喜事) would be absolutely shocking to Westerners, although the expression reflects a certain philosophic attitude towards death of the Chinese.

It should be mentioned that in translating from Chinese to English, care should be taken with Chinese terms or expressions that contain the word 白. In some cases, 白 may refer to the color, but the English equivalent of the term or expression usually does not have the word *white*, as in 白菜 (Chinese cabbage), 白熊 (polar bear), 白蚁 (termite). In other cases, 白 has nothing to do with color at all; the meaning might be something like *in vain*, as in 白费

59

事(all in vain, a waste of time and energy), 白送(give away, free of charge, for nothing). Or 白 might mean *plain*, *unadulterated*, as in 白开水(boiled water), 白肉(plain boiled pork). It might even have no generalized meaning that is apparent, as in 坦白(to confess, to make a clean breast of things), 白痴(idiot), 白话(vernacular), etc. The important thing to remember is that not all that is 白 is *white*.

BLACK In both English and Chinese there are various terms indicating that *black* is often associated with negative qualities: *blacklist*(黑名单), *black market*(黑市)*black-hearted*(黑心的)and a number of others.

Interestingly, in business English, *in the black* has a good meaning; i. e., running a business profitably. Example: *Since he became manager, the company has been running in the black.*

The opposite of this is *be in the red*, meaning running a business at a loss, not making profit. These terms came from the color of the ink used in keeping accounts. Evidently *in the red* has been taken over in Chinese, as can be seen by the term 赤字.

BLUE In English, *blue* is usually associated with unhappy feelings. *In a blue mood*, mentioned at the beginning of this chapter, *or having the blues* means a sad, gloomy or depressed mood. Similar in meaning is *a blue Monday*—the first day of work or school after a pleasant, happy weekend. Example: *It was blue Monday and he just didn't feel like going back to work.*

*Blue* is also often associated with high social position or being aristocratic. *He's a real blue blood* means he's from an aristocratic family. Also, in American English, *blue book* is a book with the names of well-known persons, especially government officials.

GREEN Besides *green with envy*, English has the term *geen-*

*eyed monster* or just *green-eyed*—both meaning jealous, envious. However, in Chinese, an expression often used to describe envy or jealousy is 眼红 or 害了红眼病—literally *red-eyed*. Quite a different color for the same feeling! Interestingly, in the old days, the Chinese expression 戴绿帽子 ( literally *to wear a green hat* or *a green head band* ) meant to be a cuckold.

In English, *green* is also often used to indicate lacking in experience, training or knowledge, as in *You're expecting too much of him. He's still green, you know*. Similar in meaning is *greenhorn*—a person lacking experience, or a newcomer who is not familiar with local customs; the term is often used for immigrants and is mildly derogatory.

YELLOW Yellow appears in such Chinese expressions as 黄色电影, 黄色书刊, 黄色音乐。How should these be translated into English? Not as *yellow movies*, *yellow books*, *yellow music*. Such terms would not be understood. For 黄色 one might use *pornographic*, *trashy*, *obscene*, *filthy*, or *vulgar*, as in *pornographic pictures*, *obscene movies*, *filthy books*, *vulgar music*.

*Yellow* does appear in the English phrase *yellow journalism*—a kind of journalism with heavy emphasis on scandals, or presenting ordinary news in a sensational manner, sometimes even distorting the facts to create a sensational effect.

Also, in most American homes one can find a big thick book called *Yellow Pages*. This is a book with the telephone numbers of different shops, businesses, organizations, etc., arranged according to different categories; for example, all the food stores, all the radio shops, all the amusement parks, all the airlines, all the hospitals. It is a most useful book. Its pages are yellow, but it is not a 黄色书 in the Chinese sense.

Other colors carry certain connotations as well, but will not be mentioned here.

It might be pointed out that colors are not always represented the same way in different languages. How they are represented has been the subject of research for a number of years. All languages seem to have terms for *black* and *white*. *Red* is found in most languages, but not all. The next most common colors seem to be *yellow* and *green*, then *blue* and *brown*. Some languages have terms that seem to be equivalent, but the boundaries differ on where to separate one color from a neighboring one on the color spectrum. Most Chinese primary colors are the same or similar to those in English. Yet even so, there are differences, as in the following two examples:

青: *qing* can be green, as in green pepper(青椒);blue, as in blue sky (青天);or black, as in black cloth(青布).

黄: *huang* is usually yellow, but may be brown, as in soy bean paste (黄酱),or golden, as in gold(黄金).

It is interesting that different languages might use different color terms to describe the same object or phenomenon. An Englishman's *black* tea is not black, but *red* in Chinese 红茶;an American might *be bruised black and blue*, but a Chinese would be 被打得青一块,紫一块(literally: be beaten *blue* and *purple*).

We shall end this chapter with a story about the experiences of an American professor who came to China on a short lecture tour. One of his topics was *Cross-Cultural Understanding in International Relations*. The lecture was interesting and full of cross-cultural bits of information and anecdotes, but he kept using the expression *cultural red flags*, a term which he had coined. He used the term to denote things that one should avoid or handle carefully in a certain culture. *Red flag* was to be itnerpreted like *red traffic light*—people should stop and not go on. One can imagine his embarrassment when it was pointed out to him that *red flag* in China and in any other socialist country has very positive associations. He was guilty of the very thing that he was warning his audience not to do!

# Chapter 8

## Allusions

In most, if not all, languages, people embellish their speech or writing with references to characters or events from their history, legends, literature, religion, etc. Such references—allusions—not only make the language richer, but also make communication much more vivid and often easier. In Chinese, 你这个人真阿 Q or 她是个林黛玉式的人物 conveys so much information that hardly any further explanation needs to be made. And how expressive of the speaker's feelings are remarks like 原来是个空城计 and 真没意思，让我们来跑龙套.

Speech and writing in both English and Chinese abound with allusions, a reflection of the rich cultural heritage of the people who speak the languages. But such allusions are not always easy to understand, and without understanding there can be little appreciation. If one has never read Lu Xun's *The Trun Story of Ah Q* (《阿 Q 正传》), he would be at a loss to understand the remark about Ah Q. Merely to know the plot of *Dream of Red Mansions* (*Dream of the Red Chamber* 《红楼梦》) is hardly enough to appreciate the reference to the heroine 林黛玉 of the story. The same reasoning applies to allusions in English.

Many English allusions involve events or characters from the treasure house of English literature, especially from Shakespeare. Native speakers of English quote him every day, often without realizing they are doing so. Although his plays were written over three hundred years ago, many lines from his plays are cited commonly in everyday English: *forgive and forget*, *that's all Greek to me*, *all's well that ends well*, *all is not gold that glitters*, *discretion is the better part of valour*, etc.

There is a story about an elderly Englishman who had never seen a play by Shakespeare. He was invited to see *Hamlet*. "Well what did you think of it?" he was asked afterwards. He shook his head. "Just a lot of quotations put together," he replied. It never occurred to him that "those quotations" came from that very play *Hamlet*, and that Shakespeare himself was the author of those sayings! Shakespeare's insight into human beings, his sensitivity to the problems of state, and his genius with words have left an everlasting mark on the English language and on the thinking of English-speaking people all over the world.

A number of characters from Shakespeare's plays have come to stand for any person having the same general traits of those individual characters. Just as calling a person in Chinese 猪八戒 means he is similar in many ways to that crude, pleasure-seeking, often erratic, but sometimes lovable pig in the novel *Pilgrimage to the West* (《西游记》), so alluding to a person as a *Romeo* implies a handsome young man passionate, dashing, who has a way with women (from Shakespeare's *Romeo and Juliet*). Other characters or names from Shakespeare's plays or later English and American literature that have also become common household terms include:

　　*a Cleopatra*—a woman of breathtaking beauty; from Shakespeare's *Anthony and Cleopatra*.

*a Shylock* — a cruel, greedy, money-grabbing person, one who will go to no ends to acquire wealth; from *The Merchant of Venice*, another play by Shakespeare.

*a Dr. Jekyll and Mr. Hyde* — a person with a two-sided character, one said good and gentle (Dr. Jekyll), the other side evil and ruthless (Mr. Hyde); originated from Robert Louis Stevenson's novel *The Strange Case of Dr. Jekyll and Mr. Hyde*.

*a Frankenstein* (often *to create a Frankenstein* — usually a monster or thing that destroys its own creator; also, a person who creates such a thing; any hideous monster or creation; from the story with the same name *Frankenstein* by Mary W. Shelley. In the book, the main character, a medical student, takes the bones of corpses and creates a man-like monster that eventually destroys its own maker.

*a Sherlock Holmes* — a detective or shrewd person who has the uncanny ability to track down any quarry or solve any mystery through careful observation, scientific analysis, and logical reasoning; Sherlock Holmes is the hero of Sir Arthur Conan Doyle's well-known detective stories.

*an Uncle Tom* — a meek person, especially a black, who submits to indignities and sufferings without any thought or act of rebelling; a derogatory term originating from the main character in Harriet Beecher Stowe's novel *Uncle Tom's Cabin*.

*A Horatio Alger story* — any "success story", often considered a myth, of a poor boy who works hard and finally rises to the top, becoming rich, successful, famous; Horatio Alger was a writer whose stories generally had the same such plot. His best-known books are the *Ragged Dick* series and the *Tattered Tom* series.

*a Catch-22 situation* — an impossible situation; one in which the solution or success depends on mutually dependent factors: A depends on B; B, in turn, is dependent on A; so it is an interlocking situation in which there is no way out; the term comes from a postwar American novel titled *Catch-22* by Joseph Heller.

Another common source of allusions in English and American

66

speech and writing is legends and mythology. Western literature and art as a whole, in fact, show the strong influence of Greek and Roman mythology, and to a lesser extent, Norse mythology:

Geographical names

*Europe*— Europa, a princess who was abducted and carried off by a bull to Crete; the bull was actually Zeus, king of the gods in Greek mythology.

*Atlantic Ocean*— Atlantis, a mythical island in what is now the Atlantic Ocean.

*Paris*— Paris, son of the king of Troy; in Greek mythology, his abduction of the beautiful Helen led to the Trojan War.

Names of days of the week

*Tuesday*—Tyr, Norse god of war noted for his bravery.

*Wednesday*— Woden, most powerful of gods in AngloSaxon mythology.

*Thursday*— Thor, Norse god of thunder.

*Friday*— Freya, goddess of music.

*Saturday*— Saturn, Roman god of agriculture.

Scientific names and terms

*Uranium* (chemistry) — Uranus, Roman mythological god of the heavens.

*Mercury* (chemistry) —Mercury, messenger of the Roman gods; also, god of commerce and science.

*Mars* (fourth planet from the sun) — Mars, Roman god of war.

*Jupiter* (largest planet in the solar system)—Jupiter, god of the sky, king of the Roman gods.

Certain stories from mythology are so common that English-speaking youngsters can recite them offhand. Some are known in non English-speaking countries as well. The story of the Trojan horse, for example, can be found in textbooks and writings in many countries throughout the world. It is often cited as a warning to be

67

alert against the enemy from the inside, against blindly accepting innocent-looking gifts under suspicious circumstances. The story of Prometheus, one of the great Greek gods, may not be so well-known, but his love of mankind, his gift of fire to men, his defiance of Zeus, the king of the gods, his unflinching determination in the face of threats and suffering —all these have been eulogized in prose and poetry by writers in different languages. Prometheus has become a symbol of love of mankind and of resistance to oppression all over the earth.

Likewise popular in many countries is the story of Odysseus (also commonly known as Ulysses), the hero of the Greek epic poem *The Odyssey* by Homer. Odysseus's many adventures, the hardships and trials he endured, the struggles agains tone enemy after another—some human, some monstrous, some fierce, some sweet and enchanting— make delightful reading in any language. In some ways *The Odyssey* is like our *Pilgrimage to the West*. There are numerous English allusions to events or people in the story, such as Cyclops, a one-eyed giant that Odysseus had to deal with; or Circe, the beautiful enchantress who charmed her victims and then turned them into swine.

Other terms or phrases alluding to mythology that have become commonplace in the English language include:

*a Herculean task*—task requiring great power of body or mind. Hercules was a powerfully-built hero of ancient Greek mythology. As punishment for a serious misdeed, he was ordered to do twelve virtually impossible tasks. Hercules succeeded in doing all and was rewarded with immortality. Example: *It was a Herculean task, but he managed to do it*.

*an Achilles heel*—the weak or vulnerable point of a person (organization, country, etc.). The story is that Achilles, one of the Greek heroes in the *Iliad*, another epic attributed to Homer, was taken by his mother when he was a child and dipped in the river Styx to make him invulnerable. The water washed every part of his body except the heel in his mother's hand. It was precisely at this vulnerable point that Achilles was later killed in battle. Example: *He would be an excellent candidate for the position. He has energy, knowledge and experience. But he's got an Achilles heel—his terrible temper. Three months ago he beat up a colleague in an argument.*

*a Pandora's box*—a present or something which may seem valuable, but which brings trouble and misfortune. In Greek mythology, Pandora was the first woman, sent to the earth by the gods as a form of punishment. Zeus (or Jupiter, in Roman mythology) gave her a box which she was to give to the man who married her. When this box was finally opened, all the evils that were in it flew out, and since then have caused trouble to mankind. Example: *The project, which seemed so promising, turned out to be a Pandora's box.*

*a Damocles sword* (the sword of Damocles) — forthcoming danger, or danger that is always present. Damocles served under Dionysius, a tyrant who ruled over Syracuse. Damocles loved wealth and pleasure and envied the life of his master. Once after excessive praise from Damocles in which such envy was all too clear, Dionysius invited him to a feast; but hanging over Damocles' head was a sword suspended by a single hair. Damocles sat through the banquet in constant fear. Dionysius wanted to show how dangerous his life could be. Example: *The terrorists had been caught and jailed. But the two leaders had escaped with machine guns and explosives. This fact hung like the sword of Damocles over the police commissioner's head.*

Religion is another source of allusions. In English-speaking countries, with Christianity as the dominant religion, one naturally expects to find a number of references to characters or events in Christianity's sacred book, the Bible:

*a messiah*—a liberator or expected liberator of an oppressed people; in

69

the Old Testament, it was prophesied that Messiah would some day come and deliver the Jews from oppression.

*like (a) Moses leading his people*—Moses was an Israelite prophet and leader (around the 13th or 14th century, B. C.), one of the greatest figures in the Old Testament; he led the Israelites out of slavery in Egypt—a trek through the desert that took 40 years.

*a Solomon*— a very wise man; Solomon was king of the Hebrews around the 10th century, B. C., and was noted for his wisdom.

*David and Goliath*—David was a shepherd boy; he killed the Philistine giant Goliath with a shot from his sling and later became king of the Hebrews; in metaphorical use, David and Goliath stand for a contest between two persons, enterprises, countries, etc, in which one is much smaller and /or weaker, but in which the smaller/ weaker one wins out.

*a Judas*—a traitor; Judas Iscariot was one of the 12 apostles of Jesus Christ; according to accounts, Judas betrayed Jesus to the Jewish priests for 30 pieces of silver.

*thirty pieces of silver*— money or other reward for an act of betrayal (see above).

*a kiss of death*— an act of affection or good-will on the surface, but which precedes or is itself an act of malice; from Judas Iscariot's kissing of Jesus in his betrayal.

Non-native English speakers often have trouble when they come across allusions to sports in English, unless they know the game which is alluded to. This is especially true of American English, which abounds with expressions from two sports games—baseball and American football—that originated in the U. S., but which are comparatively unknown in many other countries:

baseball

*to not get to first base*—to fail early or at the very beginning of an attempt; e.g., *She attracted him at first sight and he made elaborate plans to court her, but he didn't even get to first base.*

70

*to have two strikes against someone* — to be in a very disadvantageous position; e. g. , *When he applied for the job, he already had two strikes against him: he didn't have a college diploma like the other applicants, and he was ten minutes late for his interview.*

## American football

*to carry the ball* — to have the main responsibility for getting a certain task or job done; e. g. , *The negotiations are the key to the undertaking; we'd better ask Mumford to carry the ball.*

*an armchair quarterback* — person who talks about how something should be done, but who is not actually involved and has no responsibility; e. g. , *It's easy to be an armchair quarterback, but your idea wouldn't have worked at all!*

## Common figures of speech from other sports:

### boxing

*to be down and out* — in a hopeless situation after trying; e. g. , *He made one last effort, but it didn't work. There was nothing left to do but close shop — he was down and out.*

*to hit below the belt* — in a contest or in dealing with another person, to do something improper in order to hurt the other; e. g. , *How could you do a thing like that? That's hitting below the belt!*

### card games

*play one's trump card(s)* — to take a course of action in which one believes one holds the advantage (usually against an opponent); e. g. , *Just when his rivals started to rub their hands with glee, he played his trump card.*

*squeeze play* — action which puts an opponent into such a position that whatever he does, he loses or must give up something valuable; e. g. , *He was caught in a squeeze play; if he agreed to the demands, he would lose a fortune; if he didn't agree, he would have to close down his shop.*

### fishing

*to swallow the bait, hook, line and sinker* — to be taken in completely

71

by some preliminary offer or attraction; e.g., *They knew he liked to collect art goods, so when they promised him a Ming dynasty drawing, he swallowed the bait, hook, line and sinker.*

Perhaps the most troublesome of all allusions are those that involve recent or contemporary events, personalities, products, etc., of a certain society. Unless one is well-acquainted with developments in a certain country, one would be at a loss about the meaning and connotations of terms or expressions such as those below:

*a Rambo*—Rambo is the character made famous by American movies around the mid-1980s. He is a tough exsoldier of the Vietnam war, resourceful, taciturn, lonely, somewhat "odd". Rambo gets involved in numerous risky adventures or in one violent situation after another. He makes miraculous escapes from impossible situations by shooting, knifing, bombing or burning his way out. Unbelievable as his feats may seem, and repugnant as some of his violent actions may appear, he is the current hero of many American boys and young men.

*as American as apple pie*— Apple pie is one of the favorite desserts of Americans. It is often served with ice cream. Apple pie was supposedly first made by Americans, or else first made popular by them. The expression is used to emphasize that something is genuinely American.

*a Pepsodent smile*—A smile showing beautiful white teeth; from advertisements for Pepsodent tooth paste, one of the better known brands in the U.S..

*an Ivy Leaguer*—Generally a person from a well-to-do family who goes to an established and prestigious university such as Harvard, Yale, Princeton, Columbia, Pennsylvania, Cornell, Dartmouth, Brown.

*That's something for Ripley*—A number of American newspapers carry a feature titled "Believe it or not," by Ripley. It presents strange or unusual facts or happenings that are all supposed to be true and can be verified, but because they are so odd, so out of the ordinary, people find them hard to believe. The expression is generally used when referring to something that

72

seems incredible but is probably true.

In Chinese many allusions are also drawn from the same sources: literature, history, religion, sports.

From literature one finds that most allusions are characters or happenings from the novels *Dream of Red Mansions*, *Water Margin*, *Three Kingdoms*, *Pilgrimage to the West*. For example:

刘姥姥进了大观园—Granny Liu entering a palatial mansion—a country person's awe at the splendor of the environment/person overawed by the magnificence, sophistication, excellence, etc. of the surroundings.

智多星—Zhiduoxing, the nickname for Wu Yong, the resourceful strategist of the peasant army in *Water Margin* — resourceful person; mastermind.

三顾茅庐—make three calls at the thatched cottage (as Liu Bei did when he sought the aid of Zhuge Liang, a master strategist then living in seclusion) —repeatedly request someone to take up a responsible post.

万事俱备, 只欠东风—Everything is ready, all that's needed is an east wind—all is reay except what is crucial.

猪八戒倒打一耙—Zhubajie (the pig in *Pilgrimage to the West*) puts the blame on his innocent victim—make unfounded countercharges/recriminate.

China's history, with over 2 000 years of it well recorded, has provided allusions such as:

四面楚歌—hear the sounds of the Chu all around—be besieged on all sides /be utterly isolated/ be in desperate straits.

身在曹营心在汉—body in Cao, but heart in Han —in one place physically but another place in mind and heart.

围魏救赵—besiege Wei to rescue Zhao—relieve the besieged by besieging the base of the besiegers.

完璧归赵—return the jade intact to the State of Zhao —return sth. to its owner in perfect condition.

Chinese fables are another source of allusions. Phrases like the following are very common both in speech and in writing:

画蛇添足—add feet to a drawing of a snake—gild the lily (paint the lily).

守株待兔—stand by a stump waiting for hares to come and dash themselves against it—trust to chance and windfalls/waiting for gains without pains.

拔苗助长—try to help the shoots grow by pulling them upward—spoil things by excessive enthusiasm.

刻舟求剑—nick the boat to seek the sword (make a notch on the side of a moving boat to show where to look for the sword which dropped overboard)—take measures without regard to changes in circumstances.

对牛弹琴—play music to an ox—cast pearls before swine.

黔驴技穷—the (provincial) Guizhou donkey has exhausted its tricks —at one's wits' end/at the end of one's rope.

The many legends of Chinese folklore have provided such expressions as:

过着牛郎织女的生活—the Herd-boy and the Spinning Maid (mythical lovers separated by the Milky Way)—husband and wife living apart.

八仙过海,各显神通—like the Eight Immortals crossing the sea, each showing his or her special prowess — people doing the same job, but each in his own special way, and each doing it well.

Buddhism and Taoism have given rise to:

临时抱佛脚—embrace Buddha's feet in one's hour of need—seek help at the last moment/make a frantic last-minute effort.

做一天和尚撞一天钟—go on tolling the bell as long as one is a monk—do the least that is expected of one/take a passive attitude towards one's work.

道高一尺,魔高一丈—the truth grows a foot high, the evil grows to ten/as virtue rises one foot, vice rises ten—the more illumination, the more temptation/Where God has his church, the devil will have his chapel.

放下屠刀,立地成佛—drop one's cleaver and become a Buddha—

achieve salvation as soon as one gives up evil.

人面兽心—the face of a man but the heart of a beast—beast in human form /A fair face may hide a foul heart.

Allusions originating in sports or recreation:

马后炮—cannon behind the horse (Chinese chess)—belated action or advice /belated effort.

舍车马, 保将帅—give up a chariot to save the marshal (Chinese chess) —make minor sacrifice to safeguard major interests.

异曲同工—different tunes sung with equal skill—different approaches but equally satisfactory results.

一唱一和—one sings, the other harmonizes —sing the same tune/echo each other.

Interestingly, Chinese opera has inspired expressions like:

亮相—strike a pose on the stage (of Beijing opera, dancing, etc.)—declare one's position/state one's views.

跑龙套—run through the steps of the dragon dance—play a bit role/be a utility man.

唱红脸—wear the red mask of the hero—play the hero/pretend to be generous and kind.

唱白脸—wear the white mask of the villain—play the villain/pretend to be harsh and severe.

粉墨登场—make oneself up and go on stage—embark upon a venture/make one's appearance in a certain position or role (derogatory in meaning).

Obviously, most foreigners coming across allusions in Chinese will be at a loss. The suggested practice for Chinese interpreters or people conversing with English-speaking visitors is to give a rough equivalent or a brief explanation without going into details, so as not to distract from the main thread of the idea being discussed. One might say for:

将他一军—to put someone in check (exact equivalent, exact allusion).

白骨精—the White Boned Demon, an evil spirit who often took the guise of a charming young woman in the novel *Pilgrimage to the West* (a fairly detailed explanation).

此地无银三百两—a saying that means a guilty person gives himself away by conspicuously protesting his innocence.

# Chapter 9

## Euphemisms

*"Those Macedonians,"* said he, *"are a rude and clownish people, they call a spade a spade."*

　　　　　—Plutarch, *Apothegms of Great Commanders, Philip*

*"In our Victorian dislike of the practice of calling a spade a bloody shovel, it is not necessary to go to the opposite extreme of calling it an agricultural implement."*

—Robert W. Seton-Watson (from *The Great Quotations*)

Almost all cultures seem to have certain notions or things that people try to avoid mentioning directly, even when there is such a term in the language. When such a notion or thing has to be referred to, the practice will be to substitute a different term or phrase that sounds better.

One of the terms that seem to be almost universally avoided is *death*. For whatever reason, the use of a number of inoffensive substitutes is required for the word *die* or 死, or whatever the basic word for this notion may be in a particular language.

Consider the following list of such substitutes found in English and Chinese:

In English: *go* (e.g. He's gone.), *depart*, *depart from the world forever*, *decease*, *pass away*, *breathe one's last*, *go the way of all flesh*, *pay one's debt to nature*, *go to a better world*, *be in (go to) heaven*, *be with God*, *etc*.

In Chinese: 去逝,逝世,故去,病故,寿终,亡故,牺牲,作古, 谢世,弃世,与世长辞,心脏停止跳动,去见马克思,etc.

This list is not at all complete, not even of the more common ones. As for the less common ones, in English there are such as Shakespeare's *shuffle off this mortal coil*, and Mark Twain's *release: It seemed to him that life was but a trouble, at best, and he more than half envied Jimmy Hodges, so lately released.* (*The Adventures of Tom Sawyer*)

All of the phrases or expressions above show a positive or at least neutral feeling towards the deceased person. Some of them reflect different attitudes towards death and hereafter; for example, *go to a better world*, *be with God*. One or two would generally be used by a person speaking about himself, as 反正我过不了几年就 去见马克思了(In a few years I'll be seeing Marx anyway).

However, in English there are expressions such as *kick the bucket*, *be done for*, that are highly informal or slang terms. Similar Chinese expressions are: 丧命、毕命、一命呜呼, 呜呼哀哉. Obviously, they are not commendatory terms and should not be classified as euphemisms. But no matter what the differences, they are all substitutes for the same notion: *death*.

The examples above illustrate the general characteristics of euphemisms—the use of a pleasant, polite, or harmless-sounding term in the place of those considered unpleasant, rude, or offensive.

Besides *death*, there are a number of other notions often expressed in euphemistic terms. These might be grouped under several categories, some of which are mentioned here:

78

Physical shortcomings, old age, certain functions of the body, sexual acts. For example: *plain* (for *ugly*), *heavy set*, *on the heavy side* (for *fat*—usually when referring to men), *slender* (for *skinny*), *physically handicapped* (for *crippled*), *senior citizens* (for *elderly people*), *advanced in age*, *elderly* (for *old*).

Euphemisms for certain functions of the body deserve special mention here, mainly because ignorance of them may cause considerable embarrassment. As in many other languages, English has a variety of terms in this category. One does not need to explain why one has to *go to the toilet; go to the men's (ladies') room*, *rest room*, *washroom*, *lavatory*, *the John*. If one does have to explain, it would be *to wash one's hands*, *to relieve oneself*, or *to see a man about a horse*, *or because nature calls* (the last two in a humorous vein); if a woman, one does so *to powder her nose*, *to freshen up*. If one has been having trouble with one's diet, or has an upset stomach, the doctor might ask *How are your bowel movements?* and say *We need a stool specimen*. For Chinese studying abroad, or for interpreters accompanying foreigners to the doctor's, not knowing the English for such things can be quite a predicament.

Certain trends in American euphemisms should be noted. In recent years, more and more euphemisms are being used in talking about social life and social affairs. For example, there are fewer occupations called *jobs;* many have become *professions*. The names of some professions can be very misleading; the best example is *sanitary engineer*, a name for a garbage collector.

In times of economic difficulties, such as during a depression, finding a profession may not be easy, even a job of the most lowly-paid kind involving manual labor might be hard to get. Then one might become *unemployed;* or to use a more recent and sophisticated term, be *involuntarily leisured*. Of course, long periods of such "leisure" can be quite miserable, especially for the poor. The term *poor*, though, is having a struggle to survive. During the last twenty years or so, several other words have been trying to take its place, at least among educated circles and in "officialese". As some unfortunate person put it: *"At first I was poor, then I became needy, later I was underprivileged. Now I'm disadvantaged. I still don't have a cent to my name, but I sure have a great vocabulary."*

In education, euphemisms are likewise prolific. Some people prefer *educator* to *teacher*. Students are still *students*, but comments about them need to be carefully considered. "Negative expressions" have given way to "more positive" ones. The comment for a below-average student might be that *she/he is working at her/his own level*. That doesn't hurt anyone's pride, does it? *Can do better work with help* doesn't sound bad either; it's just a less offensive way of saying a student is *slow* or *stupid*. Of course it would never do to call a youngster *stupid* or *lazy;* neither the student nor the parents would tolerate that. So a lazy child is an *underachiever*. The term doesn't jolt but neither does it indicate how much or how little she/he has achieved. The student might be barely getting by, or even flunking. Other examples: *depends on others to do his / her work = cheats in class; has a tendency to stretch the truth = sometimes lies; takes other people's things without permission = steals*.

Since the purpose of using euphemisms is to reduce the unpleasantness of a term or notion, it is natural that announcements or publications of businesses, organizations or governments will often resort to them. On the New York subway a fire once broke out on the tracks and delayed the trains. This was announced as : *We have a*

80

*fire situation*. President Ronald Reagan, who had promised the American public to *cut taxes*, called for *revenue enhancements* instead of *tax increases* when he was faced with the realities of national finances. In the area of labor-management relations, at times of labor unrest, there has been talk about what steps to take in dealing with *industrial action*, meaning *strikes*. In another area, when the U.S. government explained its program to gas chickens in Pennsylvania in late 1983 in order to control a harmful disease, it was said to have *depopulated the birds*. The reason such a word was chosen was "to avoid saying *slaughter*", according to a federal information officer. Evidently *kill* was also considered as far too blunt.

In international relations, "dressed-up" expressions have become commonplace. When the Reagan administration decided to engage in "a little psychological warfare" (Secretary of State George Shultz's words) against Libya in 1986, it planted false stories about Libyan leader Muammar Gaddafi's "new plans for terrorist action and U.S. preparations to retaliate." When the true story later leaked out, there was an outcry. White House officials hurriedly explained that they had not deliberately misled the public. What they had done, they claimed, was merely to organize a "disinformation" campaign—a weak attempt to make the matter appear more acceptable. However, such efforts and the ethics of the whole affair led to a "modest dissent" by the State Department's spokesman, Bernard Kalb. He resigned, much to the embarrassment of the White House.

In 1983, after the U.S. sent its armed forces into Grenada, Reagan showed his irritation with reporters at their "frequent use of the word *invasion*." "This", he said, "was a *rescue mission*." Actually, it was Reagan himself who had first called it an *invasion*.

Grenada is a Third World country. Most such countries are poor. The term for these countries was at first *under-developed nations;* later *developing nations* and *emerging nations* took its place. The United Nations calls them *LDCs — less-developed countries*.

The military seems to have a particular fondness for euphemisms. This is natural when one considers the business it has to deal with. There are only *advances*, no *retreats;* only *victories*, no *defeats*. In this respect the most recent Commanders-in-chief of the American armed forces, Jimmy Carter and Ronald Reagan, have led the way. The helicopter raid to rescue American captives in Iran in 1980 was called *an incomplete success*. The missile known as MX for missile experimental did not really have a name until Reagan began calling it the *Peacekeeper*. At lower military levels, the wanton killing of Vietnamese was sometimes called *wasting the enemy* or *pacification* by American soldiers. This reminds one of the treatment of prisoners in Nazi Germany during World War II —some carried papers with "Rückkehr unerwünscht" (return unwanted); others were assigned "Sonderbehandlung" (special treatment). Both meant *death*. When losses are on one's own side, the natural tendency is to soften the blow. The term *light casualties* is common for loss of lives in combat. When deaths or injuries are caused by one side's own action, the need for tactful language is even greater. Many gems have been produced over the years, but few can improve on this : *accidental delivery of ordnance* for the shelling of American troops by Americans.

Most surprise attacks against an enemy are now termed *preemptive strikes*. *pre-empt* means to do something before it is done by others. A pre-emptive strike gives the impression that the action is considered necessary to deter an enemy attack. It therefore seems morally right, whereas a *surprise attack* connotes a sneaky action, morally wrong. An even newer term is *surgical strike*, giving the military action a humane tone. Surgery is generally used to remove something malignant, to correct a defect, or for treatment of injuries. A *surgical strike* thus conveys the idea that it is a necessary military action to remove an evil.

# Chapter 10

## Taboos

We have seen that certain words or notions are avoided because of unpleasantness, and roundabout expressions are substituted—thus we have euphemisms. But some words or expressions are to be avoided because tradition or social custom strongly frowns on their use. These are verbal taboos. Just as violating a cultural taboo can be quite offensive, so it is with a verbal taboo. using a certain word or mentioning a certain topic in public would be shocking or cause strong disapproval. Those who frequently violate local taboos will soon find themselves social outcasts. However, peoples of different countries do not all agree on what are taboos, therefore it is important for the foreign language learner to acquaint himself with such things.

English and Chinese have certain areas of agreement on taboos. Excreta and acts of human excretion (these are euphemistic terms themselves) are to be avoided in polite conversation. In English, if they must be mentioned, then the terms should be euphemistic ones. In Chinese, they are also taboo, but the Chinese attitude is less strict, and sometimes one will hear people say 吃喝拉撒睡 in serious public talk or conversation.

Talking about sexual intercourse and certain parts of the body is

84

taboo in both cultures. In the U. S. though, the sexual revolution of the 1960s changed this somewhat. The tendency in English-speaking countries in recent years is toward a freer, more open attitude. Thus *to make love*, *to have sex with* , etc. are not at all uncommon in writing now. But even these are slightly "dressed-up" terms. However. so-called "four letter words" ( *fuck*, *tits*, etc.) are still considered improper in most conversations, especially in mixed groups with both women and men.

In many languages, swear words are taboo. This is generally true of both English and Chinese, but here further explanations are necessary. One is that certain swear words seem to be more offensive than others and consequently the social prohibition against their use is stricter. In English, *Jesus Christ*! *Holy Mary*! *son of a bitch*! would be such terms, whereas *Damn*! *Damn it*! *Hell*! would be less so. Notice that most English swear words have to do with Christian religious terms or names. In Chinese, which seems to have fewer set swear words, 他妈的 seems to be the most common, one that doesn't arouse too strong disapproval. Another qualification would be the age, sex and occupation of the people involved. Swearing by a child will often bring quick scolding from an elder; swearing by a woman would be considered indecent; swearing by a teacher would be regarded as highly improper. A third qualification would have to do with the setting or environment. The taboo is stricter in public speaking, in the classroom, or at gatherings of people with a certain social status. It would be less strict at home, at one's work place, or in one's office, and in buses, subways and crowded market places.

It should be mentioned that people's reactions to swear words may change. Some swear words become rather common and gradually lose their shock value. They are no longer so offensive. Some of the swear words mentioned above are now frequently heard in young people's conversation. For non-native speakers, though, it is better to be cautious in using profanity.

Now, turning to the dissimilarities, we might begin with the little incident below.

An American teacher in her early fifties was invited to the home of a young Chinese colleague for dinner. When she arrived, the 4-year old daughter of the hostess was presented to her. "Hello Auntie," the little girl chirped in English. This was how her mother had taught her to greet grown-up women.

"No, no, not Auntie," the mother hurriedly corrected. "Say Granny!"

"No, not Granny, please. Just call me Auntie."

"But that's not polite for her. You're so much older than I am."

The American woman's face flushed a second, then she smiled and said, "Just have her call me Auntie; I'd prefer that."

What was the reason for the awkwardness in this situation?

It was one of different attitudes towards age.

Age, to most British and Americans, is one of the things considered improper to ask a stranger or a person that one does not know well. Besides age, other such matters include one's income, marital status, politics and religion. Some people may not mind and will readily talk about such things, but it is not polite to ask unless the other person shows that he/she will not be offended. Thus questions like the following, although inoffensive to Chinese, should be avoided when conversing with English-speaking people:

How old are you?

What's your age?

How much do you make?

What's your income?

How much did that dress cost you?

How much did you pay for that car?

Are you married or single?

How come you're still single?

So you're divorced? What was the reason? Couldn't you two get along?

Are you a Republican or a Democrat?

Why did you vote for—?

Do you go to church?

What's your religion?

Are you Catholic?

If for some reason such information is absolutely necessary, one might give the reason before asking the question; for example, at a hotel, hospital, or when filling out a form:

"For registration purposes, I need certain information. Would you mind telling me your—(age, marital status, etc.)?"

"These people need some information about you. Could you tell me—?"

Sometimes, one may want personal information about another person in order to know how to handle or deal with that person, not for curiosity's sake or registration purposes. In such cases, the matter should be handled tactfully. Talking about oneself first and then leading up to the other will often get the desired results. This might be done in the manner below:

"I'm married and we have one child, a daughter. We're a closely knit family, but I find I have so little time to spend with my wife and daughter. It's so frustrating at times..."

The other person might then say, "I have the same problem too. My children often complain that..."

87

If one is interested in another's political views, for example, one might lead up to the matter in an offhand general manner:

"There's been quite a bit of news in the papers about the coming American presidential elections. I find it quite interesting but sometimes a bit confusing, especially because I was told that Americans don't feel that strongly about politics. Maybe I'm wrong. How do Americans feel about such things? And do most Americans belong to a party?"

The other person will often answer such questions, or make some comments, and in the process, may talk about himself:

"Well, not really. They might register as a Democrat or a Republican, but they don't feel that they *belong* to that party. In fact, they might vote any way in an election. For instance, I generally consider myself a Democrat, but in the last elections, I voted Republican because..."

Thus the desired information comes out.

One of the reasons behind the taboo on questions about personal matters is that English-speaking people place a high value on *privacy*. The English have a saying *A man's home is his castle*, meaning a man's home is sacred to him; no one should come in without permission. So it is also with his life and personal affairs. To ask questions such as those mentioned above would be considered prying into an individual's personal life, which is another form of invading a person's "castle".

The whole matter of *privacy*, as understood in the West, is alien to many Chinese—in fact, there is no equivalent Chinese term for *privacy*. This may be due, in part, to the close living arrangements of the Chinese. Villages with scores or a hundred or more families densely packed in a small area have been typical of the Chinese countryside for centuries. Even in towns and cities in the north of China, the 四合院, a quadrangle with several households around a single courtyard, meant continual contact among members within

88

the compound. With such arrangements, privacy would be hardly possible. This is quite different from the individual houses —often with a sizeable surrounding yard or garden for each—that have been characteristic of Western countries until comparatively recent times. Another reason may be the communal spirit or spirit of brotherhood that has long prevailed among the Chinese. Close contact and a certain amount of mutual dependence and mutual concern mean that one person's affairs are also very much the affairs of one's family, one's neighbors, and even the larger community that one belongs to. How different this is from the *privacy* so treasured in the West!

In connection with Western feelings about *privacy*, there are certain English expressions meant to be deliberately vague. If a person says *I'm going out*, one should not ask where. If he /she says *I have an appointment*, it would be improper to ask with whom or what kind of appointment it is. Likewise, if a woman claims she has a headache, it would not do to be over-solicitous and ask what the trouble is, or whether or not she needs some medicine. If she really is in distress, she will probably say so. A non-native speaker should know that the expressions mentioned above are often excuses for not doing something or not accepting some offer or invitation. They are "defensive" expressions to stop further questions.

In recent times, there has been a growing tendency to regard as taboo language that reflects a demeaning attitude towards certain groups in society. Many people are sensitive to what is called sexist language and racist language. We shall say a few words here about each of these.

Sexist language in its present day connotation means primarily language demeaning to the female sex. In some cultures, there are distinct male and female languages. In other cultures, there may be different levels of language—high prestige and low prestige; females may use only the one with low prestige. Studies of sexism in the English language—begun by American women concerned with the effects of language on people's attitude towards women—showed that English is male-centered, biased in favor of men, derogatory towards women. In speech and writing, for example, a person of unknown sex is referred to as *he*, not *she;* the person presiding over a meeting is the *chairman*, even if she is a woman, thus leading to such forms of address as *Madame Chairman*. The history of our world is the history of *mankind*, not *womankind*. There are farmore words denoting a sexually promiscuous female than there are for a promiscuous male. Similarly, synonyms for *prostitute* far outnumber those for *whoremonger*, reflecting greater tolerance towards men in the matter of sexual liberties. *Sissy* is a term of light contempt for a girlish boy or a womanish man, whereas *tomboy*, for a girl who behaves like a spirited boy, carries pleasant connotations.

The Chinese *Han* language reveals similar sexism. In the old days, women were often regarded as ignorant, lowly; 妇人之见 and 男子汉不同妇人一般见识, for example, virtually ridicule a woman's point of view. A wife was little more than one who did the household chores, as indicated by names like 家里的, 内人. What's more, her lot and her place in society were wholly dependent on her husband, as this common saying shows: 夫唱妇随(literally: the husband sings and the wife follows; or: the wife keeps harmony, while the husband sets the tune).

A sexist bias is even more noticeable in the Chinese written language; that is, in its characters. The number of Chinese characters denoting negative qualities that contain the female radical 女 is astounding. Here are just a few: 奸 (evil, wicked, treacherous); 婪

90

(greedy, avaricious); 嫉 (jealous, envious); 媚 (flatter, fawn on). Likewise, the character 阴 (*yin*, in Chinese philosophy or medicine, symbolizing the feminine or negative principle in nature) is used to form a number of terms of negative meaning: 阴毒 (sinister, insidious); 阴森 (gloomy, ghastly, gruesome); 阴谋 (plot, scheme, conspiracy).

In the last few decades, with the great change of women's status in China, certain corresponding changes have taken place in the language. Demeaning terms such as 内人, 家里的 are no longer common. Married women retain their surname, rather than losing it and being known simply as 刘太太 or 张太太 (Mrs. Liu or Mrs. Zhang). Women as well as men are addressed as *Comrade*, implying equality as well as other positive connotations. Outright expressions of ridicule or contempt are likely to be frowned on or censured.

Racism is the belief that some human races are inherently inferior to others (Light and Keller, 1985). Racist language is that which shows a bias against certain racial or ethnic groups; it is language that degrades or belittles them. In the English language, much of the bias is against blacks, whether intentional or not. In an earlier chapter it was mentioned that the color *white* generally stands for innocence, purity, cleanliness, chastity—all words with positive, pleasant connotations. On the other hand, the color *black* is associated with wickedness, evil, filth; e. g., *blackguard*, *blacklist*, *black mark*. A member of a family that the others are ashamed of is called a *black sheep*, not a *white sheep*. Even a lie, if it is a *white lie*, is not so bad as an ordinary lie, or *black lie*. Small wonder that some blacks have complained that even semantics have conspired to make *black* seem ugly and degrading. Besides these, there are terms like *nigger*, *boy* (for an adult black man), which are outright offensive. These are seldom heard now, except by people with racist views, used deliberately to be insulting or as a term of contempt.

However, it is not just blacks who are called degrading names in the U. S. There are names for other racial or ethnic groups as well: Italians are called *dagos;* Jews—*kikes;* Poles—*polacks;* Chinese —*chinks;* Japanese—*japs;* just to mention some. All of these are insulting names, reflecting strong racial prejudice.

Sometimes, one will hear slurring racial remarks or "ethnic jokes"—jokes about the supposed stupidity, ignorance, oddities, of certain groups. Such jokes may appear funny, but they are offensive nevertheless.

The Chinese *Han* language likewise shows trace of racism, although there have been considerable improvements since the People's Republic was set up. Prior to that, belittling or outright degrading terms for non-*Han* people were not uncommon: virtually calling certain Chinese ethnic groups barbarians, such as 蛮人; derisive expressions such as 蒙古大夫(Mongolian doctor —a quack or incompetent doctor) to show off the assumed superiority of one's own ethnic group. Since the middle of the century, with the equality of the different nationalities adopted as national policy and expressly stated in the Constitution, such racist terms and expressions have largely disappeared from the language, but not completely. Today, one can still hear foreigners referred to as 鬼子 (devils), or 洋鬼子(foreign devils). The term 大鼻子(big nose ) may not be quite so offensive, but it is hardly one of respect.

In Chinese, the color *black* is also used in a number of undesirable or negative terms, such as 黑心(black hearted—wicked, evil) 黑帮 (black gang—counter-revolutionaries), 黑话 (black talk—language of the underworld or of counter-revolutionaries). This does not reflect a Chinese prejudice towards blacks. Nor is there a favorable bias towards whites. A white face in Beijing opera stands for a villain; and in socialist terminology, terms like 白区 (white area), or 白色恐怖 (white terror), indicate areas controlled by, or terror caused by, reactionary forces. Nevertheless, blacks in China who understand Chinese are often sensitive to such terms. They have been known to complain about such language and people should be aware of their feelings. There should be discretion in using these terms, even though no offence is intended.

In spite of the changes mentioned above, and in some respects the progress has been considerable, both English and Chinese still retain traces of sexism and racism. Unless one is careful, one can easily offend without realizing it. Keeping up with the language changes in these respects is needed of course. More important, though, is developing a sensitivity to the feelings of those who suffer from the bias, whether women or ethnic groups unfairly treated. Understanding the injustice of social inequality is perhaps the best guarantee against racist or sexist behavior, whether intentional or not.

# Chapter 11

## Language of Respect and Humility

An English woman in a Chinese park came across an eiderly Chinese one morning. Attracted by his long flowing white beard she approached him and asked politely in Chinese: 爷爷, 你几岁啦? The old man looked at her in surprise. Turning to people nearby, he exclaimed somewhat indignantly: 您瞧! 她问我几岁啦! 几岁啦! The young woman had not expected such a reaction at all. Later, the misunderstanding was cleared up: her question would have been all right if she were asking a child, but addressing an elderly person she should have asked: 您高寿? or 您多大年纪啦?

This amusing incident illustrates a cultural as well as a language problem that sometimes comes up when Chinese and English-speaking people attempt to communicate. When addressing one's elders or superiors, Chinese have traditionally used language that is more respectful than that used for people of one's own generation or of "lower status". Certain terms or expressions of respect are used. To use the same language could be interpreted as disrespectful, as improper or impolite, or perhaps even as a sign of conceit. On the other hand, when referring to oneself while speaking or writing to one's elders, it has been customary to use terms of humility or self-effacing expressions. Not to do so would also imply the same atti-

94

tude of disrespect mentioned above.

While things have changed considerably during the last few decades, this practice has not disappeared; honorific language is still used today, although it is less widespread than before.

This matter of honorifics is especially troublesome for English-speaking people trying to communicate in Chinese. The reason is that English has very few such terms, and of these, even fewer are commonly used in present times. In English, speaking or writing to one's superiors might call for a more respectful *tone*, but not for any special expressions. *You* is *you*; *me* is *me*, no matter what the other person's age, rank or position.

For Chinese, on the other hand, even when communicating with native English speakers, the idea of using more or less the same language, direct and unadorned, for elders, guests, and people of importance is hard to accept and even harder to abide by. The natural tendency of Chinese is to use "polite" terms—expressions of respect or humility.

A comparison of two actual invitations will illustrate the difference:

"...will you please honor me by coming to my humble home for a simple meal this Sunday evening? We will be very pleased if you can come at 6 o'clock..."

"Frank, we'd like you and your wife to come over for dinner this Friday evening. Six-thirty at our place. Can you make it?"

One is dripping with politeness, whereas the other is simple and direct.

This is not to say that all English invitations are so informal. Some can be quite formal:

Dr. and Mrs. John Q. Smith

request the pleasure of the company of

Mr. and Mrs. Wang Xiaotang

at a reception

in honor of the arrival of the — delegation

4:30 p.m., October 6

Pacific Room, Continental Hotel

R.S.V.P.


The more formal tone is reflected in the use of the names of the hosts and of the guests, rather than using *you*, *we*. Also the form of the invitation is more or less standard.

Below is a list of some of the more common Chinese honorifics or terms of humility. Equivalents in English are provided for comparison.

(Addressing or speaking to a guest, elder, ete.)

| | |
|---|---|
| 您,您老人家 | you |
| 先生,伯父,叔叔,大婶, | you (or the person's name) |
| 局长,经理,师傅,老师等 | Mr. (Mrs.)— |
| 敝人 | I, me |
| 贵姓,尊姓大名 | Your name? |
| | Could I have your name? |

(Referring to members of the other person's family or relatives, or to one's own)

| | |
|---|---|
| 令尊,令兄 | your father, your brother |
| 家严,家慈 | my father, my mother |
| 师母,伯母,嫂子 | your wife, Mrs.— |
| 舍亲,舍侄 | my relatives, my nephew |
| 令郎,令爱 | your son, your daughter |
| 我那个丫头 | my daughter |
| 我们那个小子 | our son |

96

(The last two above would be used more in the countryside)

(Referring to another's or one's own home, work place or organization that one belongs to, etc.)

| | |
|---|---|
| 府上 | your home, the place you're from |
| 贵校(店) | your school (shop) |
| 敝厂(所) | this (our) factory (institute) |
| 敝处 | my home, my place |

Notice that the Chinese use "prefixes" to denote *honorable, esteemed, respectful*, such as 贵, 令; and others to denote *humble, unworthy*, 家, 舍, 敝, etc. In fact, in times past, teachers of Chinese letter-writing had their students memorize a rhyme to help them keep the prefixes straight: 家大舍小令他人。However, no such prefixes or equivalents are used in English. In translating the above terms from Chinese to English, it would probably be better to use the simple terms *home, shop, school, organization*, etc., without any modifier. *Please come to my humble home*, or *We would like to visit your honorable organization* sounds very stiff and unnatural in English.

During the last few decades, with the growing emphasis on equality and the gradual de-emphasis on highly formal and mainly ceremonial trappings in everyday life, many of the very formal honorifics have gradually passed out of use. Some are still heard, but are used mainly among older, more educated people. A few of these are given below, as examples, with translations to show how they might be rendered into acceptable English.

| | |
|---|---|
| 久仰,久仰大名 | I've heard a lot about you. |
| | Your name is well-known here (to us). |
| 欢迎光临 | Welcome. Welcome to (name of place). |
| 欢迎指导 | Welcome (to a person on a professional or business visit). |

|  | We're very pleased to have you come and visit us. |
| 您有何高见? | What's your opinion? |
|  | We'd like to have your opinion. |
| 请提宝贵意见 | Please give us your comments or suggestions. |
|  | Could you give us your comments or suggestions? |
| 拜读了大作 | I've read your book (article, report, work, etc.). |
| 拙作 | My book (painting, literary work, research paper, etc.). |
| 敬请指正 | (A remark which means literally *I respectfully request that you point out the mistakes;* often nothing more than a polite remark when showing or presenting one's own book or work as a gift.) |
| 敬请光临 | You're invited to come.... |
| …惠存 | To (for)... (name of receiver of gift). |
| …敬赠 | From... (name of giver). |
| 请教 | to ask for advice. |

The still widely-used self-deprecating expression 不敢当 needs special mention here. The way it should be translated depends on how it is used. If 不敢当 is the answer to a polite comment or request such as 请您指教 (Kindly give us [me] your advice) then it might be translated as *I'll be glad to* or *Thank you* or possibly *I'm honored, but I'm not sure I'm the right person.* If in answer to praise such as *You're one of the top scholars (authorities) in the field,* then 不敢当 might be rendered as *Not really* or *It's such a small field.* If it is said as a reply to a comment like *That was a magnificent speech. I found it very stimulating,* one might translate 不敢当 as *That's very kind of you to say so* or simply *Thank you.* Quite a difference between the English and Chinese! *Thank you* implies acceptance of the praise, whereas 不敢当 implies

98

that he or she is not worthy of the praise.

The Chinese expression 哪里！哪里！ is another common reply to praise. How to translate it also depends largely on the context and situation in which it occurs. However, we shall not take up this term in detail here.

In officialese—the language of communications between different government agencies, or between different levels of organization with the same agency or unit—both English and Chinese show certain similarities in distinguishing between a superior or subordinate, a higher or a lower level in the hierarchy. English has terms like *hand down a directive*, *issue orders*, *submit a report*, just as Chinese has 发布命令，下达指示，呈报，呈递，呈请. English may have fewer such terms, but the overall tone of a communication can occasionally be equally stiff or unnatural, sometimes dripping with "humility" on the one hand, sometimes quite abrasive in its tone of authority on the other.

# Chapter 12

## Some Differences in Writing Style

*"Words, words, mere words, no matter from*
*the heart."*
　　—William Shakespeare, *Troilus and Cressida*
*"Words are like leaves, and where they most abound,*
*Much fruit of sense beneath is rarely found."*
　　—Alexander Pope, *Essay on Criticism*, Ⅱ

Why is it that the English writings of Chinese students read so much like translations of Chinese? Why is it that one can fairly easily tell whether an article was written by a Chinese or by a native speaker of English?

Is it because most Chinese students have not yet mastered the language?

Is it because of Chinese and Westerners think differently?

Is it because of differences in Chinese and English writing styles?

The answer is probably "yes" to all of the last three questions. If students of English had a better command of the language, they probably *could* write more like a native English speaker. Westerners probably *do* approach or look at matters in a different way from

100

most Chinese in many situations. And there *are* stylistic differences in English and Chinese writing.

It is the last question—differences in style—that this chapter will deal with. Specifically, we will examine some of the most obvious stylistic differences that reflect *cultural* differences.

Before beginning, it should be pointed out that both Chinese and English writing are similar in stressing in-depth knowledge of one's subject, well thought-out ideas, careful choice of materials, and presentation with sincerity, directness and simplicity. The following remarks—of unknown origin—apply not only to English, but to Chinese as well, and probably to all languages:

> "He that will write well in any tongue... must speak as the common people do, but think as the wise men do."

> "A man's style in any art should be like his dress—it should attract as little attention as possible."

With the above remarks in mind, let us now take up certain differences.

1. Narration and description in Chinese seem to be a bit more ornate, or "flowery", than in English. The following passage from a student's composition is typical of this kind of faulty writing in English:

> "I walked joyfully along the path that was lit up by the golden rays of the morning sun. Beautiful flowers of many colors were blooming. How fragrant they smelled! Little birds were singing in the trees, as if greeting me 'Good morning! Good morning!'... my heart was bursting with happiness..."

One of the common faults in this matter is the tendency of Chinese students to use too many adjectives. Adjectives, of course, are necessary in good writing. They are like paints that brighten and bring scenes and events to life. But if not used with care, they can have the opposite effect —quickly kill interest and produce boredom.

The story is told of the well-known American Daniel Webster, whose speeches during his youth were quite bombastic. But he came to realize that effective speech and writing was that which was simple and direct, that it was the meaning that gave power to a statement. Daniel Webster changed. He concentrated on his ideas, on how to present them effectively. He used as few adjectives as possible. When he did use one, he usually chose the simplest and the most precise. His speeches became sharp and powerful, like a magnificent sword. Even today he is remembered for his eloquence...

Overuse of adjectives is bad. Indiscriminate use is also bad. These are marks not only of students learning a foreign language, they are also signs of immature writers. All too often, such people try to dress up their work by resorting to a host of adjectives and adverbs. And all too often, such modifiers are those that have become tired from overwork and have long lost flavor, like *great*, *marvelous*, *wonderful*, *very*. Some may have been chosen after careful thought; they may have some effect, but the effect is not always a pleasant one. Such writers try to prettify rather than inject vigor. But what appeal can writing have that does not inform or stimulate but merely glitters?

A study of English writing will show that good writers are often those who choose their words with precision. Their verbs especially ignite one's imagination. Here, for example, are sentences and passages from Shakespeare:

A poor player/That *struts* and frets his hour upon the stage/And then is heard no more.

But *screw* your courage to the sticking-place,/And We'll not fail.

Daffodils /That come before the swallow *dares*, and take the winds of March with beauty.

102

This by Ophelia from *Hamlet* is especially illustrative:

Now see that noble and most sovereign reason, /Like *sweet* bells *jangled*, out of tune and harsh.

Could there be a better choice of words—the unusual choice of *jangled* following the delightful use of *sweet*—to suggest the incongruity of reason and madness in the same person? Or to reflect the torment in Ophelia's mind?

Of course not everyone is a Shakespeare, and most Chinese will not be producing verse or plays in English. Equally true, poetry is more concise and demands more precision. But the same general rule about words applies to prose. Study this passage, for example, from *The Crisis* by Thomas Paine (1737—1809):

"These are the times that try men's souls. The summer soldier and the sunshine patriot will, in this crisis, shrink from the service of their country, but he that stands it now, deserves the love and thanks of man and woman. Tyranny, like hell, is not easily conquered; yet we have this consolation with us, that the harder the conflict, the more glorious the triumph. What we obtain too cheap, we esteem too lightly: it is dearness only that gives everything its value. Heaven knows how to put a proper price upon its goods; and it would be strange indeed if so celestial an article as freedom should not be highly rated."

2. Chinese and English-speaking people seem to look differently on the use of set phrases and expressions. Good English writing discourages what are called "clichés" or "trite expressions". Chinese writing, on the other hand, gives its approval to well-chosen "four-character expressions." To a native English-speaker, the following sentence would be frowned on as an example of poor writing: *He slept like a log and woke up at the crack of dawn, fresh as a daisy.*

The fault is not that the sentence isn't vivid, but that it contains three clichés: *sleep like a log, at the crack of dawn, and*

103

*fresh as a daisy*.

Trite expressions and clichés originally caught people's attention precisely because they were and are so colorful and express an idea so well. But overuse caused them to lose their charm and freshness. The English language is full of these, as for example: *last but not least*, *it goes without saying*, *by leaps and bounds*, *in our day and age*, *as busy as a bee*, *happy as a lark*.

Chinese "four-character expressions," however, have their place in Chinese writing even though they have been used over and over again. One seldom finds a piece of Chinese expository writing without a number of them. For example, one could hardly pass judgment on an essay or speech without using some of the following: 一气呵成, 别具一格, 引人入胜, 慷慨激昂, 栩栩如生, 言简意赅, 咬文嚼字, 油腔滑调, 强词夺理, 牵强附会. They often add the touch that brings the passage to life—画龙点睛—to use such a Chinese expression as illustration. Of course, even in Chinese writing, excessive use should be avoided.

3. In persuasive writing such as social or political essays and editorials, English-speaking writers tend to be less militant in tone and language than most Chinese. The idea is *to let the facts speak for themselves*. In other words, the facts themselves should be able to convince the reader. Thus in such types of writing, one finds rather sparing use of such phrases as *we must*, *we should not*, *it is wrong to*, *it is absurd*, *cannot be denied*, *resolutely demand*. The tone is usually restrained; the language is generally moderate. In present-day Chinese social and political writings, facts are of primary importance, of course, but considerable stress is also laid on militancy, on making one's stand clear. This difference in attitudes is an important one. Experience has shown that a hard-hitting essay or

editorial in Chinese does not always have the effect intended when translated into English. Instead of convincing people, the blunt tone and language often antagonize people or arouse suspicion that the writer does not have a strong case and must resort to fiery language, rather than rely on facts and reasoning.

Similar to the above, good English persuasive writing is generally that which presents the facts convincingly, without the writer stating specifically the conclusion he would like to have the reader draw. At most, the conclusion should be stated briefly, for English-speaking people do not like "to be sold an idea"; they shy away from "being told what to think."

On this matter, Dr. Annette Rubinstein writes this about the Chinese students in her American Literature class when she was teaching Nathaniel Hawthorne:

"...their criticism of Hawthorne was that at the end of the story he does not tell you what you are supposed to think. They said that when a Chinese writer writes a story you know exactly what he wants you to think. I said that... we Americans feel it is much better if the writer makes you start thinking for yourself. Then they asked, 'But how do we know what is right and what is wrong?'" (Rubinstein, 1984)

While this attitude may not be universal in China, it certainly is true of many people.

Besides the three points of differences mentiond above, there are others. The whole matter of Chinese-English differences in writing style would require far more detailed treatment and could take up a whole book. The intention of this chapter is merely to call attention to this phenomenon, and provide a few illustrations. The hope is that some readers will explore the matter further on their own.

A few words here about "Chinglish", or Chinese-English,

which is really not a matter of style but will be put here for convenience. Chinglish is speech or writing in English that shows the interference or influence of Chinese. Some sentences may be little more than word for word translations of Chinese expressions. Chinglish may be grammatically correct, but the choice of words or phrases and the manner of expression do not conform to standard English usage. Although understanding may not be a problem, Chinglish is unacceptable.

The following are samples from student writings or conversations:

1. *His body is very healthy.*
2. *We are difficult to finish all this tonight.*
3. *His sick condition is much better. He is no longer dangerous.*
4. *We must spend bitter work to master knowledge.*
5. *He only said a few sentences. He made us very disappointed.*
6. *Recently she doesn't study well. All day she talks love.*

No. 1 is an exact translation of the Chinese 他身体很好。But in English, people simply say *He's very healthy*. Adding the word *body* makes the sentence sound queer.

No. 2 is also translated directly from the Chiense. The problem lies in the faulty handling of the word *difficult*. The correct way would be *It'll be difficult for us to finish all this tonight*.

No. 3 contains two mistakes. In Chinese we might say 病情好转，but English-speaking people generally say *His condition is much better*, or simply *He's much better*. To say person is *dangerous* means that the person is in some way a threat to others. Here, improper use of the term changes the meaning entirely. What is meant, of course, is that the person's condition is no longer criticial, that he is "out of danger."

106

In the 4th sentence, *bitter work* literally means work that is bitter. The intended meaning of the Chinese is hard work and perseverance. Also, *spend* is incorrect. One does not *spend* work. Evidently the student had in mind *spend a lot of time on . . . .  To master knowledge* may be acceptable in certain contexts, but many Chinese students tend to equate *master* with 掌握 and use it in almost all situations involving the Chinese term. It would be far better to say *We must work hard and try to learn as much as possible*.

A better way to express No. 5 would be: (1) *We were quite disappointed that he said only a few words.* (2) *He only made a few comments (remarks.) We were quite disappointed. (It was quite a disappointment.) Say a few sentences* is heard in English and is not wrong, but far more common is *Say a few words. Make someone disappointed* is marginal—not wrong, but seldom found in English usage.

In No. 6, the first sentence is grammatically wrong. *She hasn't been studying well recently* would be the grammatically correct version. However, the suspicion is that the student had in mind 好好学习, which is more *studying hard* than *studying well*. As for the second sentence, there couldn't be a more literal translation of 谈恋爱. *Talk love* is not the English for 谈恋爱. It might be acceptable in a very special context, perhaps in one-to-one conversation, with a slight touch of humor, as in *Enough of such things. Let's talk about something more interesting. Let's talk about love.* Even so, this would be rare. So the idea of the two sentences could be better expressed as *She hasn't been studying hard because she spends most of her time with her boyfriend.*

Another common phenomenon in Chinglish involves the Chinese phrases 吃饭, 读书, 唱歌, 跳舞, 付钱, etc. In these Chinese

107

verb-object constructions, the object is almost always mentioned. In English, however, the object is understood and is generally omitted. Chinese students who do not realize this, often produce awkward-sounding sentences such as the following:

      \* Let's go and eat our meals.

      \* They're reading books.

      \* He's going to sing songs at the concert.

      \* We danced some dances last night.

      \* Have you paid the money?

It would be much more natural to express the above as:

      Let's go and eat.

      They're reading.

      He's going to sing at the concert.

      We danced last night.

      Have you paid yet?

Some Chinglish expressions involve parts of the body. In Chinese, we say 腰痛, but in English there is no such expression as *waistache*, there is only *backache*, *Oh*, *my aching back*! When something is uproariously funny, Chinese will 捧腹大笑, but English-speaking people, will *hold their sides with laughter*, not *hold their stomachs or bellies*. Interestingly, *stomachache* can be either 胃痛 or 肚子痛: in English, there is no distinction between the two, which often causes Chinese to grope around for a proper English equivalent for 胃痛. Turning to other parts of the body, *His two eyes are blind* would sound ridiculous in English for 双目失明, English speakers would ask *How can one be blind except in the eyes*? One could say *He's blind*, *He's completely blind*, or *He's lost his eyesight*.

Certain Chinese phrases or expressions contain modifiers that are perfectly natural and entirely appropriate in Chinese. However, if translated into English, the result would be quite the contrary. When a person with some professional status comes to an institution, organization, or company for a visit, it is customary to say 请提宝贵意见. If this is rendered into English as *Please give us your valuable opinions*, the visitor would be put in an awkward situation. He/she would probably think: *How do I or they know whether my opinions are valuable or not*? To offer one's opinions under such circumstances would hardly be modest; it would be equivalent to saying *Yes, my opinions are valuable, here they are*. To avoid this, he/she might decide not to say anything at all. Actually, the Chinese 宝贵 in this expression really means *Your opinions will be appreciated*.

Similarly, 毫无根据的捏造 is a good, sound Chinese expression. 毫无根据 is for emphasis, not a qualifying condition. It would not do to translate the Chinese as *groundless lies*, or *groundless fabrications*. To the English or American mind, lies or fabrications are by definition groundless. To accept *groundless lies*, implies that there can be *well-grounded lies or fabrications*, which is absurd. So adding *groundless* is not only superfluous, but also illogical—as the Chinese saying goes: 画蛇添足 (adding feet to the serpent).

A number of other common Chinese sayings need similar care when rendered into English: 不切实际的幻想 (impractical illusions) —can there be practical illusions? 残酷的迫害 (cruel persecution) —is there persecution that is *not* cruel? etc.

In dealing with such chinese sayings, one should consider whether or not to keep the modifier in English. If the modifier does not strengthen, but instead detracts or diverts attention from the meaning, then it should be omitted. Such omission or adjustment is not only permissible, but a necessity.

Another point is the titles of articles. While titles must by nature be short, yet inform the reader of what the article is about, there are certain differences in English and Chinese titles, especially for scholarly papers and articles in learned journals. Here, one of the more noticeable differences will be discussed.

The practice in English is generally to be straightforward, as the following actual titles indicate:

> *Science and Linguistics*
> *Filmmaking in Contemporary America*
> *Women vs. Men in the Work Force*
> *Art History in a New World*
> *The Farm Revolution Picks up Speed*

Chinese titles, in addition to conveying information about the main contents, often try to show the author's humility about his work, thus:

> 《浅谈……》(*A Superficial Discussion of . . .*)
> 《试论……》(*An Attempt to Discuss . . .*)
> 《……初步分析》(*Preliminary Analyses of . . .*)
> 《……初探》(*Preliminary Exploration of . . .*)
> 《……之我见》(*My Understanding of . . .*)
> 《……刍议》(*My Humble Opinions on . . .*)

Such titles are especially common by authors whose work is comparatively unknown. They avoid giving the impression that the author regards himself/herself as an authority on the subject matter. Also, if certain points or parts in the article are later shown to be faulty, the author can explain that the work was "a preliminary analysis", "a superficial discussion", "an attempt to probe" as indicated in the title. He/she thus has a built-in excuse. Unfortunately, this is sometimes a convenient way out for sloppy thinkers and irresponsible writers.

110

Until one has a good command of a foreign language, one's speech and writing is bound to be affected by one's native language. Until one can think in English, his ideas will often be expressed in word for word renderings of Chinese into English. The lower a student's proficiency in the foreign language, the truer this will be. So a certain amount of Chinglish is inevitable at a certain stage or stages of the Englsih-learning process. Being able to put an idea into an acceptable equivalent requires considerable knowledge of English—of the words, phrases and expressions avail-able to him, of their linguistic and social appropriateness. He must correlate all this with the ideas that he has in mind in Chinese. He should then try to select the closest possible equivalent. But please note that real equivalence is equivalence in meaning, tone, connotation, style and association.

# Chapter 13

## Varieties of English

"*When I read Shakespeare I am struck with*
*wonder*
*That such trivial people should muse and*
*thunder*
*In such lovely language.*"
—D. H. Lawrence, *When I read Shakespeare*

The story is told of the queen of a European country who visited the city of Chicago as part of her trip to the U. S. Everything went off well, with the usual pomp and ceremony that would be due a visiting monarch. It was time for the royal entourage to leave. The mayor of Chicago was present, of course, at the farewell ceremony, making the expected remarks and good wishes. As the gathering listened attentively, he concluded in an outburst of enthusiasm and goodwill, "*The next time you come, bring the kids along.*"

The change in the atmosphere was electric. Some stared wide-eyed in disbelief. Here and there was a titter; it was hard to suppress laughter, even with royalty present. Those responsible for protocol were red-faced, either with embarrassment or indignation, depending on whether they were Americans or members of the

112

queen's party.

What was the reason for the shock? Why the disbelief, amusement, anger or embarrassment?

The answer lay in the use of the word *kids*. One does not use such a word for the descendants of a reigning monarch, the *princes* or *princesses*. The effect of the mayor's words was equivalent to a person saying to a Chinese dignitary：下次您老人家光临，带上您的丫头和小子。

This story, which is supposed to be true but which the author could not verify in detail, illustrates that the *same* language may carry different meanings or produce different results in different circumstances. As linguists point out, language has different functional roles in different communities; also, within the same community, people use more than one style or variety of the same language.

It is this general aspect of American English that this chapter will deal with: differences within the language that may be important to Chinese speakers of English. Specifically we shall take up regional differences, differences in medium, and social differences.

## Regional Differences

Regional differences in the same language may be in pronunciation, intonation or rhythm; or the differences may be in the choice or usage of certain words and idioms; sometimes, even in syntax, although this is not so common. Regional differences are found in the Chinese *Han* language as well as in English — in British English, American English, Canadian or Australian English. The speech of Shanxi, Sichuan or the northeastern provinces does not sound the same as that of Beijing. People in Shanxi would pronounce

113

the name of their province, for example, with the final *n* in *Shanxi* not very distinct, somewhat similar to the final *n* sound in French. Sichuanese would pronounce the first character of the term 解放军 (the People's Liberation Army) as *gai*, rather than *jie*, and some of the tones would also be different. And the word 人 (man, person) would be pronounced as *yin*, rather than *ren*, by many people in the northeastern provinces. As examples of terms or expressions with a regional flavor, we could cite 滚水 (boiled water — Shanxi), 打牙祭 (have a feast — Sichuan), 老鼻子 (many, a lot — north-eastern China), 贼 (very, quite; e. g. 那灯贼亮贼亮 — that light is very, very bright — north-eastern provinces). As for the dialect spoken in Shanghai and that spoken in Guangdong Province, the differences are so great as to be incomprehensible to outsiders.

In American English, regional differences are not so great, but there are dissimilarities that should be mentioned. People in New England — the northeastern states in America — tend to pronounce certain words the way the British do. People in the South — the dozen or so states in the southeastern part of America — tend to speak with a drawl; they speak slowly and the vowel sounds are greatly prolonged. Also, for a number of objects they use terms that are different from those commonly used in other regions; for example, a *bag* in other states would be called a *poke* in the South; a *purse* would be called a *pocketbook*.

Regional differences in English may be quite a problem for Chinese who are used to hearing the more standard or more common forms of English. There is no easy solution. One must gradually accustom oneself to the differences through frequent hearing and trying to figure out the meaning. Fortunately, most native English speakers who come to China do not pose this problem. Their English is

114

generally standard.

The whole matter of regional differences could take up much space. It will not be dealt with further here. It is enough to call the reader's attention to this.

## Differences in Medium

——Written English, Spoken English

Sometimes, one will hear the comment *He talks (speaks) like a book*, or 他说话文绉绉的. Such comments indicate that the person is not speaking the way most people would speak in such situations. The comment indicates also that the language itself — whether it be English, Chinese, or some other language — is diverse, and that the spoken form may not be identical with the written. In Chinese, this is a fact understood by all literate people. Classical Chinese, with its 之、乎、者、也 is quite unlike colloquial Chinese, nor is it like the *baihua* (vernacular) of modern Chinese writing. Although expressions such as 何许人也, 公之于众, 绳之以法 are still found in contemporary writing, they would definitely be out of place in ordinary conversation.

English is similar, although the gap between formal written English and colloquial English is not as wide as that between classical Chinese and the *putonghua* (literal meaning: common speech) that is spoken in daily conversation. A quick study of the following excerpts will show this. One is from expository writing, the other from informal conversation.

1. In his book *Future Shock*, Alvin Toffler writes:

"In the three short decades between now and the twenty-first century,

**115**

millions of ordinary, psychologically normal people will face an abrupt collision with the future. Citizens of the world's richest and most technologically advanced nations, many of them will find it increasingly painful to keep up with the incessant demand for change that characterizes our time. For them, the future will have arrived too soon. . .

"Western society for the past 300 years has been caught up in a fire storm of change. This storm, far from abating, now appears to be gathering force. Change sweeps through the highly industrialized countries with waves of ever accelerating speed and unprecedented impact. It spawns in its wake all sorts of curious social flora — from psychedelic churches and 'free universities' to science cities in the Arctic and wife-swap clubs in California."(Toffler, 1970)

2. Below is part of a conversation overheard by Dr. Matthew P. Dumont, a physician. The setting is a typical working-class tavern in a major American city:

Don: Cancer is from too many cigarettes.

John: John Wayne smoked five packs a day and they took a piece of his lung out.

Don: I just take a couple of drags from each butt.

Tom: I heard a guy who got cirrhosis of the liver and he never took a drink in his life.

Jack: Yeah, but most of it's from too much booze and no food.

Don: You get holes in your liver.

(Dumont, in Henslin, 1981)

In the tavern conversation between several men out of work for some time, who habitually go to the tavern to spend their hours just to be together and chat, the subject matter is loosely about the effects of smoking and drinking on people's health. The conversation starts with cancer and moves on to cirrhosis. Only two remarks seem to have direct relevance to what the previous speaker said: John's remark about John Wayne, and Jack's short comment. And

116

in these two, there are omissions of words that show connection with previous remarks. Yet there is no problem in understanding what the conversation is about. Grammarians might say that the sentence *I heard a guy who got . . .* is ungrammatical, that it should be *I heard about a guy who got . . .* And some people might frown on the use of such slang as *booze*, *drags*, and the word *butt*.

Toffler's passage offers a marked contrast: the longer, more carefully constructed sentences, the use of "learned" words or expressions such as *abrupt collision*, *incessant demand*, *abating*, *unprecedented impact*, the liberal use of figurative speech such as *fire storm of change*, *waves of ever accelerating speed*, *spawns in its wake*, *social flora*.

The differences between the written and the spoken language are due mainly to the fact that one is generally planned, whereas the other is more or less spontaneous. In writing, one has time to think, to deliberate, to choose one's words carefully, to use different devices of rhetoric in order to make the final product more colorful, more appealing, or more convincing. The writer has time to edit and polish. If necessary, he can revise or do the whole thing over again. In speaking, however, one's words and even one's ideas often emerge in the course of the conversation; little is planned or deliberated. There are hesitations, backtracking, changes in the middle of an idea or sentence. There are omissions as there are repetitions. The choice of words tends to be mainly from the short, most common ones that come easily to mind. There is generally no attempt or even thought of how to "touch up" what one says.

The obvious differences between the planned and unplanned, between writing and speech have produced distinctive characteristics in the style of each. English writing tends to be more carefully constructed, tends to use longer words of Latin origin, and often relies on rhetorical devices for effectiveness. Conversational English tends to ramble; sentence constructions are often loose, sometimes "ungrammatical", frequently with incomplete expressions and ellipses; and in choice of words, there are plenty of colloquialisms and slang.

What has been said above about the characteristics of writing refer mainly to the more formal, standard type of writing. English writing, like the writing of many other languages, including Chinese, consists of more than one style. Different styles have different characteristics or standards. The stiff, formal language of official documents or legal papers, such as legal contracts, is quite unlike instructions on how to bake a cake. The carefully chosen language of a philosophical dissertation does not read the same as a newspaper sports story discussing the merits of two teams in a championship match. Nor does a person writing a letter of recommendation use the same tone as he would in a chatty letter to a close friend.

There are differences in each, which should be noted and studied by those who need to write often in English. However, details about these differences go far beyond the scope of this book and will not be taken up here. For those interested, there is plenty of reading matter available on stylistics.

## Social Differences

Linguistic research has shown that in many languages, people will change their speech from one variety or style to another, depending on the situation. Different languages have a different number of varieties. In general, if there are two varieties, one will be more formal while the other will be more informal. Some linguists

118

classify the differences as classical and colloquial, or "high" and "low". If there are more than two varieties, they will fall within a hierarchy ranging from informal to formal.

Such distinctions are true of both Chinese and English, as well as of many other languages, such as Arabic, modern Greek and German, to mention just a few.

Using the right variety in the right situation is very important. Obviously, it would be as absurd to greet a child of four with *How do you do, Mr. Mullins* or 您好, 毛毛先生, as it would be improper to greet a minister of a government or the chairman of a multinational corporation for the first time with "*Hi, Jim. How're things goin'*'? or 嘿, 老兄您混得怎么样?

Occasionally, non-native speakers with a good command of the foreign language may also make mistakes in this. For example, an American professor mentioned how surprised she was when the slang word *bucks*, meaning dollars, was used when discussing her salary — by one of the best English speakers at the Chinese university where she was teaching. This was like asking a Chinese professor 您每个月挣几张'大团结'? — totally inappropriate.

The variety of speech that one used depends on a number of circumstances:

1. The setting, or situation — at a public gathering, an official reception, a formal dinner, an informal party, a chance meeting on the street, etc.

2. The subject matter — whether the conversation is about philosophy or some minor ailment, an interview for a job or borrowing some sugar, making a complaint or telling the latest gossip.

3. Persons involved — the persons in the conversation and the relationships between them; whether strangers or acquaintances,

family or friends, intimate or distant; whether persons of authority and of high social position or otherwise.

4. Mood — the mood and feelings of those involved; whether joyful, excited, nervous, irritated, angry, depressed, etc.

All of the above must be taken into account in choosing the variety of language to use.

How many varieties of speech does American English have? What are the options that Americans have to choose from in different situations?

Different linguists have different answers to this. We shall go by the study made by Martin Joos, a well-known linguist whose views on this matter are widely quoted throughout the world. He cites five different varieties of American English speech: 1. frozen (or oratorical), 2. formal (or deliberate), 3. consultative, 4. casual, 5. intimate. Explanations of each are given below:

Frozen: Used by professional speakers, for public address. Sentences are constructed with the utmost care, and elaborate rhetorical devices are used. The words or phrases are generally very precise, often "learned" words of Latin origin.

Formal: For audiences too large for effective interchange with the speaker, as lectures by college professors, or scholarly talks at professional conferences. Such speech is planned, although generally with less precision and elaborateness than in the frozen variety. If used in speaking to a single person, it indicates a certain distance between speaker and listener; the distance may be because of different occupational or social status — such as a subordinate speaking to a superior, or it may be the result of personal feelings, such as contempt.

Consultative: For conducting most business matters, but not

120

among close friends. Such conversation tends to be more or less spontaneous; the words are generally those that come to mind without too much deliberation.

Casual: For situations in which no social barriers are felt by the parties involved, such as close friends in informal situations. Casual conversation is spontaneous; sentences are often short and clipped, with auxiliary verbs and pronouns frequently left out. Colloquialisms and slang are fairly common.

Intimate: Used among members of the family or very close friends; intimate language is completely spontaneous, with hardly any restraint. Such language often assumes shared knowledge between the participants and therefore is at times unintelligible to outsiders.

It might be said that the five varieties represent five degrees or levels of formality. An example of each expressing the same idea is given below:

> Frozen: Visitors should make their way at once to the upper floor by way of the staircase.
>
> Formal: Visitors should go up the stairs at once.
>
> Consultative: Would you mind going upstairs right away, please?
>
> Casual: Time you all went upstairs, now.
>
> Intimate: Up you go, chaps!
>
> (Strevens, in *English Studies*, Vol. 45, NO.1)

Let us now turn to two illustrative passages from actual life. The first is the famous speech made on August 28, 1963, at the civil rights rally in front of the Lincoln Memorial in Washington, D.C., by the Reverend Martin Luther King, Jr.

"Five score years ago, a great American, in whose symbolic shadow we stand today, signed the Emancipation Proclamation. This mo-

121

mentous decree came as a great beacon of light and hope to millions of Negro slaves who had been seared in the flames of withering injustice. It came as the joyous daybreak to end the long night of captivity.

"But one hundred years later, the Negro still is not free. One hundred years later, the life of the Negro is still sadly crippled by the manacle of segregation and the chain of discrimination. One hundred years later, the Negro lives on a lonely island of poverty in the midst of a vast ocean of material prosperity. One hundred years later, the Negro is still languishing in the corner of American society and finds himself an exile in his own land. So we have come here today to dramatize a shameful condition..."

(King, in Renshaw, 1975)

This speech, delivered to over 200 000 people, is very much like a piece of formal writing. In the speech, one finds a number of words not commonly found in informal English: *withering, seared, captivity, manacle, languishing,* etc.; one finds rather literary expressions such as *in whose symbolic shadow;* the use of parallel constructions in his four uses of *one hundred years later...* But perhaps the most striking feature is the extensive use of metaphors: *a great beacon of light and hope, the long night of captivity, the life ... is crippled by..., a vast ocean of material prosperity, a lonely island of poverty, in the corner of American society,* etc. All these show the utmost thought that went into the preparation of the speech.

In the passage below, we find something quite different. Studs Terkel spent three years interviewing Americans from all walks of life and in various occupations, having them talk about their work. From recordings taken during the actual interviews he produced the book *Working*. The language of the interviews is entirely conversa-

122

tional — informal or casual, straight from the heart, natural and unadorned.

A New York policeman, Tom Patrick, talks about his experiences:

> "I worked in Harlem and East Harlem for three years. There was ten, eleven cops and they were all black guys. I was the only white cop. When they saw me come into the office they started laughin'. 'What the fuck are they sendin' you here for? You're fuckin' dead.' They told me to get a helmet and hide on the roof.
>
> "My father's a great man. I see what he went through and the shit and hard times. I don't see how he lived through it. I used to lay awake when he was drinkin' and listen to him talk all night. And I used to cry. He talked about the shittin' war, all the money goin' for war. And the workers' sons are the ones that fight these wars, right? And people that got nothin' to eat... I tell ya, if I didn't have an income comin' in... These kids hangin' around here, Irish kids, Italian kids, twenty-five years old, alcoholics, winos. One guy died of exposure. He went out with my kid sister and he's dead now."

(Terkel, 1974)

There are no long complex sentences here, no literary words or expressions. The whole passage is made up of short, simple constructions using the most common everyday words, among which are slang words like *winos*, and "four-letter" words such as *shit*, *shitting*, *fuck*, *fucking*. The language is direct, concise, vivid.

Here several points might be raised: Is the English of casual or intimate conversation good English? Is it the kind of English that Chinese speakers should use when conversing with Westerners? Should such English be taught to Chinese students learning English?

In answering the first question, we might consider what the linguists have to say. According to majority opinion, the variety or style of language is not good or bad in itself but depends on the occasion in which it is employed. If the language that a person uses is commonly spoken by most people for such occasions, then it is proper and good.

Conversely, if the style is not one that is generally used in such situations, then it is not proper, no matter how correct, good, or even elegant it may be by other standards. For example, while many of the features of the interview with the policemen or the tavern conversation may be looked on with disapproval by most teachers of English or grammarians, it would be wrong to consider them as "shortcomings" or "errors". They are an essential part of a certain variety of level of conversational English and can only be considered "wrong" according to the standards of formal or written English. In fact, to use formal English in a tavern, or an amusement park or shopping place, or any place for informal gatherings would make one the object of ridicule. The choice of the proper variety, then, demands care.

In answering the second question, it is obvious that if the variety or style of language that a person uses should fit the occasion, then this rule should apply equally to Chinese conversing in English, or for that matter, for people of any country doing the same thing. The problem, however, is that most non-native speakers of English do not know the language well enough to adapt to the situation. Being able to use several different styles requires a high degree of fluency in the language. Without such, the results could be disastrous. Improper ellipses, poor choice of idiom or slang, inconsistencies in style or tone, etc., can have a ludicrous effect. Nothing sets off a

124

foreigner more than trying to sound like a native speaker without the native speaker's command of the language. For Chinese, whose native language and whose culture is so totally different from English, the problem is made even more difficult.

It should be mentioned that knowing the different styles alone is not enough. One should also be acquainted with the customs that govern their use — when, where and how to use what style. One should also know the rules of shifting. Although not very common, people may shift from one style to another, sometimes during the same discourse and occasionally even within the same sentence. However, custom limits such shifting only to a neighboring style, either "higher" or "lower". A shift to a style more than one level apart would not be acceptable.

Should casual or intimate English be taught to students learning English? Clearly, if maximum communication is expected by and between people using a foreign language, and if proper pes of the different varieties is an essential aspect of effective communication, then at least some exposure to the different varieties should be helpful. This exposure should come before actual need arises, preferably as part of the student's training in the language.

We should realize that the English taught in most schools — whether at the secondary or college level — is what might be called "the common core" of the language, or the features that are most common to all varieties. This "common core" can be used on almost all occasions, for almost all purposes. In other words, one can write a letter of application or a quick note to a personal friend, converse with a high-ranking company offical or chat with an intimate friend using more or less the same "core" of language. It can be used without offending others or bringing embarrassment to oneself. It is safe language — perhaps dull and colorless, but inoffensive. Such language, used by a nonnative speaker, will be tolerated. Communication is achieved, although not much more can be said for it.

This "core language" is a necessity for all learners. But it is not enough if one wishes to have the most effective communication with others. One does not really have a good command of the language unless one can use the style suited to the occasion, unless one can be formal or intimate as the situation demands.

For students of English, then, as well as those whose work involves contact with Westerners, exposure to different varieties or registers should begin early. Sensitivity should be developed. If possible, there should be training and practice to recognize and understand the differences.

# Chapter 14

## Body Language — Nonverbal Communication

*"There's language in her eye, her cheek,
        her lip."*

　　　—William Shakespeare, *Troilus and Cressida*

When a Chinese converses with a Canadian or American friend of the opposite sex, would it be indecent to be looking at the other person?

If two young friends of the same sex walk with their arms around each others' shoulders or hold hands, would this be regarded by English-speaking people as proper?

Does nodding the head mean "yes", and shaking the head mean "no" in all cultures?

These are not questions about language, but about body language, about nonverbal communication.

Although we may not realize it, when we converse with others we communicate by much more than words. By our expressions, gestures and other body movements we send messages to those around us. A smile and an outstretched hand show welcome. A frown is a sign of displeasure. Nodding one's head means agreement — "Yes". Waving an outstretched hand with open palm is the ges-

127

ture for "goodbye". Leaning back in one's seat and yawning at a talk or lecture shows lack of interest, boredom. These gestures have come to be accepted in general as having the meanings mentioned, at least to Chinese and Americans. They are part of the way in which we communicate. This "body language", like our verbal language, is also a part of our culture.

But not all body language means the same thing in different cultures. Different peoples have different ways of making nonverbal communication. The answers to the questions at the beginning of this chapter are all "no". Even nodding the head may have a different meaning. To Nepalese, Sri Lankans, some Indians and some Eskimos it means not "yes", but "no". So in order to communicate effectively in a foreign language, one should know also the gestures, body movements, mannerisms, etc., that accompany a particular language.

Watch an Arab and an Englishman in conversation. The Arab, showing friendliness in the manner of his people, will stand close to the Englishman. The latter will move back, wanting to keep a certain distance considered proper by the English. The Arab will then move forward to be closer; the Englishman will keep moving backward. By the end of the conversation, the two may be quite a distance from the place where they were originally standing!

Here, distance between the two is the key factor. Different people have different ideas about the proper distance between people conversing. According to studies, it seems there are four main distances in American social and business relations: intimate, personal, social, and public. Intimate distance ranges from direct physical contact to a distance of about 45 centimeters; this is for people's most private relations and activities, between man and wife, for example. Personal distance is about 45—80 centimeters and is most common when friends, acquaintances and relatives converse. Social distance may be anywhere from about 1.30 meters to 3 meters; people who work together, or people doing business, as well as most of those in conversation at social gatherings tend to keep a distance of about 1.30—2 meters. Public distance is farther than any of the above and is generally for speakers in public and for teachers in classrooms.

The important thing to keep in mind is that most English-speaking people do not like people to be too close. Being too far apart, of course, may be awkward, but being too close makes people uncomfortable, unless there is a reason, such as showing affection or encouraging intimacy. But that is another matter.

The appropriateness of physical contact varies with different cultures. Figures from a study offer interesting insight into this matter. Pairs of individuals sitting and chatting in college shops in different places were observed for at last one hour each. The number of times that either one touched the other in that one hour was recorded, as follows: London, 0; Gainesville, Florida, 2; Paris, 10; San Juan, Puerto Rico, 180. These figures speak for themselves. (Robinett, 1978).

In English-speaking countries, physical contact is generally avoided in conversation among ordinary friends or acquaintances. Merely touching someone may cause an unpleasant reaction. If one touches another person accidentally, he/she usually utters an apology such as *Sorry, Oh, I'm sorry, Excuse me*.

In China, a common complaint of Western mothers is that Chinese often fondle their babies and very small children. Such behavior — whether touching, patting, hugging or kissing — can be quite embarrassing and awkward for the mothers. They know that no harm is meant, and that such gestures are merely signs of friendliness or affection, therefore they cannot openly show their displeasure. On the other hand, such actions in their own culture would be considered rude, intrusive and offensive and could arouse a strong dislike and even repugnance. So the mothers often stand by and watch in awkward silence, with mixed emotions, even when the fondling is by Chinese friends or acquaintances.

Going beyond the milder forms of touching, we shall take up the matter of hugging and embracing in public. This practice is fairly common among women in many countries. And in most of the more industrialized countries, it occurs frequently between husband and wife and close members of the family when meeting after a period of absence. Hugging and embracing among men, however, is a different matter. Among Arabs, Russians, French, and in several of the East European and Mediterranean countries, a warm hug and a kiss on the cheeks are a standard way of welcome. The same is true with some Latin Americans. In East Asia and in the English-speaking countries, though, the practice is seldom seen. A simple handshake is the custom. The story is told of what happened not long ago when the Japanese Prime Minister at the time, Mr. Fukuda, went to the U. S. on a state visit. When he stepped out of his car in front of the White House, he was greeted by the American President with a"bear hug". The Prime Minister was flabbergasted; others of the Japanese delegation were amazed; many Americans were surprised — it was so unusual and so unexpected. If the President had bowed low in Japanese fashion, it would have been less a surprise than to be greeted in a way so uncommon in either country!

The matter of physical contact between members of the same

sex in English-speaking countries is a delicate one. Once past childhood, the holding of hands, or walking with an arm around another's shoulder is not considered proper. The implication is homosexuality, and homosexuality generally arouses strong social disapproval in these countries.

Eye contact is an important aspect of body language. One could draw up quite a list of "rules" about eye contact: to look or not to look; when to look and how long to look; who and who not to look at. These passages from the book *Body Language* (Fast, 1971) are amusing as well as informative:

"Two strangers seated across from each other in a railway dining car have the option of introducing themselves and facing a meal of inconsequential and perhaps boring talk, or ignoring each other and desperately trying to avoid each other's glance. A writer, describing such a situation in an essay, wrote, 'They re-read the menu, they fool with the cutlery, they inspect their own fingernails as if seeing them for the first time. Comes the inevitable moment when glances meet, but they meet only to shoot instantly away and out the window for an intent view of the passing scene.'"

He points out that with people who are unfamiliar:

"We must avoid staring at them, and yet we must also avoid ignoring them ... We look at them long enough to make it quite clear that we see them, and then we immediately look away.

"There are different formulas for the exchange of glances depending on where the meeting takes place. If you pass someone in the street you may eye the oncoming person till you are about eight feet apart, then you must look away as you pass. Before the eight-foot distance is reached, each will signal in which direction he will pass. This is done with a brief look in that direction. Each will veer slightly, and the passing is done smoothly."

In conversations with people who know each other, however, American custom demands that there should be eye contact. This applies to both the speaker and the listener. For either one not to look at the other person could imply a number of things, among which are fear, contempt, uneasiness, guilt, indifference. Even in public speaking there should be plenty of eye contact. For a speaker to "bury his nose in his manuscript", to *read* a speech instead of looking at and *talking* to his audience, as some Chinese speakers are in the habit of doing, would be regarded as inconsiderate and disrespectful.

In conversation, a person shows that he is listening by looking at the other person's eyes or face. If the other person is speaking at some length, the listener will occasionally make sounds like "IIꭐꭐ", "Ummm", or nod his head to indicate his attention. If he agrees with the speaker, he may nod or smile. If he disagrees or has some reservations, he may slant his head to one side, raise an eyebrow, have a quizzical look.

Staring at people or holding a glance too long is considered improper in English-speaking countries. Even when the look may be one of appreciation — as of beauty — it may make people uneasy and embarrassed. Many Americans travelling abroad find the stares of the local people irritating. They become extremely self-conscious and often end up quite indignant about the "rudeness" of the people there, not realizing that the practice may be quite common in the country and may be nothing more than curiosity. Many English-speaking people in China have been heard to complain about this. In fact, a young American woman who is a good friend of the author's, decided to leave China partly because of this. Although she liked her teaching in Beijing and had strong feelings of affection towards China and the Chinese, she decided she could no longer stand the constant staring, the rude gaping, wherever she went. The fact that she is unusually tall and large partly explains the behavior of many of the Chinese passersby. When she left China, it was with some reluctance; nevertheless, she left before she had planned to. The feelings aroused by staring can be that strong!

"The language of the eyes"— one of the most common and ancient ways of exchanging feelings between boys and girls, men and women — is especially elaborate in the United States. Much study has been made of this: how people of the opposite sex show interest or indifference, encouragement or discouragement, approval or disapproval, affection or aversion. However, there are many differences even within the United States. Men use their eyes in different ways than women; there are differences of age, class or social status and geographical region; there are differences of ethnic background.

The ability to look someone straight in the eye is considered significant in a number of countries. A well-known Soviet film about Lenin has a scene in which a Cheka agent who had turned traitor refuses to meet the eye of his chief, Dzherzinsky, when being questioned. By this his guilt seems to be confirmed. The same significance is attached to such eye contact by many Americans, but not by all ethnic groups in that country.

The story is told of a teen-age Puerto Rican girl in a New York high school who was taken with a number of other girls to the principal for suspected smoking. Although there was no proof of any wrongdoing and although she had a good record, the principal decided she was guilty and suspended her. "There was something sly and suspicious about her," he said in his report. "She just wouldn't meet

133

my eye. She wouldn't look at me."

When she was questioned by the principal it was true that she kept staring at the floor and refused to meet his eye. And in English there is a saying "Don't trust anyone who won't look you in the eye."

It so happened that one of the teachers had a Latin American background and knew about Puerto Rican culture. After talking with the girl's parents, he went to the principal and explained that according to Puerto Rican culture, a good girl "does not meet the eyes of an adult." Such behavior, he explained, "is a sign of respect and obedience."

Fortunately, the principal accepted the explanation, admitted his mistake and the matter was settled properly. This difference in interpreting a simple eye gesture was a lesson in cultural diversity that he would not easily forget.

Rules about eye-language are numerous and complex. What has been mentioned gives a good idea of this; we shall not go further into detail.

Smiles and laughter usually convey friendliness, approval, satisfaction, pleasure, joy, merriment. This is generally true in China as well as the English-speaking countries. However, there are situations when some Chinese will laugh that will cause negative reactions by Westerners. To illustrate, here is an excerpt from a letter by an American to the author on nonverbal gestures that often cause cross-cultural misunderstanding:

> "…One is the different meanings of laughter in China and America. When an American is parking his bicycle, for example, and the bicycle accidentally falls over, he feels embarrassed at his awkwardness,

and is quite angered and humiliated when Chinese onlookers laugh. I have seen the same thing happen in the dining room, when a foreigner drops a plate quite by accident and feels badly and Chinese onlookers laugh, compounding his discomfort and causing anger and bad feeling."

Such laughter, of course, is not *at* the person or his misfortune — whether he be a foreigner or a Chinese. It can convey a number of feelings: don't take it so seriously; laugh it off, it's nothing; such things can happen to any of us, etc. However, for people unaware of this attitude, the reaction to such laughter is usually quite unpleasant and often generates ill feeling towards those laughing.

Gestures can be particularly troublesome, for a slight difference in making the gesture itself can mean something quite different from that intended. A wrong interpretation of a gesture can arouse quite unexpected reactions.

A well-known case is a gesture made by Winston Churchill, the doughty Prime Minister who led Britain through the Second World War. As he appeared before a large crowd, he was greeted with cheers and applause. The occasion was a momentous one and Churchill flashed the "V for victory" sign — with the forefinger and middle finger raised to form a "V". Whether by mistake or ignorance, instead of facing the palm of his hand to the front, he made the "V" with the back of his hand towards the audience. Some in the crowd applauded; some gasped; some broke out in laughter. The Prime Minister's gesture, as given, meant quite something else. Instead of "V for victory", it meant something dirty; it was an obscene gesture!

Another case involved Nikita Khrushchev, the irrepressible leader of the U.S.S.R. in the late 'fifties and early sixties. During his tour of the U.S., he aroused quite a bit of controversy by a number of his remarks and some of his behavior. One of his contro-versial gestures was raising his clasped hands in a sort of handshake over his head. It apparently was meant to be a greeting and a sign of friendship, but it did not go over well with many who saw him in person or over TV. The gesture was familiar in the United States — the sign of victory after a boxer has defeated his opponent. Khrushchev had made earlier remarks about the burial of American capitalism, and many Americans regarded his as a boastful gesture signifying he had already won. Many, of course, were offended.

A comparative study of Chinese and American body language shows a number of similarities; for example: men don't hug or em-brace when meeting; a handshake is the most common gesture that goes with a greeting; waving a hand to say "goodbye" is the same; a frown shows displeasure, and the wrinkling of one's nose is a sign of dislike, disgust or disapproval; nodding means "yes", and shak-ing one's head means "no"; pouting has the same meaning — dis-pleasure, bad humor, resentment; a pat on the back of a man or boy indicates approval, praise, encouragement; gritting one's teeth may express anger, fury, or determination.

The charts on the following pages provide examples of some of the differences:

The examples in the charts are by no means complete, but are enough to illustrate the diversity of body language and to show the importance of knowing the specific gestures that go with a language.

The study of body language should be complementary to the study of language. The understanding of one should be helpful in the further understanding of the other. Some authorities feel that the two are dependent on each other. This is certainly true in most situ-ations. But it is also true that in certain situations body action con-

136

# A

## Same Body Language in Two Cultures,
## but with Different Meaning

| Meaning in China | Body Language | Meaning in U.S. |
|---|---|---|
| anger, irritation, frustration, remorse | stamping one's foot | impatience |
| thank you; mutual positive feelings | speaker or performer clapping at same time audience applauds (See Drawing 1) | applauding oneself; improper, immodest |
| curiosity, sometimes surprise | staring, gaping (See 2) | considered impolite; makes people embarrassed, self-conscious |
| disapproval, hissing | "Shhh"(See 3) | calling for silence |
| seldom used; occasionally adults may pat head of children to show affection; patting the head of a teenager or adult would cause displeasure and can be insulting (See 4) | pat on head | giving comfort, consolation or encouragement; also shows affection |

# B

## Different Body Language, Same Meaning

| Meaning | Body Language in China | Body Language in U.S. |
|---------|------------------------|-----------------------|
| "Come here" (beckoning someone to come) (See 5) | hand extended toward person, open palm, palm down, with all fingers crooked in a beckoning motion | hand extended toward person, closed hand, palm up, with forefinger only moving back and forth (in China, this same gesture would be considered offensive by many) |
| "Shame on you!" (semi-joking gesture) (See 6) | forefinger of one hand extended, tip touches one's own face several times quickly; similar to scratching, but with the forefinger straight (usually with the remark "Shame on you!") | forefinger of each hand extended, palms down in front of one's body; one forefinger makes several brushing movements over the back of the other forefinger |
| "I'm very full" (after a meal) (See 7) | one or both hands open, lightly patting one's own stomach | hand raised to throat, fingers extended, palm down (often with the remark "I'm full up to here.") |

# C

## Body Language and Meaning in One Culture;
## No Equivalent in Other Culture

### (1)

| Body Language | Meaning in U.S. |
|---|---|
| chewing one's fingernails (See 8) | emotional stress, worried, doesn't know what to do |
| thumbing one's nose (one thumb on tip of own nose, fingers curled and moving together) (See 9) | defiance, contempt |
| wagging one's finger (forefinger of one hand raised, other fingers clasped, the raised forefinger is wagged from side to side) (See 10) | warning not to do something; indicating that what the other person is doing is wrong |
| thumb down (arm crooked in front of body, closed fist, thumb extended down, one or several downward movements (See 11) | rejection of a proposal, idea, person; nonverbal way of saying a strong "No" |
| winking (quick closing of one eye, generally with a smile and slight nod) (See 12) | may show several feelings: understanding, approval, encouragement, trying to get across a message, solidarity |

## (2)

| Body Language | Meaning in China |
|---|---|
| touching or pointing to tip of one's own nose with raised forefinger (See 13) | "It's me" "I'm the one" (To Westerners, the gesture would seem slightly funny) |
| using an open hand to cover one's mouth while speaking (generally used by older people) (See 14) | to show confidentiality and secrecy; sometimes no meaning |
| using both hands (when one would be enough) in offering something to a visitor or another person (See 15) | respect |
| (When one's tea cup is being refilled by the host or hostess putting one or both hands upright, palm open, beside the cup (See 16) | "Thank you" |
| upraised forefinger of each hand coming together in front of the body until the two touch (See 17) | boy and girl in love; a good match |

140

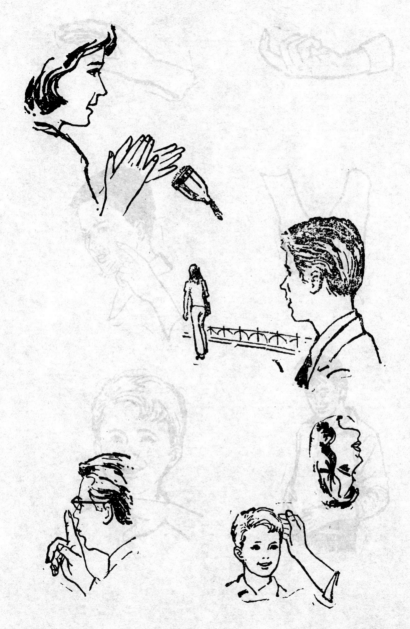

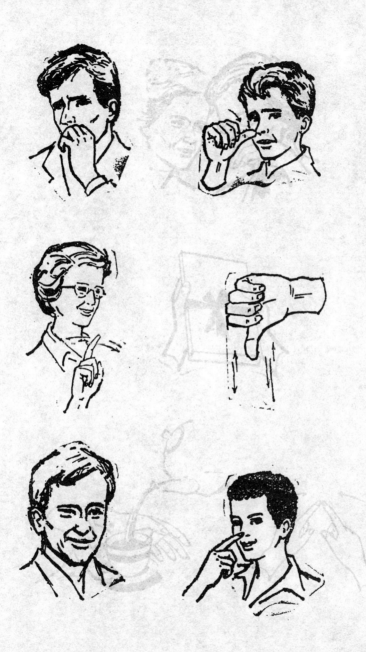

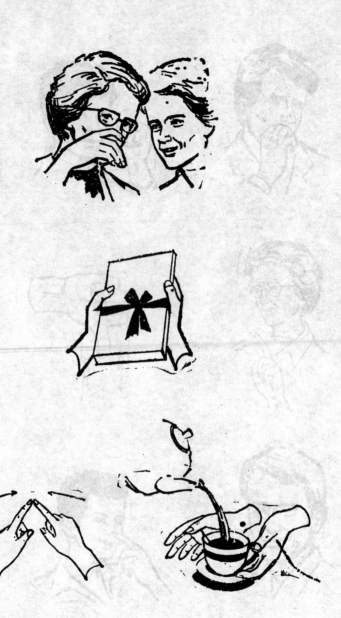

tradicts what is being said, just as the spoken words may mean something quite different from what body language communicates. When this occurs, one must try to get further information, or guess the meaning from the context of the situation. In a sense, all body language should be interpreted within a given context; to ignore the overall situation could be misleading.

A word of general advice: When one communicates in a certain language, it is generally advisable to use the nonverbal behavior that goes with that particular language. Observation shows that a truly bilingual person switches his body language at the same time he switches languages. This makes communication easier and better.

# 第一章

# 引　论

　　有一次，几个中国人到一位比较富裕的美国人家里去作客。主人引他们参观自己的住所，中国客人说："你们的房子多好啊。非常漂亮。"主妇听了十分高兴，按美国习惯笑着回答说："谢谢。"有些中国客人对她的回答感到意外。后来，在餐桌上谈话时，主人对大学毕业不久的中国女翻译说："你的英语很好，很流利。"女翻译谦虚地说："不！不！我的英语说得很不好。"主人没想到她会这样回答，感到有些迷惑不解。

　　那位美国主妇的回答是否像有些中国人认为的那样"不够谦虚"呢？

　　那位年轻的中国女翻译的回答是否像美国主人听起来那样"不够诚恳"呢？

　　其实，美国主妇的回答并非不谦虚，中国女翻译的回答也不是不诚恳。讲英语的人听到别人赞扬，一般说"谢谢"，表示接受，说明自己认为对方的赞扬是诚心诚意的，所赞扬的事是值得赞扬的。因此，不应"假装自卑"或"故作谦虚"。但是，对中国人来说，听到别人赞扬时，通常要表示受之有愧，做得很不够；或者说自己的成就不过是由于侥幸，或者说是客观条件造成的，等等，而接受赞扬则意味着有骄傲自满情绪或缺乏教养。因此，上述两种回答引起不同反应是由于双方语言习惯不同。他们都根据各自的风俗去理解别人所说的话。

文化背景不同,说不同语言的人在交谈时,常常发生下列情况:由于文化上的不同,即使语言准确无误,也会产生误会。对于不同的人们,同一个词或同一种表达方式可以具有不同的意义。由于文化上的差异,谈一个严肃的问题时,由于一句话说得不得体,可以使听者发笑,甚至捧腹大笑;一句毫无恶意的话可以使对方不快或气愤;由于文化上的差异,在国外演讲的人经常发现听众对他讲的某个笑话毫无反应,面无表情,鸦雀无声;然而,在国内,同一个笑话会使听众笑得前仰后合。

读者也许已经发现,此处所说的"文化"有特定的涵义。我们所说的"文化"指什么呢?

显然,这里所说的"文化"二字与"他没有文化"或"文化班"中的"文化"有所不同,与英语中的 culture 一词(狭义指文学、音乐、美术等)的涵义也不一样。我们这里所说的"文化"的涵义更广泛。这是一个社会学的术语,按照社会学家和人类学家对"文化"所下的定义,我们所说的"文化"是指一个社会所具有的独特的信仰、习惯、制度、目标和技术的总模式。

"文化包括一切人类社会共享的产物。"它不仅包括城市、组织、学校等物质的东西,而且包括思想、习惯、家庭模式、语言等非物质的东西。简单地说,文化指的是一个社会的整个生活方式,"一个民族的全部活动方式。"

语言是文化的一部分,并对文化起着重要作用。有些社会学家认为,语言是文化的冠石——没有语言,就没有文化;从另一个方面看,语言又受文化的影响,反映文化。可以说,语言反映一个民族的特征,它不仅包含着该民族的历史和文化背景,而且蕴藏着该民族对人生的看法、生活方式和思维方式。

关于文化与语言的关系,这里不再多谈。但应指出,语言与文化互相影响,互相作用;理解语言必须了解文化,理解文化必须了解语言。

社会学家告诉我们,一切文化都是独特的,互不相同的。文化是形形色色的,语言也是多种多样的。由于文化和语言上的差别。互相了解不是一件容易的事,不同文化间的交流常常遇到困难。

学习一种外语不仅要掌握语音、语法、词汇和习语,而且还要知道操这种语言的人如何看待事物,如何观察世界;要了解他们如何用他们的语言来反映他们社会的思想、习惯、行为;要懂得他们的"心灵之语言",即了解他们社会的文化。实际上,学习语言与了解语言所反映的文化是分不开的。

本书粗略探讨英语国家的人(或以英语为本族语的人)与中国人之间的文化差异。这种文化上的差异是多方面的,我们只围绕语言交际这一方面进行考察。至于其他,如生活方式、衣着打扮、举止行为、饮食习性等等与语言交际无关的差异,则不赘述。即使在语言交际范围内,我们也只能探讨一些最常见的差别。

这里"以英语为本族语的人"(或"英语国家的人")这个词主要指英国、美国、澳大利亚、加拿大、新西兰等国的居民。虽然他们的语言一样,但各自的文化却有所不同。实际上,他们的语言也不尽相同,尽管乍一听,区别并不明显。例如,在英国,"卡车"叫 lorries,在美国就叫 trucks。别人说 Thank you 之后,美国人回答 You're welcome,而英国人回答 Not at all 或 Don't mention it 或 It's a pleasure。这些都是相当于汉语"别客气"、"不用谢"之类的客套话,但用语不同。本书不可能论述所有讲英语的人的语言、文化习惯,仅限于探讨美国英语和美国文化。一方面是因为美国在英语世界所处的政治、经济、文化地位重要;另一方面是笔者比较熟悉美国英语和美国文化。

美国幅员广大,社会复杂,显然难于就整个国家进行概括。何况,在美国境内,还有因民族、阶级、地域、职业、性别、年龄之不同而形成的语言、文化的差异。然而,对某些事物来说,大多数美国人的看法和态度是基本相同的;对某些社会习惯、行为准则和社交方式,大多数美国人也是接受的,是遵守的。当然会有例外。我们在本书中将研究这些一般的看法、态度、习惯、准则和方式。

谈到中国,问题同样复杂。我们所说的中国语言指的是现代汉语,中国文化指的是现代汉族的文化。中国有很多民族,各有不同的文化,又有很多语言和方言,进行全面探讨是不可能的。甚至汉语和汉族文化也因地域而有所不同,因此我们把对汉语语言的研究范围限于以北京方言为基础的普通话(包括语言及文字)和以北京地区为主的汉族居民的文化。

　　本书对象为学习英语的学生、英语教师和英语翻译,即常与讲英语的人交往或常使用英语的人。这不是一本学术著作,我们进行了一些调查和探讨,但远非全面。希望以下各章的内容对多数读者有实用价值,对一些读者能有所启发,有助于他们作进一步的研究,而这一切我们希望会有助于国际间的相互了解。

# 第二章

## 论词:是同义,是相似,还是貌合神离?

把英语词、语译成汉语词、语时,它们的意义是否完全相等? 能否在汉英词典或英汉词典中查出汉语词的确切英语意义或英语词的准确的汉语对应词?

或许有人认为,这些问题有些奇怪。英语中的 book 就是汉语中的"书", tiger 就是"虎"。汉语中的"总司令"就是英语中的 commander-in-chief, "哲学"就是 philosophy, 这还用说吗?

但是,对上面所提的几个问题,回答都是绝对肯定的吗? 不同语言中的对应词的意义完全相同吗? 比如说:

汉语的"周末"相当于英语的 weekend。但是美国人或欧洲人对 weekend 的理解同中国人对"周末"的理解完全一致吗? 汉语的"知识分子"与英语的 intellectual 意思是一样的吗?

对这两个问题的回答似乎都是肯定的。所有的英汉词典上都用"周末"来注释 weekend, 用"知识分子"来注释 intellectual。然而,它们不尽相同,确实存在一些差别。

在中国,每周工作六天,"周末"指星期六晚上和星期日。在西方工业国家,每周工作五天,所以"周末"从星期五晚上开始,包括星期六和星期日。一个中国人刚到美国,不知道这种差别,当他看到有些商店的牌子上面写着 T.G.I.F., 听人说过 T.G.I.F. parties, 就问道:"T.G.I.F. 是什么意思", 别人告诉他说,这几个字母代表 Thank God it's Friday. 他一听感到奇怪,又问道:"为什么偏选星期五？为什么不说星期一、星期二或其他任何天呢？美国人正要解释，他忽然想起：在美国星期五是一周工作的最后一天。人们都盼望离开自己的工作岗位，享受两天的娱乐和休息。

同样，"知识分子"和 intellectual 在各自的文化背景中含意也大不相同。在中国，"知识分子"一般包括大学教师、大学生以及医生、工程师、翻译人员等一切受过大学教育的人；而且，中学教师也是知识分子。在中国农村有许多地方，连中学生也被认为是"知识分子"。但在美国和欧洲，intellectual 只包括大学教授等有较高的学术地位的人，而不包括普通大学生，所以这个词所指的人范围要小得多。此外，还有其他区别。在美国 intellectual 并不总是褒义词，有时用于贬义，如同我国文化大革命中叫"臭老九"一样。关于这一方面的区别，暂不在此讨论。

这两个例子说明，切不可以为双语词典上的注释都是词义完全对应的同义词，不要以为在不同的语言中总能找到对应词来表示同一事物。

我们在本章和下一章中探讨部分英语词和汉语词的语义差别。有以下几种情况：

1．在一种语言里有些词在另一语言里没有对应词。

2．在两种语言里，某些词语表面上似乎指同一事物或概念，其实指的是两回事。

3．某些事物或概念在一种语言里只有一两种表达方式，而在另一语言里则有多种表达方式，即在另一种语言里，这种事物或概念有更细微的区别。

4．某些词的基本意义大致相同，但派生意义的区别可能很大。

一

汉语中有个谚语："夏炼三伏，冬炼三九"。激励人们坚持锻炼

151

身体。"三伏"和"三九"在英语里是什么呢？一个年轻翻译对几个加拿大人说 three fu 和 three nine。听的人当然莫名其妙。他只要说 In summer keep exercising during the hottest days; in winter do the same thing during the coldest weather 就可以了。

一个中国青年到附近游泳池去游泳，一会儿就回来了。和他同住一室的中国人和一个外国朋友都感到奇怪。他解释说："游泳池里人太多，水太脏，早该换了。简直像芝麻酱煮饺子。"这个比喻很别致，很生动，和他同住一室的中国朋友笑了，而那个外国人既没有吃过"芝麻酱"也没有见过"煮饺子"，丝毫不觉得这个比喻幽默，难怪他显出一副茫然不解的神情。西方人形容某地人多、拥挤不堪，常说 It was packed like sardines（塞得像沙丁鱼罐头一样，拥挤不堪）。这种比喻有些中国人可以理解，但不一定能欣赏其妙处，因为见过打开的沙丁鱼罐头的人很少，看到过一个又小又扁的罐头盒里，紧紧塞满整整齐齐的几排手指头长的沙丁鱼的人是不多的。

还可以举出很多例子说明某些事物或概念在一种文化中有，在另一种文化中则没有。

例如，汉语中的"干部"这个词译成英语时往往用 cadre。但是英语的 cadre 与汉语中的"干部"不同。而且 cadre 不是常用词，许多讲英语的人都不知道它是什么意思。即使认识它的人，在说到它时，发音也不一样——有三四种读法。因此有人建议用 official（官员；行政人员；高级职员），functionary（机关工作人员；官员），administrator（行政官员）等代替 cadre，但这些词没有一个与汉语中的"干部"完全相同。

同样，汉语中没有表达 cowboy 和 hippie（或 hippy）的意思的对应词。这两个词是美国社会特有的产物。cowboy 与美国早期开发西部地区有关，关于他们的传说总带有浓厚的浪漫主义和传奇色彩。在汉语中译为："牧童"或"牛仔"，反映不出这些意义。汉语中把 hippie 音译成"希比士"或"希比派"也没反映出 60 年代那些中国人觉得行为古怪的美国青年的特点。译成"嬉皮士"可能稍好一些,不过这个词也会造成误解,因为那批青年并不都是"嬉皮笑脸"的人,其中有不少人对待社会问题很严肃,对社会怀有某种不满情绪,尽管他们的生活方式与众不同:往往蓄长发,身穿奇装异服,甚至行为颓废,染上吸毒恶习,等等。这就要在词典上或译文中加解释性说明了。

在社会活动和政治活动方面的用语中也可以举出不少例子。例如汉语中的"斗争会"这个词可以译成 struggle meeting,但这种译法说明不了这种会的内容。反过来,美国的 revival meeting 是什么样的活动,中国人很难猜测,除非亲自到现场看过这种宗教气氛极浓、歇斯底里般的信仰复兴集会。同样,中国人对 bingo party和 bingo game 往往一无所知,有些词典中 bingo 的汉语注释是:"一种用纸牌搭成方块的赌博"(《新英汉词典》),"排五点[一种赌博性游戏]"(《英华大辞典》),读者查到此词仍然不得要领。

日常生活中的用语也有类似现象。多数英美人从来没有睡过中国的"炕"(kang, a heatable brickbed),没有吃过"冰糖葫芦",(candied haws on a stick),也没有用过中国的"秤"(steelyard)。大部分中国人没有住过美国的 motel (专为开汽车的游客开设的、有停车场的旅馆),没有吃过 hamburger (牛肉饼;汉堡牛排;汉堡包),也不需要在上班时由 time clock (出勤记录钟)证明他们是否按时上班。类似这样的英语词在汉语中都找不到对应词,连词义相近的词也没有,因为根本没有这种概念。这种情况十分普遍,无需在此多说。

在表示自然现象的语言中,汉语中"节气"的概念在英语中是没有的。(应当指出,把"节气"译成 solar terms,大部分西方人仍然不懂。)如一部常用的现代《汉英词典》中,把"雨水"译成 Rain Water (2nd Solar Term),把"惊蛰"译成 Waking of Insects (3rd Solar Term),把"清明"译成 Pure and Brightness (5th Solar Term)。这些名称不另加解释就没有什么意义。但有些"节气"的名称在英

153

语中确实有对应词:春分 = Spring Equinox;夏至 = Summer Solstice;秋分 = Autumnal Equinox;冬至 = Winter Solstice。

在表示自然力和宇宙方面,汉语里有些传统的古老的词,如"阴"和"阳",在英语里没有对应词,《朗曼现代英语词典》对"阴"和"阳"的解释是:"按道教的宇宙观,'阴'和'阳'是两种力量,这两种力量的本质产生了宇宙,保持宇宙和谐。'阴'表示黑暗、雌性、消极的。'阳'表示光明、雄性、积极的。"

"阴"和"阳"的概念作为中医治疗基本原理的一部分已沿用了许多世纪,然而,这些原理却很难对西方人讲清楚。中医理论里所说的"寒"、"上火"等概念,也很难用英语词表达,只能做些解释。如"上火",就说是"内热过多",然后再描写一下症状。在《汉英词典》中"阴"、"阳"两词只好分别注释为:(in Chinese philosophy, medicine, etc.) *yin*, the feminine or negative principle in nature; *yang*, the masculine or positive principle in nature 与《朗曼现代英语词典》一致,但西方人还是不易明白。

以上例证足以说明差别之大。造成这些差别原因是多方面的,或是由于环境和传统有所不同,或是由于工业和技术发展的水平有差异,或是由于政治制度和社会制度不一样,等等。

遇到这些问题应该怎么办呢?

1. 释义:例如英语中的 brunch 一词在《新英汉词典》中是这样解释的:"晚吃的早餐;早吃的午餐;早餐和午餐并作一顿吃的一餐。"在《英华大词典》中是这样解释的:"(早点与午餐并作一顿吃的)晚早餐,早中饭"。

2. 译音:例如英语中的 radar 译成"雷达"; coffee 译成"咖啡";汉语中的"大字报"译成 dazibao;"气功"译成 qigong (chigong);鲁迅就曾把 fairplay 译成"费厄泼赖"。

3. 造词:例如汉语中的"武术"在英语中称为 martial arts; 英语中的 computer software 和 hardware 分别称为"软件"和"硬件"。但是,这种新造的词往往一时不为一般群众所知,不易被人接受,至少最初使用时是这样。所以有时还需要酌加解释,例如:splashdown 称为:"(宇宙飞船在水面上)溅落。"

4. 综合:一种注释法表达不清楚时,可采用两种或几种办法综合处理,如可以又译音,又释义。《朗曼现代英语词典》在注释汉语词"磕头"或"叩头"时是这样的:*kowtow*;... to kneel, touching the ground with the forehead as a token of homage or deep respect among the Chinese。(中国人下跪并以前额触地,表示臣服或深深的敬意。)再如"锅"这个汉语词,《新编韦氏大学词典》的释义是:*wok* ... a bowl shaped cooking utensil used esp. in the preparation of Chinese food。(炊事用具,形状像碗,多用于烧中式菜。)人们也许会说, wok 的发音不像普通话中的"锅"。其实,它来自广东方言。

《英汉大词典》中 engine 的汉语释义是:"引擎","蒸气机","发动机"。

二

有这样一个故事:罗马有一家鞋店,门口挂着一个牌子,招徕懂英语的顾客。牌子上写道: Shoes for street walking. Come in and have a fit。这个牌子引起许多懂英语的游览者的注意,他们聚在店前——不是看橱窗里所展出的商品,而是看牌子上的字,看后都哈哈大笑。店主是意大利人,会说一点英语,但他不知道 street walker 不是"逛大街的人",而是"在街头拉客的妓女", to have a fit 也不是"试穿",而是"勃然大怒"。过路人看了这块牌子当然感到滑稽可笑了。

有些懂一些英语的中国人介绍自己的爱人时用 lover 一词,外国人对此颇为惊讶(因为 lover 表示情夫或情妇的意思)。外国人不理解,一向在这类问题上谨慎小心的中国人,为何公开声明自己有 lover 呢? 应该记住,相当于汉语中"爱人"这个词的英语词就是：husband（丈夫）或 wife（妻子）；fiancé（未婚夫）或 fiancée（未婚妻）。

美国总统的夫人和州长的夫人常称为 First Lady，有时译作"第一夫人"，但一些中国人看到"第一夫人"字样会发生误解，以为既然有"第一夫人"就有"第二夫人"甚至有"第三夫人"、"第四夫人"等，从而得出一种错误的印象："白宫的主人居然搞了好几个老婆！"

中国人问别人的"籍贯"时，可能指 place of birth 或 where a person is from（本人的出生地或来自某地），也往往指 where a person's parents or ancestors came from originally（父母或祖先来自何地）。有时这两个地方是相同的，但也常常不同。在英语中没有与"籍贯"对应的词。place of birth 只表示本人出生的地方，与祖先的任何情况无关。这种差别有时会造成混乱，填写身份证、个人履历表、护照等时尤其如此。

下面再举一些英汉两种语言中"貌合神离"的词语的例子。

指"处所"、"机构"等的词语：

high school ≠ 高等学校

　　high school 是美国的中学。英国的中学叫 secondary school。

service station ≠ 服务站

　　service station 是给汽车加油及进行简单维修的地方。

rest room ≠ 休息室

　　在美国英语中，rest room 是剧院、大商店或大建筑物中的一间房子，里面设有厕所、盥洗设备等，供顾客、雇员等使用。这是浴室、厕所的委婉说法。汉语中的"休息室"应译为英语中的 lounge 或 lobby。

指"人"的词语：

busboy ≠ 公共汽车上的售票员或司机

　　busboy 与公共汽车没有任何关系，它指的是在餐馆中收拾碗碟、擦桌子的杂工。（美国英语）

goldbrick ≠ 金锭

　　goldbrick 不是用以称赞人的词，它是美国英语中的俚语，指逃避工作

156

的人,尤其是爱偷懒的士兵、懒汉。

## 大忙人 ≠ busybody

英语的 busybody 相当于汉语的"爱管闲事的人"。汉语中的"大忙人"可译为 a very busy person,也可以直接说:He/She is always busy. He/She is always busy with something.

从词的组成看,人们会认为 goldbrick 和 busybody 是褒义词,其实都是贬义词。

## 指"政治活动"、"社会活动"等的词语:

## political campaign ≠ 政治运动

political campaign 指英美政府职务的候选人为了树立自己的形象,争取选票而组织的活动,即竞选活动。

## 改善生活 ≠ improve one's standard of living

在英语中 improve one's standard of living 表示"提高生活水平"的意思,而汉语中的"改善生活"则不然;《人民日报》(1984 年 2 月 26 日)一则新闻中说:"我的邻居是一位六十多岁的老太太,隔三差五,到街头饭馆改善一次生活。但每次都是去一家私人饭馆。她说,原因不是别的,就是这家小饭馆服务态度好,总听到一声'里边请'。"按中国的习惯用法,"改善生活"在一般情况下指吃一顿或几顿比常吃的伙食较好的饭菜等。

## 成语,谚语,常用语法:

## 令人发指 ≠ to make one's hair stand on end

前者用于看到或听到某种暴行等而十分"气愤"的场合,后者用于看到或听到某种可怕的事物而十分"害怕"的场合,相当于"令人毛骨悚然。"例如:The sight made his hair stand on end —— he thought it was his dead brother's ghost. (这个景象使他毛骨悚然,他以为这是他哥哥[或弟弟]的鬼魂出现了。)英语中有 to bristle with anger 一语,表示"气得毛发竖起来",但多用于动物,不用于人,除非用作比喻。《英华大辞典》上举了两个例子:His hair bristled on his scalp with anger. (他气得头发都竖起来了。) The hog bristled up. (猪的鬃毛竖起了。)

## 自食其言 ≠ to eat one's own words

前者指说了话不算数,答应了的事不去做。后者指收回自己说的

157

话,一般多用于强迫别人收回所说的话,使他丢脸。例如:He told every-
one he was absolutely certain that his article would be published by the
*Times*, but when the letter of rejection came, he had to eat his own
words.(他逢人就说《泰晤士报》必将发表他的文章。退稿之后,他只好
收回自己的话。)

## to get a kick out of something ≠ 被踢出去

前者是非常道地的英语成语,多用于口语,意思是"欣赏……或
从……中得到极大愉快"。如:I got a kick out of watching those kids
perform; their play made me realize how strange and funny we grown-ups
must seem to them.(我非常欣赏孩子们的表演。他们演的戏使我意识
到,在他们看来,我们这些成人多么古怪和可笑。)这与"踢"这一动作本
身毫无关系。

## to blow one's own horn (or trumpet) ≠ 各吹各的号

前者是个成语,表示"自吹自擂",一般用来形容某人炫耀自己的成
就、技能、智力等。很像汉语中的"老王卖瓜,自卖自夸"。如:If he's so
successful, why does he have to keep blowing his own trumpet?(既然他
干得很出色,干吗要整天自我吹嘘呢?)汉语中的"各吹各的号,各唱各
的调"则表示两个或几个人各干各的事或各自坚持自己的看法,不能协
调一致,与英语中的 each doing his own thing 相近。

# 第三章

## 再论词：文化差别和词的涵义

### 一

同一个事物、生物或概念，在某些语言中可能只用一个词来表达，在另一种语言中可能有几个或更多的词来表达。一般地说，表示同一概念的词越多，词义就区分得越细。如汉语中只有"骆驼"一个词，它相当于英语中的 camel，也可细分为 dromedary(单峰骆驼)和 Bactrian camel(双峰骆驼)。但据说，阿拉伯语中有四百多个词表示"骆驼"，因为骆驼曾是大多数阿拉伯人的重要交通工具。这四百来个词可以区分骆驼的年龄、性别、品种、大小等，甚至还可以区分骆驼能否驮重物。据说最少有一个词指怀了孕的骆驼。

在用汉语和英语与不同文化背景的人进行交际时，表示亲属的词语常常在彼此理解对方的意思方面会造成很大困难，因为不是所有的称呼都能找到令人满意的对应词。英语中 Linda's brother married Michael's sister 这句话都很难译成汉语，因为不知道 brother 是指 Linda 的哥哥还是弟弟；sister 是指 Michael 的姐姐还是妹妹。在汉语中，则有许多称呼来指各种具体的关系。请看下表：

| 汉语词 | 英语词 | 必要的英语解释 | | |
|---|---|---|---|---|
| 祖父(母) | grandfather (mother) | paternal grandfather (mother) | | |
| 外祖父(母) | | maternal grandfather (mother) | | |
| 父 | father | | | |
| 母 | mother | | | |
| 兄,(姐) | brother (sister) | elder brother, (sister) | | |
| 弟,(妹) | | younger brother (sister) | | |
| 伯父 | uncle | paternal uncle | father's brother | elder brother |
| 叔父 | | | | younger brother |
| 姑父 | | | husband of father's sister | |
| 舅父 | | maternal uncle | mother's brother | |
| 姨父 | | | husband of mother's sister | |
| 姐夫 | brother-in-law | husband of elder sister | | |
| 妹夫 | | husband of younger sister | | |

上表仅列出部分亲属关系,至于"姨公(婆)"、"堂(表)兄弟(姐妹")、"嫂子"、"弟妹"、"小舅子"、"侄"、"外甥"等用更细致的方式来区分的亲属关系,在交际中所造成的困难更大。西方人对这些汉语称呼束手无策。relative(亲戚)一词简单得多,就用它来表示一切亲属关系,多么省事。

应该指出,在不用名字而用表示亲属关系的词称呼长辈时,按英语习惯,往往降一辈来称呼。例如:greatuncle(指与祖父同辈的男亲属)可称 Uncle 或 Uncle Jim, Uncle Henry 等。实际上,用 Greatuncle Liu, Greatuncle Chen 之类来称呼一个人,听起来不太顺耳,而且许多西方人也不喜欢别人用 grand-或 great-之类来强调自己上了年纪。

在汉语中一般只用"公"和"母"(或"雌"和"雄")二字来区分禽

兽的性别。在英语中则往往各有单独名称,小动物也另有名称。
见下表:

| 总　　称 | 雄性名称 | 雌性名称 | 小动物名称 |
|---|---|---|---|
| chicken 鸡 | cock, rooster | hen | chick |
| duck 鸭 | drake | duck | duckling |
| goose 鹅 | gander | goose | gosling |
| horse 马 | stallion | mare | foal |
| cattle (cow) 牛 | bull | cow | calf |
| pig 猪 | boar | sow | shoat |
| dog 狗 | dog | bitch | puppy |
| sheep 羊 | ram | ewe | lamb |
| deer 鹿 | stag | doe | fawn |

　　并非所有禽兽都要用特殊名称来区分雌雄。人们对某些特殊名称并不熟悉。要用不常见的区分禽兽雌雄的词时,常用 bull 或 cow, cock 或 hen 来代替。如 bull seal(公海豹),cow seal(母海豹);bull elephant(公象),cow elephant(母象);cock pheasant(公野鸡),hen pheasant(母野鸡);cock sparrow(公麻雀),hen sparrow(母麻雀)。也可用 male 和 female 或 she 再加上原名。如:male leopard(公豹),female panda(母熊猫),she wolf(母狼)。
　　再举一些例子:
　　机关名称和职务名称在汉英两种语言中也不是一对一的对应关系。例如:

　　各国国会的名称:

| 汉　　语 | 英　　语 |
|---|---|
| 国　　会 | Parliament (英国和其他国家) |
| | Congress (美国和其他国家) |
| | Diet (日本和其他国家) |

161

副职的名称:

| 汉 语 | 英 语 | 英 语 实 例 |
|---|---|---|
| 副（职） | vice | vice-chairman, vice-president |
| | associate | associate professor, associate director |
| | *assistant | assistant manager, assistant secretary |
| | deputy | deputy director, deputy chief-of-staff |
| | lieutenant | lieutenant governor, lieutenant general |
| | under | undersecretary (of State, U.S.) |

*assistant 在汉语中常译为"助理"。但在英语中与副职的地位和称呼一般并无区别。

# 二

现在谈谈词的涵义。什么是词的涵义呢?《朗曼现代英语词典》上说:涵义是"一个词的基本意义之外的含义"。

《新编韦氏大学词典》上说:涵义是"一个词明确指称或描写的事物之外的暗示的意义"。

这两部词典的定义说明:词的涵义不同于它的字面意义——基本的或明显的意义。涵义是词的隐含或附加的意义。对于学外语的学生来说,不仅要掌握词的字面意义,而且要知道词的涵义。不了解词汇涵义,会在言语上犯严重错误;有时误把好言当恶语,引起谈话者的一方或双方不快;有时误把嘲讽当称赞,被人暗笑。

谈起中国农村时,在华的一些讲英语的外国人有时问道:"你们为什么要用 peasant 一词? 我想,农民的社会地位不是已经变了,他们不是得到尊重了吗?"

很多中国人会认为这个问题提得莫名其妙。为什么不能把农民叫 peasant 呢? 用了这个词为什么就意味着不尊重他们呢?

比较敏感的中国人会从外国人提的问题意识到:英语中的

peasant 与汉语中的"农民"所体现的意义并不完全相同，可能有不同的涵义，英语中的 peasant 很可能有贬义。其实，查一下词典就清楚了。下面是两部词典给 peasant 一词所下定义中的一部分：

《新编韦氏大学词典》："一般指未受过教育的、社会地位低下的人"。

《美国传统词典》："乡下人，庄稼人，乡巴佬"；"教养不好的人，粗鲁的人"。

既然 peasant 有这种涵义，美国人和英国人自然会认为：在一个强调平等的国家里，为什么把广大农村居民称为社会地位低下、没有教养的人呢？为什么称他们是"无赖和流氓"呢？（见《牛津英语词典》）

汉语中的"农民"一词当然毫无贬义。我们现在把"农民"这个词译作 peasant 时，用的是它的基本意义：

"农民阶级的一员，包括农场主、有土地的农民、雇农等"（《美国传统词典》）；

"广大雇农和小农都很穷困的国家里的农场主、有土地的农民、佃农和雇农"（《朗曼现代英语词典》）。

谈到 peasant 这个词，我们不妨讨论一下讲英语的人对下面这句话的反应：The poor peasants talked about their happy life today.（贫农谈到他们现在的幸福生活。）

了解中国农村 1949 年后发生的巨大变化的人很容易理解这句话。不过，许多讲英语的人不知道 poor peasant（贫农）和 rich peasant（富农）有特别的意义。他们不了解这两个词是用来区分解放前阶级成分的用语。他们认为，poor 就是"缺钱，缺物，无奢侈品"。既然如此，贫苦农民还有什么幸福生活可言呢？当然觉得不可思议了。

进一步说，在中国，poor peasant（贫农）和 laborer（劳工）含有正面的、积极的涵义，但对许多西方国家的一些人来讲，却有某种反面的、消极的意味。相反，landlord（地主），capitalist（资本家），

163

boss(老板)对中国人来说有一定的贬义,而在资本主义国家对许多人来说却不是这样的。这些词的某种涵义反映了人们对不同社会阶级的不同态度。但无论赞同与否,必须承认这种语言事实,才能使交际双方彼此间真正互相了解。

下面我们再举一些例子来说明词的不同涵义、词的不同文化内涵和某些词使人产生的联想等问题。

首先,idealist 和 materialist 这两个英语词常常被人误解。如果没有具体的上下文,前者通常译作"唯心主义者",后者通常译作"唯物主义者"。在哲学著作中,这种译法可能是对的。不过,这两个词常常用来表示完全不同的意思。请看下面在实际对话中引出的一段:

> "She has always been an *idealist*. So you can understand why she turned down a good job offer to work among refugee immigrants and low-income groups after she got her degree in social studies."("她一向追求自己的理想。因此,可以理解,她得到社会学学位之后,拒绝了一项很不错的工作,却到逃难来美国的移民中和低收入的阶层中去工作。")

显然,这段话中的"她"是致力于实现自己的理想的人,不是一味追求高薪工作、追求金钱或物质享受的人。可以把"她"叫做"理想主义者"或"追求理想的人",但不是"唯心主义者"。根据实际情况,也可以说"她"是个脱离实际的"不现实的人",因为英语中的 idealist 这个词也有这种涵义。

英语中的 materialist 也有同样的问题。请看笔者参加的谈话中所听到的一段话:

> "Quite frankly, I'm a *materialist*. I've got a good-paying job and I want to keep it. I've bought a home near Westlake, and me and my wife want to enjoy the comforts of life. I had a hard time when I was a kid and I don't want to go through all that again."

> (老实说,我是个讲究实际的人。我有一个收入不错的工作,希望能干下去。我在西湖买了一所房子,我和我的老伴儿要享受享受了。我年轻的时候很苦,我不想再过那种日子了。)

lectual 一词带有强烈的贬义……它意味着极端势利或高傲自大。）

显然,使用 intellectual 这个词时要十分小心,必须考虑上下文、语言环境及所指的人。

还有一些词在一种语言的常用意义中有贬义、在另一种语言中却没有贬义或只是中性词,例如:

**1**

| 中国人(贬义) | 词　语 | 美国人(褒义) |
|---|---|---|
| 野心勃勃的 | ambitious | 有雄心的<br>有抱负的 |
| 平均主义的<br>"大锅饭"的 | equalitarian<br>(egalitarian) | 平均主义的<br>平等主义的 |

**2**

| 中国人(褒义) | 词　语 | 美国人(贬义) |
|---|---|---|
| 宣传 | propaganda | 传播带有偏见的消息<br>以使人赞成或反对某<br>种观点 |
| 做好事的人 | do-gooder | 空想的社会改良家 |

美国安乃特·鲁宾斯坦博士曾在北京外国语学院任教。许多学习英国文学的中国学生都知道她的著作《英国文学的伟大传统——从莎士比亚到萧伯纳》。她谈到她 1982～1983 年在中国教 ambitious 这个词的体会:

"我曾在中学和大学里教过 89 次或 90 次《凯撒大帝》,在美国授课时,每次都要解释一下安东尼为什么在形容凯撒时,将 ambitious 作为

167

一个贬义词来用。如安东尼提到凯撒时曾说：'他是我的好朋友，对我忠实，待我公正。但布鲁特斯却说他有野心（he was ambitious），如果真的是那样，那是严重的错误'。这次在北京外国语学院授课时，我准备对这个词做第91次解释。但学生没有就此提出一个问题。他们认为 ambition 理所当然是贬义词。我实在不明白为什么。他们认为 ambition 是什么意思呢？他们把 ambitious and greedy（有野心和贪婪的）或 ambitious and ruthless（有野心和残忍的）联系在一起。我问学生：'你们不说 poor but ambitious（人穷志不穷）或 ambitious and hardworking（壮志满怀，勤奋努力）吗？'他们说：'不，不。'——他们认为 ambition 的含义是不会与这些词相联的。"

英语中的 do-gooder 是贬义词，从字面上看，可能有不少中国人感到奇怪。"干好事的人"怎么会有贬义呢？参看《韦氏国际大词典（第三版）》的定义有助于弄清这个词的涵义：

"真心实意有志于为社会谋福利或进行改革，但通常是不现实的人道主义者——一般带有过于天真或浮躁鲁莽、徒劳无功等贬义。"

在英汉词典上一般译为"空想的社会改革家"。

把一位不谋私利、乐于助人的人叫做 do-gooder，这是多么大的错误！

读者可能会注意到，本节所举例词大部分来自社会科学，这是很自然的，这不仅反映了文化上的差别，还体现了政治上的一些差别。

其实，英语中的 social sciences 一词本身也值得注意。在汉语中这个词译作"社会科学"。这两个词概括的语义范围是否完全一样呢？根据现代汉语的用法，"社会科学"包括除自然科学和应用科学以外的一切学科，也包括英语所称的 the humanities（人文学科）——语言、文学、哲学等学科。英语中的 social sciences 一词概括的范围较小，包括政治学、经济学、历史学（历史学有时列入人文学科）、社会学等，即一切研究人类社会，尤其是社会组织和社会成员之间的关系的学科。

# 第四章

## 日常谈话中的文化差别

### 一 打招呼和告别

一天中午, 一个在中国学习的美国留学生有个约会。他刚要骑上自行车, 一位中国朋友从旁边走过, 问他:"吃了吗?"这是中国人在吃饭前后打招呼的常用语。美国留学生笑着点点头, 挥挥手表示告别, 就走了。他知道, 中国朋友的话等于英语中的 Hello 或 Hi。但如果照字面译成 Have you eaten yet? 或 Have you had your lunch? 外国人听起来就很怪。

美国人会以为, 这种打招呼似乎是说:"我也没有吃。走吧, 我们一起去吃点东西吧。"或者说:"没有吃的话, 我正要请你到我家去呢"。总之, 这样打招呼有时意味着邀请对方去吃饭。

发生过这样的事。有一次, 一个刚到中国不久的外国留学生结结巴巴地用汉语说:"你们为什么老问我吃了饭没有? 我有钱。"他以为人们总问他"吃饭了吗"是因为怕他没钱吃饭。他显然对这种问法感到生气。

再如, 汉语中的"上哪儿去啊?"和"到哪儿去啦?"这样打招呼的话直译成英语就是 Where are you going? 和 Where have you been? 用这两句英语来打招呼, 大部分讲英语的人听了会不高兴, 他们的反应很可能是:It's none of your business! (你管得着吗!)

幸而,打招呼的话并不都令人感到奇怪或者引起对方反感。有许多打招呼的话是相似的,有些只是说法不同。在许多语言里,打招呼的话往往与时间有关,但即使在一种语言中也有不一致的地方。英语中有 Good morning, Good afternoon, Good evening(都相当于汉语中的"您好",只是说的时间不同而已),但不说 Good noon。而 Good night(晚安;明天见;再会)根本不是打招呼的话(大多数讲英语的人不会这样说)。这只是告别时说的话。

两个中国人初次见面时,没有什么特别的汉语说法,而多数讲英语的人初次见面总要说 I'm pleased to meet you.(认识你很高兴)之类的客套话。分手时,他们还要说句 It's nice meeting you 或 It's nice to have met you.(能认识你很高兴)之类的话。

人们分手时通常说 Good-bye, Bye-bye, Au revoir, Hasta la vista, 相当于中国人说"再见"。几乎所有语言中都有类似的说法。但在说 Good-bye 或"再见"之前,还有些客套语很有意思,各种语言也不尽相同。如有贵客或不大熟的人来访或串门儿,客人离开时,按中国的习惯,主人要把客人送到房门口或大门口。客人对主人说"请留步",主人最后要说"走好"、"慢走"、"慢点儿骑(自行车)"之类的客套话。这些说法都不能直接译成英语。如果说 Stay here, 听起来十分别扭。如果说 Go slowly, Walk slowly 或 Ride slowly, 也很不自然。其实,微微一笑并作个表示再见的手势就可以了。

## 二 各种称呼

近年来,许多讲英语的人常常用名字称呼别人(如: Tom, Michael, Linda, Jane 等),而不用某某先生、某某太太或某某小姐(如:Mr Summers, Mrs Howard, Miss Jones 等)。这种做法在美国人中尤为普遍,甚至初次见面就用名字称呼。不仅年龄相近的人之间这样称呼,年龄悬殊的人之间也这样称呼,没有不尊重对方的意思。可以听到孩子叫年长的人 Joe, Ben, Helen, 等。甚至孩子对父母或祖父母也可以这样称呼。社会地位不同的人也是这样的。例如,许多大学生叫老师的名字。老师们对这种做法并不反感,也不认为学生不尊重自己或过于随便;他们反而认为学生能这样做,正好说明自己待人友好,平易近人。这当然与中国的习惯完全相反。中国孩子对祖父母,学生对老师,若直呼其名,成年人的反应是可想而知的;孩子会挨一顿骂,甚至会挨几巴掌。

中国人称呼家庭成员、亲戚或邻居时,往往用"二哥"、"三姐"、"四婶"、"周大伯"之类。这些称呼不可用于英语。用英语称呼时不论对男人还是女人,一般直呼其名就行了。主要的例外是:称父母为 Dad, Mom, Mum, Mother 等,称祖父母为 Grandpa, Grandma 等,有时称年长的亲戚为 Aunt Mary 或 Uncle Jim(注意:一般用名字,不用姓)。就连对这种亲属关系,美国人也倾向于用名字相称,不用表示亲属关系的词语。应当指出,Brother Joseph 或 Sister Mary 之类的称呼只用于天主教团体和某些别的宗教或职业团体。

中国人称呼别人时,有时称此人当时所担任的职务,前面加上他的姓,如"黄局长"、"林经理"、"马校长"之类。但是,很少听到讲英语的人称别人为 Bureau Director Smith(史密斯局长), Manager Jackson(杰克逊经理), Principal Morris(莫里斯校长)。只有少数职业或职务可用于称呼。如医生或有博士学位的人称 Doctor—;有权主持法庭审判的人可称 Judge—。州长和市长可称 Governor—和 Mayor—,但往往只称 Governor 或 Mayor,省去其名;Professor 一词也有类似用法。

应该指出,对军官的称呼在汉语两种语言中也有所不同。在汉语中用姓加职务,如"陈司令"、"郝团长"、"梁排长"等。在英语中则用姓加军衔,不用姓加职务,如可以说 Captain Johnson(约翰逊上尉),却不说 Company Commander Johnson(约翰逊连长);可以说 Admiral Benjamin(本杰明海军上将),却不说 Fleet Commander Benjamin(本杰明舰队司令官)。

汉语作品译成英语时,常常将某些称呼直译成英语词,如把"爷爷"译成 Grandpa,"姑姑"译成 Auntie,"嫂子"译成 Sister-in-law,讲英语的人听起来不顺耳,实际上也不完全对应。有些人用英语写中国的事情时,用这些称呼使文字带有中国色彩,这是无可非议的。不过,有些称呼使人为难。例如,如何称呼教师,就一直是个问题,是直接叫 Teacher(老师),还是叫 Teacher Zhang(张老师)?这两种叫法都不符合英语习惯。称老师为 Comrade(同志)或 Comrade Li(李同志),合适吗?Comrade 一词在非社会主义国家不大用。如果让中小学生就按英语习惯,称教师为 Mr Wang(王先生)Mrs Yang(杨太太)或 Miss Fei(费小姐),中国人又觉得有些刺耳。

再有就是"师傅"、"警察叔叔"、"解放军叔叔"等称呼。把"师傅"译成 master,就带有"主仆关系"的味道,不是目前汉语"师傅"二字所表达的意思。更难办的是,原来"师傅"只用来称呼老手艺人、工人、厨师、汽车司机等。现在却成了一种很普遍的称呼,不问职业,不分男女,都可以称"师傅"。把"解放军叔叔"译成 P.L.A. Uncle,把"警察叔叔"译成 Uncle Policeman 都不妥。第一,很多外国人不知道 P.L.A. 代表"中国人民解放军";第二,在西方,军队和警察与人民的关系不像在中国这样亲密,不明白为什么要称他们为"叔叔"。

还有一种现象也很有趣。英语中没有一个笼统的称呼用来引起陌生人或不知姓名的人注意。汉语则很方便,用"同志"就可以了,现在更时髦的是叫"师傅"。碰到这种情况要用英语时怎么办?这要根据情况而定。按英语习惯,有时可以说 Excuse me, Pardon me, I say there(英国英语)等用语,显得比较客气。有时说 Hey;或 Hey, you;或 you, there 等用语,但不大客气。实际上,人们常常不用任何称呼,不用任何语言,就靠清清嗓子,或随便哼一声,或做个手势,以引起对方注意。

172

### 三 祝贺和赞扬

第一章曾说过,听到别人赞扬,美国人和中国人的回答不同:美国人一般表示接受赞扬,中国人则一般表示受之有愧。

关于这种差别,可以再多谈几句。请看下面几个例子:

1. 一位中国青年妇女在美国,身上穿着一件漂亮的服装。当别人对她说:这件衣服真雅致,颜色美极了。这位中国青年妇女很高兴,但有些不好意思,就按中国习惯回答说:"这是件普通的衣服,我在中国国内买的。"

2. 一位中国学者刚到美国,到一所大学去参加招待会。女主人是他的老朋友。两个人正在谈话,女主人的一个熟人走过来。她对那个人说:"罗恩,我来介绍一下,这位是陈先生,他是杰出的物理学家,是一位很了不起的人。"陈先生同刚走过来的人握手,看看女主人,笑着说:"叫我脸红呢,还是跟他说您只是开个玩笑呢?"

在这两个例子里,两位中国人的回答都可能被人误解。别人也许以为青年妇女的回答是说对方不识货,对一件普通衣服如此大惊小怪,可见美国妇女鉴赏能力有问题。那位姓陈的物理学家的回答,如果不是带着笑,别人可能认为他的意思是:"你这么说,不过是表示客气,不是真心话。"第一例中说对方鉴别能力差,第二例中说女主人言不由衷。二者都有责备赞扬者的意味,说话人的意图和所传达的信息之间有很大差距。

还有一些话,在汉语中很得体,在同外国人谈话时,说了这些话却会起相反的作用。这里举两个例子:

1. 一个外国人到中国人家里作客,看到主人养的花儿长得很好,有几盆花儿开得很茂盛,流露出赞赏的神情,主人却不好意思地说:"我喜欢养花,但不太会养。"

2. 一位中国美术教师认识一位加拿大妇女。有一天,那位加拿大人拿了自己写的一篇有关中国画的文章,请他过目。他答应了,但谦虚地说:"其实我也不大懂。"

在这两种情况下,即使他们说的是真心话,别人都会怀疑是在故作谦虚,以便博得赞扬。因为,在第一种场合,外国客人不得不说:"不,这花非常美"或"我要是能养成这样就好了"之类的话。在第二种场合,加拿大人只好说:"得了!得了!你还不是行家!"也许会说:"你不懂,还有谁懂!"像这样逼人家说恭维话是很不得体的,使人反感,况且,这种恭维有什么价值呢?

在称赞什么人的问题上,也反映文化方面的差异。人们常听到美国妇女谈她丈夫工作如何努力,干得怎样出色,历次提级,得到奖励,等等。她也会夸自己的子女多么聪明,学习成绩怎样好,在集邮小组里多么积极,在什么地方的音乐会上演出过,等等。在中国,人们就会认为这样做未免太俗气。他们不会在外人面前夸自己家里的人。

中国人还忌讳夸别人的妻子长得漂亮。许多中国人认为说"你的妻子真漂亮"这样的话近乎下流,对中、老年人来说尤其是这样。然而,对西方人来说,却很自然,被夸奖的人颇为欣赏。

## 四 其他社交礼节

汉语和英语中都有表示感激、歉意的固定说法,请别人帮忙前,也要先说点什么,例如汉语里的"谢谢"、"对不起"、"请……",英语里的 Thank you, I'm sorry, Excuse me 等。总的来说,这些表达方式十分相近,不会造成什么麻烦。但是,尽管相近,仍有差异。

英语里的 Thank you 和 Please 比汉语的"谢谢"和"请……"用得更加广泛。如果求人帮点小忙,比如借枝铅笔,问个路,传个话,叫人来接电话等,中国人常常不说这些客气话,特别是对亲属和好朋友,更不用这样客气。许多中国人认为,西方人过于喜欢说Thank you 和 Please,没有必要,甚至叫人不耐烦。另一方面,中国人相信对方知道自己的感激之情,因此不必多言;但在西方人看来,不说这些客气话就有些失礼,对别人不够尊重。

对方说了 Thank you 或"谢谢"之后,英语的回答是 Not at all,
Don't mention it 或 You're welcome;汉语的回答是"没什么"或
"不用谢"。导游人员和服务人员为外宾做了什么事,外宾说
Thank you 后怎么回答呢? 有人会说:"这是我应该做的。"如果把
这句话直译为 It's my duty,就会含有下列意思:服务员或导游本
人并不想做这件事,但这是他(或她)的职责,所以不得不做。这与
汉语所要表达的原意有很大出入。适当的回答是 I'm glad to be
of help 或 It's a pleasure 表示"我很乐意(为您效劳)"之类的客套
话。

人们往往认为汉语中的"请"相当于英语中的 Please。但在某
些场合却不宜用英语 Please,比如让别人先进门或先上车时,不说
Please,一般都说 After you。(初学英语的人常用 You go first,这
是不对的。)在餐桌上请人吃饭吃菜、喝酒或请人吸烟时,一般用
Help yourself (to something),也不用 Please。

在求人办事或打断别人的话时,先得笼统地说一声 Excuse
me(对不起)。但汉语中这个笼统说法要用不同的方式表达。求
别人办事时,一般用"劳驾";请别人让路时一般用"借光"或"请让
一让";询问某事时一般加"请问"。不懂这些区别的外国人常常在
一切场合中都用"对不起"。

汉语中的"辛苦了"是一句很热情的话,表示对别人的关心。
有时用"辛苦了"来肯定别人付出辛勤的劳动和所做出的成绩,并
表示慰问。用英语表示这种意思时要十分注意。"辛苦了"这句话
适用范围很广,而英语却没有完全对应的说法,把它直译成
You've had a hard time 或 You've gone through a lot of hardships
都是不贴切的,有时还会引起误解。对一个经过长途旅行后刚刚
到达中国的外国人,可以说 You must have had a tiring journey 或
You must be tired from such a long trip 或 Did you have a good trip?
表示"路上辛苦了"、"一路好吗"之类的客套话。对正在进行或刚

刚完成一项艰难任务的人，可以说：Well done. That was（You've got）a hard job.（干得不错，你辛苦了。）不过这几种英语说法都表达不出汉语中"辛苦了"的意味和感情。

　　有人打了个喷嚏，旁边的人有时会说点什么。中国人可能会说"有人想你了"、"有人说你了"或开玩笑地说"谁在骂你"；英国人或美国人则说 God bless you（上帝保佑你）。

# 第五章

## 成语、谚语和格言

### 一

成语(或习语)、谚语和格言是一个社会的语言和文化的重要组成部分。这部分语言,尤其是成语,不仅难于理解,更难于运用得当。然而能否正确使用成语、谚语、格言,往往是一个人的语言水平的标志。不论说话还是写文章,如果完全不使用成语、谚语和格言,就会显得语言文字枯燥无味,缺乏文采,用得过多或使用不当,就会使语言文字显得矫揉造作,不大自然。据说,使用外国语的人(如中国人用英语,美国人用汉语)最明显的特点之一就是成语、谚语用得过多。

有这样一个故事:一个在美国学习的外国学生坐在窗前看书。她听见有人喊 Look out!(当心!)她以为人家说"往外看"呢,就把头伸到窗外去看。上面掉下一块板子,差点儿砸着她。她又生气,又害怕,往上一看,见一个人在修屋顶。那个人说:Didn't you hear me call 'look out'?(你没有听见我喊'look out'吗?)她回答说:Yes, and that's what I did.(听见了,所以我才向外看呢。)

不管这个故事是真是假,它说明了学习成语的困难。从字面上看,成语的意义简直体现不出来。成语中的每个词可能都认识,但组成成语之后,词义就变了。就英语成语而言,同样几个词在不

177

同的上下文中意思不一样。除上面举的 look out（往外看；把头伸到窗外看；当心；留神）外，像 make up 在不同的上下文中可以表示"弥补"、"赔偿"、"拼凑"、"配制"、"编排"、"编制"、"虚构"、"捏造"、"组成"、"调解"、化妆"等几十种意思。set off 可以表示"出发"、"动身"、"使爆炸"、"引起"、"使开始（做某事）"、"衬托"等十几种意思。同样，turn out 也可以表示多种意思，如：*Turn out* the light. （关灯）*Turn out* the guard. （派出警卫）The whole town *turned out* for the event. （为此全城人都出动了）This machine can *turn out* 300 copies a minute. （这台机器每分钟能复制 300 份。）It *turned out* to be a mistake. （结果证明是个错误/误会。）

在各种英语成语中最难学的可能是四十来个最常用动词和十来个介词或副词（如：up, down, in, out, on, off）组成的成语了。这种成语也可以叫做动词短语。这些词搭配起来可以表示好几百种不同的意义，使学生感到十分困难，弄不清它们的意思。

因此，学生首先不要因为这些成语是由简单、容易学的词组成的而轻视它们。学生应在文章里注意找出这些具有各种不同意义的短语，若无把握，就查词典。在头几次使用这些成语时，必然会碰到不少困难，但应继续学习，不要退缩。坚持学习一段时间，就一定可以弄懂，可以准确地掌握它们。

So, first of all, a student should learn not to *look down on* such idioms just because they're *made up of* such simple and easy words. He should *look out for* identical phrases with different meaning and *look them up* in a dictionary if he's not sure. He's bound to *run into* a lot of trouble when he first uses them, but he shouldn't *give in*, much less *give up*. If he keeps trying and *keeps at* it long enough he'll *make out* and things will *turn out* well in the end.

在这一段英语说明文中有下列成语：

look down (on)　　　　看不起

178

| | |
|---|---|
| made up of | 由……构成 |
| look out (for) | 留心(找) |
| look...up | 查(词典) |
| run into | 遇见 |
| give in | 屈服;让步 |
| give up | 放弃;让步 |
| keep at | 坚持(做某事) |
| make out | 理解;了解 |
| turn out (well) | 结果获得成功 |

除上列动词短语外,还有一些成语,学生也感到难于理解,但也许并不难记。学生在熟知这些成语的用法前,一定会犯不少错误。有些错误会使人发笑。但不必着急,对这种事要有耐性。可以说,学好外语,就得这样。

Before he *gets the hang of* how to use them he'll make a lot or mistakes. Some mistakes will cause people *to hold their sides with laughter*, but that shouldn't *put him in a stew*. He should learn to *put up with* such things. You might say that's *part of the game*.

在这一段英语说明文中有下列成语:

get the hang of 熟悉;得知

hold one's sides with laughter 捧腹大笑

put someone in a stew 使某人烦恼(或为难,着急)

put up with something 忍受(某事)

part of the game 事情就是这样

再谈谈汉语成语。汉语成语同其他语言的成语一样,也不能按其中一个一个的字的意思而望文生义。外国人学汉语时,在成语方面,同样困难,说错了同样闹笑话,出洋相。

一所美国大学开办汉语口语训练班,由一男一女两位教师来教。他们的本族语都不是汉语。在初学阶段,教师用实物来教某些用语,他们用各种实物演示来教"这是什么? ——这是书桌(椅子等)"之类的句子后,就着手教"这是东西吗? ——是,这是东西"

179

这样的句子。随后他们又教否定式的回答。这位男教师指指自己说:"我是东西吗?"女教师摇摇头说:"不,你不是东西。"男教师又指指女教师问:"你是东西吗?"女教师又摇摇头说:"不,我不是东西。"

当时有个中国人在教室里听课,他几乎忍不住要笑起来。事过后,当有人告诉两位教师汉语中说人"不是东西"是什么意思时,他们的脸马上红了,很难为情。

成语的翻译问题素来十分复杂,如果两种语言的历史、文化背景相距甚远,更是如此。在编写《汉英词典》(CED)时,编译人员对此深有体会。许多人认为此部词典是迄今为止同类中最好的。主编之一王佐良教授在《一部词典的编后感》一文中写道:

> "翻译者的任务首先是理解原文之意。不懂原文当然就找不到对等词语。林语堂把'吃软不吃硬'译为 bully the weak but yield to one who fights back,不仅英译文晦涩,而且说明他根本不懂这个短语的真正含义。……正确理解原文之后,就看译者的外语水平了,看他的英语底子是否雄厚,是否了解当今英语国家的发展变化。例如,把'布衣蔬食'直接译为 wear cotton clothes and eat vegetable food,在今天就会引起误解。布衣蔬食在中国标志着生活俭朴。但在英、美也是如此吗? 现在,蔬食远非穷人所专用,已是西方医生给饮食过量的百万富翁们开的药方了。'

这部词典最后把"布衣蔬食"译为 coarse clothes and simple fare。这种译法"不仅保持了原义,而且 fare 一词略带古色,正好反映出原文的风格"。

王佐良教授说,词典经过三次大的修改,"每次修改都是漫长、痛苦的过程,每次都使译文有所改进"。文章中,他举了不少例子来说明修改的过程。下面引用三例:

害人虫: an evil person/an evil *creature*

> 修改虽小,但意义却大;它保持了汉语原文的风格,英语译文也更

地道。

自投罗网: throw oneself into the trap/ *walk right* into the trap
　　第一种译法比较符合原文;第二种译法比较符合英语习惯。

奇花异木: rare flowers and trees/ *exotic* flowers and *rare* trees
　　第二种译法在语体上有所改进,也更加符合原文的语气。

# 二

现在谈一下谚语和格言。谚语和格言就是民间流传的至理名言,措辞简练,便于记忆。谚语内容精辟,寓意深邃,因而有广泛的感染力。学生喜欢学习谚语。初学外语的人能用上一两句谚语会感到很得意。

谚语往往多少能反映一个民族的地理、历史、社会制度、社会观点和态度。比如,有些民族住在沿海一带,靠海为生,他们的谚语往往涉及海上航行、经受风雨、捕鱼捉蟹。像阿拉伯人这样的游牧民族的谚语则多涉及沙漠、草原、羊、马、骆驼和豺狼。尊敬老人的社会就会有颂扬老人足智多谋的谚语。妇女地位不高的社会就有许多轻视、贬低妇女的谚语。

人们的经历和对世界的认识在不少方面是相似的。因此,尽管中国人和讲英语的人文化背景不同,但在英语和汉语中相同或相似的谚语却很多。请看下列谚语:

Strike while the iron is hot. 趁热打铁。

Many hands make light work. 人多好办事。

Haste makes waste. 欲速则不达。

Out of sight, out of mind. 眼不见,心不烦。

Birds of a feather flock together. 物以类聚,人以群分。

Look before you leap. 三思而后行。

Where there's smoke there's fire. 无风不起浪。

Where there's a will there's a way. 有志者事竟成。

Give a person a dose of his own medicine. 以其人之道还治其人之身。

All good things must come to an end. 天下没有不散的宴席。

由于文化对语言的特征有重大影响，英汉谚语的差别自然十分明显。同英语的谚语相比，汉语的谚语有以下特征：第一，谚语为数极多，几乎一切方面——不论是人与自然的关系，还是人与人之间的关系——都有谚语或格言。第二，许多谚语有明显的中国特征。如："小卒过河，意在吃帅"来自中国象棋；"挂羊头，卖狗肉"与中国肉店的特点有关。第三，许多谚语反映社会中的不平等和被剥削者、被压迫者的感情。如："卖花姑娘插竹叶，卖线姑娘裙脚裂"；"只许州官放火，不许百姓点灯"。第四，有些谚语反映了佛教对中国习俗、思想的影响，如："远看菩萨，近看泥巴"；"平时不烧香，临时抱佛脚"，而英语的谚语反映的是基督教的影响。最后，汉语中反映互助、友爱、与人为善精神的谚语也相当多。如："前人栽树，后人乘凉"；"一人掘井，众人吃水"；"一个篱巴三个桩，一个好汉三个帮"。

以上所谈的区别并非全部，但读者可从中对类似现象有所认识。

许多汉语谚语没有对应的英语说法，因篇幅有限，不能一一列举。下面选的几个例子，有的精辟简练，可能会使讲英语的人感兴趣；有的表达了与英美人不同的观点；有的与英语谚语的涵义相似，但字面意思西方人颇为生疏，因此难以理解。下列汉语谚语的英译文都是作者译的。

良药苦口利于病，忠言逆耳利于行：Frank advice is like good herbal medicine; hard to take, but ultimately beneficial.

含义明白，无需解释；只是有许多西方人没有尝过中草药，只能设想其味苦难吃。

瓜田不纳履，李下不整冠：Neither adjust your shoe in a melon patch; nor your hat under a plum tree.

182

为了押韵,可译成:nor straighten your hat 'neath an apple tree. 许多西方人不会立刻理解其中含义,不过,一旦明白,必发出会心的微笑。

要知朝中事,乡间问老农:Ask the common folk if you want to know how the country is faring.

语无新奇之处,却含有一些民间普遍的哲理。

衙门自古朝南开,有理无钱莫进来:Court doors may open, but not to the poor.

英语译文只存大意,未留细节,为什么"衙门朝南开",就要多费笔墨加以解释。

一人得道,鸡犬升天:Even the dog swaggers when its master wins favor.

许多人看了这个谚语都会苦笑一下,点头赞同。英译文中没有"鸡"字,无损原义,可使英语精练顺畅。

同样,有些常见的英语谚语似乎也没对应的汉语谚语。下面举的几个例子中,有的反映出不同的生活习惯,有的显示了对事物的不同看法,有的表明不同的人生观和处世态度。

Absence makes the heart grow fonder. 越是不见越想念。

An apple a day keeps the doctor away. 常吃苹果少得病。

You can't have your cake and eat it too. 两者不可兼得。

Let sleeping dogs lie. 莫惹是非。

You can't teach an old dog new tricks. 年逾花甲不堪教。

应特别注意下列四个谚语,英汉两种说法貌似对应,意义却不同:

It takes two to make a quarrel 很像汉语中的"一个巴掌拍不响"。二者有相同之处:表示双方都有缺点。但汉语谚语中还有另一层意思:一件有意义的事情不能靠一个人去完成。

A miss is as good as a mile 很象汉语的"差之毫厘,失之千里"。不过,汉语谚语另有一种寓意:小错误不及时纠正,最后会出大错,闯大祸,告诫人们要防微杜渐。英语谚语只说明一个事实、一种态度、一种看法:没有打中就是没有打中,小失误也是失误,差一毫米和差一公里一样。《新英汉词典》译为:"毫末之错仍为错;死里逃生总是生。"(指程度虽有不同,性质都是一样。)

Gilding the lily 似乎与"锦上添花"的意思相近,其实相差甚远。此处的英语谚语的意思倒近似"画蛇添足",指对很完美的东西作不恰当而且过分的修饰,表示不赞成这种弄巧成拙的做法。而"锦上添花"是比喻好上加好。

Life begins at forty 可与两句汉语谚语相比。一句是"人到四十五,正如出山虎",寓意相近,但年龄相差五岁。第二句是"潮怕二十,人怕四十"。意思是潮水一过阴历二十日就要落下去,人一到四十岁就走下坡路,年龄相同,观点相反。

**把汉语谚语和格言译成英语同样困难,因为谚语中的文化因素更重要,译好就更加不易。现在分析几个例子:**

盲人瞎马:A blind man on a blind horse—rushing headlong to disaster.(《汉英词典》)

前半句是直译,英美人士会有各种不同理解,而后半句才点出谚语的寓意。

黄鼠狼给鸡拜年,没安好心:The weasel goes to pay his respects to the hen—not with the best of intentions.(《汉英词典》)

在直译译文之后点明寓意,形象生动,体现了原句风格和韵味。

挂羊头,卖狗肉:Hang up a sheep's head and sell dogmeat—try to palm off sth. inferior to what it purports to be.(《汉英词典》)

另一种译法是:The sign says mutton, but the meat is dogmeat—try to peddle something under false claims. 西方人对 sheep's head 和 dogmeat 都有反感,英译文对此应有所考虑。

芝麻开花节节高:A sesame stalk puts forth blossoms notch by notch, higher and higher.(《汉英词典》)

英语部分是汉语谚语的直译文;这个汉语的寓意是形势越来越好。西方人很少见到正在生长的芝麻,所以从译文中体会不到这个比喻的妙处。

一个和尚挑水吃，两个和尚抬水吃，三个和尚没水吃：There's
a Chinese saying about monks fetching water:

One monk, two buckets; two monks, one bucket; three
monks, no bucket, no water——more hands, less work done.

还可以进一步解释说：这有点像英语中的 Too many cocks spoil
the broth. (厨子太多难烧汤)。英语中只有 carry 一词，无法区分"挑"
和"抬"，这是难译的原因之一。此外为什么这个谚语里偏挑"和尚"为
例？这也是个问题。

看来，翻译谚语时，最好先按原文的语气和风格直译，然后附
加起画龙点睛作用的词语，点出谚语寓意，后者最好用道地的英语
说法，这样可以给人以深刻印象，效果较好。

# 第六章

## 比喻和联想

"快像狮子般从梦中醒来，
你们有的是无法征服的数量，
快把你们瞌睡时被加在身上的
链锁，像露水一样甩掉——
你们人多，——他们人少。"

英国诗人雪莱这首诗曾激励了数以百万计的劳动人民，挣脱身上的锁链，拿起武器，同压迫他们的人斗争。

"像狮子般……醒来"——这是多么恰当的比喻！

在所有的语言中都有比喻。比喻使语言生气勃勃，形象鲜明。英语中的比喻手段非常丰富。在下列各句中都有比喻性的表达法：

She's like a *rose*—fresh, delicate, beautiful. (她像一朵玫瑰花，鲜艳，娇嫩，美丽。)

He went about the job like a *bull* in a china shop. (他干这活儿就像公牛进了瓷器店那样莽撞。)

We shall not be moved—just like a *tree* standing by the water. (我们会像水边的树那样屹然不动。)

What a dull speech! He's merely *parroting* what many others have said. (多么枯燥的讲话！不过是鹦鹉学舌，重复许多人说过的话而已。)

One look at his face and we realized that a *thunderstorm* was about to break.（一看他的脸色，就知道暴风雨要来了。）

在以上例句中，我们看到用鲜花、树木、动物和自然现象作比喻，通过鲜明的对比，获得显著的效果。如果不用这些比喻，这几句话就会显得平淡无味。

然而，理解另一种语言的比喻往往并不容易。学习英语的学生可能碰上这样的句子：

"You *chicken*!" he cried, looking at Tom with contempt. ("你这个胆小鬼!"他轻蔑地看着汤姆嚷道。)(不是"你这只鸡"。)

The *stork visited* the Howard Johnstons yesterday. (霍华德·约翰斯顿家昨天添了一个孩子。)(不是"有鹳鸟做客"。)

学生遇到这样的句子，如果不知道 chicken 指"懦夫"或"胆小鬼"，不知道 a visit by the stork 指"孩子诞生"，就可能会感到迷惑不解。讲英语的人学汉语时也会对下面的句子感到费解："你真熊!""那个家伙简直像条泥鳅!"

讲英语的人和中国人对于熊的联想很不一样。他们认为熊是很凶猛、危险的动物，也可能认为动物园或野生动物园林里的熊调皮淘气，滑稽可爱；但决不会像中国人那样，认为熊愚笨、无能、无用。在一定的上下文中"你真熊"可能相当于"你真笨"、"你真没用"、"你真软弱"、"你真窝囊"等义。

大部分英语国家里都没有泥鳅，人们不过把泥鳅看作是一种鱼，不会认为它很滑，并理解"滑"的转义："圆滑"、"狡猾"、"不老实"、"不可靠"等。不过，在英语中的确有一种说法跟汉语中的"滑得像泥鳅"这种比喻在意义上和感情上完全一样：slippery as an eel(滑得像鳝鱼)。

从上列论述可以看出，人们时常把某些品质或特性与某些动物或物体联系起来。这些品质或特性又往往能使人产生某种反应或情绪，尽管这种联想很少或根本没有什么科学根据。联想到的特性和所引起的情感也往往因民族不同而各异。在本章中，我们只讨论一些与禽兽有关的比喻，以及在不同文化的环境中这些比喻所引起人们的相同或不同的联想。

先举几个联想相似的例子。

He's as sly as a *fox*. He's *foxy*. You've got to watch him. (他滑得像个狐狸。他很狡猾。对他你可要当心点儿。)

You *ass*! You stupid *ass*! How could you do a thing like that?! (你这头驴! 你这头蠢驴! 怎么会干出那种事儿来?!)

He doesn't have an idea of his own. He just *parrots* what other people say. (他没有自己的观点,只会鹦鹉学舌。)

The children were as busy as *bees*, making preparations for the festival. (孩子们准备过节忙得像蜜蜂一样。)

中国人对上述动物的联想同美国人、英国人、加拿大人一样。实际上,在汉语中也有"蠢驴"、"鹦鹉学舌"、"像狐狸一样狡猾"等说法。

在这两种文化中,联想相似的其他动物还有: 鹿是胆小温顺的,小羊是讨人喜欢的,猪是肮脏贪吃的,猴子是顽皮淘气的,豺是贪婪卑鄙的,狼是凶残好杀的。

现在谈一下联想不同的情况。这种情况可分为两类: 第一,在一种文化中提到某些动物时往往可以联想到某种特征,而在另一种文化中却联想不到任何特征。第二,有些动物在两种文化中人们会联想到某种特征,但所联想的特征却不同。

第一类举 bull(公牛), beaver(河狸,海狸), crane(仙鹤)和 tortoise(乌龟)为例。

对中国人来说,公牛和河狸不会引起什么联想,不论是否常见,有用无用,无非是动物而已。中国人也许猜得出 a bull in a china shop(瓷器店里的公牛)是什么意思,但想像不出说英语的人心目中的形象:一头喷着鼻息、怒气冲冲的公牛闯进摆满精致瓷器的店里。因此中国人对这个说法的生动性体会不深。这种说法的意思是:在一个需要举止灵巧得体、细致周密的场合闯进一个行为粗鲁、手脚笨拙、会惹麻烦的人。

河狸主要产于北美洲,在中国很少见。河狸经常积极活动,有啮树筑巢的习性,在筑巢这一方面,河狸有很高的技艺和独创性,因此有 eager beaver(卖力的河狸)之称。在喻义方面 eager beaver 则指"急于做成某事而特别卖力,但有点急躁的人"。这个比喻有时略带贬义,则指"为讨好上司做事过于卖力的人"。

鹤在中国文化中是长寿的象征,因此父母常常给孩子起名为"鹤年"、"鹤龄",说明他们希望孩子长大成人,长命百岁。鹤常与象征坚定长寿的松联在一起。绘画和图案常以松鹤为题材,并以"松鹤延年"题词。上年岁的人在过生日的时候,喜欢人们赠送画有松鹤图案的礼物。但对西方人来说,鹤不会引起这种联想。如果有的话,大概同《伊索寓言》中的鹤有点关系吧。

在中国文化中,龟有两种象征意义。一方面龟象征长寿。古代的府第、庙宇、宫殿等建筑物前常有石龟,作为祈求长寿的象征。另一方面,龟也用来比作有外遇者的丈夫。骂人"王八"或"王八蛋"是极大的侮辱。在西方文化中没有这种联想,乌龟不过是行动缓慢、其貌不扬的动物而已。中国人听说英语词 turtle-neck sweater(龟脖式毛衣,即翻领毛衣)时,往往免不了作个鬼脸。

第二类举 owl(猫头鹰), bat(蝙蝠), dog(狗), tiger(虎), petrel(海燕)为例。

英语中有 As wise as an owl(像猫头鹰一样聪明)这样的说法,表明讲英语的人把猫头鹰当做智慧的象征。在儿童读物和漫画中,猫头鹰通常很严肃、很有头脑。禽兽间的争端要猫头鹰来裁判,紧急关头找猫头鹰求教。有时人们认为猫头鹰不实际,有点蠢,但基本上是智慧的象征。然而,中国人对猫头鹰的看法不同,有些人很迷信,怕看到猫头鹰或听到它的叫声;以为碰上它要倒霉。汉语中的"夜猫子进宅"意味着这家厄运将至,夜猫子就是猫头鹰。

有位美国妇女刚到中国来,不了解中国人对猫头鹰的看法,常戴着她喜爱的猫头鹰别针。她发现人们常停下来看着或指着她的别针，有好几次还问她为什么戴这种别针，她觉得很奇怪；后来有人告诉她中国人对猫头鹰的看法，她才知道戴猫头鹰别针不太合适。

西方人对 bat(蝙蝠)无好感，通常联想到坏特征。英语中有 as blind as a bat(瞎得跟蝙蝠一样，眼力不行，有眼无珠)，crazy as a bat(疯得像蝙蝠)，he's a bit batty(他有点反常)，have bats in the belfry(发痴；异想天开)。有时还有更坏的比喻。提到蝙蝠，人们就会想到丑陋、凶恶、吸血动物的形象。这也许因为吸血蝠的缘故。所以，西方人对蝙蝠的感情很像中国人对猫头鹰的感情，又怕它，又讨厌它。

对中国人来说，蝙蝠是吉祥、健康、幸福的象征。这些联想很可能来自蝙蝠的名称——"蝠"与"福"同音。有些图画或图案把蝙蝠和鹿画在一起，颇受欢迎，因为"蝠鹿"读起来同"福禄"一样，象征吉祥、幸福、有钱、有势。

英语中有 Man's best friend(人之良友)的说法。有多少中国人知道指的是什么动物呢？说"人之良友"是狗，许多人会感到奇怪，想不到狗会有这样的荣誉。在中国，狗往往使人们联想到令人厌恶的东西，如"狗东西"、"狗娘养的"、"狗改不了吃屎"等。当然，西方人所喜欢的狗的某些品质，中国人也喜欢，如狗忠实、可靠、勇敢、聪明等。但在中国，狗首先是看家的动物，不是供玩赏的动物；人们养狗是因为它有用，并非因为它是个好伴儿。就是说，狗是有用的动物，但并不可爱。

不过，应该指出，讲英语的人也并非总说狗的好话：You dog!(你这狗东西!) That cur!(那个狗东西!) Son of a bitch!(狗娘养的!)这些都是常说的骂人话。不过这些骂人话并不影响狗的地位。在英国和美国狗仍然是："人之良友"。

对英国人和大部分西方人来说狮子是"百兽之王"。从 regal as a lion(狮子般庄严)，majestic as a lion(像狮子一样雄伟)等用语可以看出，狮子享有很高的声誉。12 世纪后期英王理查一世因勇

190

武大胆而被誉为 lion-hearted（狮心理查）。本章开头引用的雪莱的诗中号召被压迫者像狮子般醒来（rise like lions）。难怪英国人选狮子作为自己国家的象征了。

在中国文化里，人们对狮子一般没有那么多的联想。狮子不过是一种凶猛强大的动物，不见得庄严雄伟，倒是老虎往往会引起类似的联想。

在中国文化中，人们对虎的联想有好坏两个方面。从好的方面说，虎英勇大胆，健壮有力，坚决果断。如："虎将"、"干起活来像小老虎"、"虎老雄心在"、"虎虎有生气"等词语和男人的名字"大虎"、"二虎"、"小虎"等。从坏的方面说，虎凶猛残忍，冷酷无情。如："拦路虎"、"狐假虎威"、"苛政猛于虎"等。

近来中国人往往把海燕（petrel）看作值得学习的榜样。"海燕"这个词在人们心目中的形象是：一只孤零零的小鸟冒着风雨，英勇顽强地在大海上空飞翔。许多年轻人把自己比做海燕，不畏艰难险阻，不屈不挠，在茫茫人海中拼搏，奋勇前进。少年的日记里常提到海燕，青年的作品中常描写海燕，许多商品用海燕作商标。殊不知，西方人对海燕并无好感。1976 年出版的《朗曼现代英语词典》中说：暴风雨的海燕有"预示灾难、纠纷、暴力行动即将出现的人或幸灾乐祸的人"之义。可见两种联想的差别有多大。

最后讲一讲传说或神话中的禽兽。在中国封建皇朝时代人们把龙（dragon）和凤（phoenix）作为皇权的传统象征。龙代表帝王，凤代表后妃，毫无贬义。时至今日，这两种传说中的动物仍偶尔在传统的中国图案中出现。龙是一种象征吉利的动物，所以汉语中常说家长"望子成龙"，即希望孩子长大后能有所成就。给男孩子起名字也常用"龙"字，如"龙翔"、"一龙"等。

西方人却认为 dragon（龙）是邪恶的象征，认为龙是凶残肆虐的怪物，应予消灭。在一些描写圣徒和英雄的传说中讲到和龙这种怪物作斗争的事迹，多以怪物被杀为结局。最有名的也许是公元 700 年左右盎格鲁—撒克逊人关于贝奥武尔夫事迹的叙事诗。

诗中主人公贝奥武尔夫打败妖怪格伦代尔后,与恶龙搏斗,两者同归于尽。有趣的是,中国画上的龙没有翅膀,西洋画上的龙却是有翅膀的怪物。

在西方神话中,phoenix(凤)与复活、再生有关。根据希腊传说,凤能活许多年——有一种说法是 500 年。在这一时期结束时,凤筑一巢,唱支挽歌,拍着翅膀扇起火来,把巢烧掉,凤烧成灰烬,灰烬中又飞出一只新凤。因此,当一个城镇、一个场所或某团体的主要建筑物失火或因其他原因而毁坏时,好心人会祝愿它"像传说中的凤凰那样,以崭新的面貌从废墟中升起"。

在中国神话中,凤凰被看作是鸟中之王。雄性称"凤",雌性称"凰"。虽然中国没有像古希腊那样家喻户晓的神话传说,凤凰却是吉祥的动物。因此,中国女性的名字中常有"凤"字,如:"凤莲"、"金凤"。凤凰还比喻某种罕见、珍贵,例如:"凤毛麟角"。

# 第七章

## "颜色"在语言中的运用

### ——再谈比喻和联想

英语中 *green* with envy 是什么意思? 人们忌妒或羡慕时脸色真的变绿或发青吗?

英语中说 Paul was in a *blue* mood; Paul(保尔)是什么情绪? 高兴、激动、悲哀,还是什么?

在上列两句中,green(绿)和 blue(蓝)都不指颜色。两个词都有别的意思——某种文化方面的联想——从字面上看这种意思不明显。在词典上,green 这个词有"(脸色)变绿"的意思,但 green with envy 是个固定词组,不过表示"十分妒忌"而已。blue 这个词与 mood 之类的词连用体现某种情绪时,表示"沮丧的"、"忧郁的",如:Paul was in a *blue* mood. (保尔情绪低落。)

本章将以汉语和英语如何运用表示"颜色"的词语为例,讨论某些颜色在不同文化中的联想。

red(红色):无论在英语国家还是在中国,红色往往与庆祝活动或喜庆日子有关。英语里有 red-letter days(纪念日, 喜庆的日子),在西方一般指圣诞节或其他节日,因为这些日子在日历上是用红色标明的,所以 red-letter 的转义就是"可纪念的"、"喜庆的"。(普通的日子印的是黑色,但 black-letter day 却不是"平常的日子",而表示"倒霉的一天"。)又如 to paint the town *red* 表示"狂欢"、"痛饮"、"胡闹",多指夜生活中的狂欢作乐,饮酒胡闹,不是"把全城染红"。此外, roll out the *red* carpet for sb. 的意思是:"(铺展红地毯)隆重地欢迎某人"。如:He was the first European head of state to visit their country, and they *rolled out the red carpet for him*. (他是第一个访问该国的欧洲首脑,他们用隆重的礼仪来欢迎他。)

以汉语中"红双喜"为例——这是传统的喜庆象征,原指举行婚礼时在门窗或墙上贴的"喜"字。"开门红"中的"红"代表好运气。不过"开门红"这个用语不能按字面意义译成英语,应释义为 to begin well, to make a good start, 表示"一开始就取得好成绩"。有时相当于汉语中的"旗开得胜"的转义:win victory in the first battle—win speedy success。

红色也用来表达某些感情。英语中的 become *red*-faced 或 Her face turned *red* 同汉语中的"脸红"一样,表示"不好意思"、"难为情"或"为难"、"困窘"。不过,英语中有些包含"红色"字样的说法就不那么容易为中国人所理解。如 to see *red*, waving a *red* flag 到底是什么意思,就不好懂。二者都与"生气"、"发怒"有关。前者的意思是:"使人生气"或"发怒"、"冒火"。后者中的 red flag 指"使人生气的东西", waving a red flag 指"做惹别人生气的事",如:The mere mention of his hated cousin's name was like *waving a red flag* in front of him. (只要一提他那个讨厌的表兄弟的名字,他就生气。)

怎样把汉语中的"你红光满面"译成英语呢? 显然不是 Your face is very red. (你脸红了。),否则表示对方"不好意思"或"处于窘境"。如果译成 A ruddy complexion, 虽带有"身体健康,面色红润",但不表示汉语含有的因"精力充沛"(energy and vigor)而"红光满面"之义。可以说:You look so healthy and full of pep 或 You look the very picture of health and energy. 两者都表示"你红光满面"之义。根本不必把"红"字译出来。有的词典上把"红光满面"

194

译作(one's face) glowing with health；或 in ruddy health 都是从"身体健康而面色红润"这个角度来考虑的。

红色象征革命和社会主义。在汉语和英语中都有用 red(红)表示这种意义的词语,如:red guard(红卫兵)。英语中的 Red (大写 R)一词本身常用作"共产主义者"或"共产党员"的同义词,但有贬义。不过,有些带"红"字的汉语词语译成英语的 red 并未表达原有的含义。例如,把"又红又专"译作 red and expert 表达不出汉语词语的原义,不如译为 both socialist-minded and professionally qualified。同样,把"一颗红心"译为 a red heart,不好懂,除非再解释一下,如 loyal to the Party, having socialist virtues(忠于党,具有社会主义的道德品质)。

white(白色):对多数中国人和西方人来说,白色所引起的联想有一些是相近的:purity(洁白), innocence(清白无辜)。但英语中的 white lie 这个短语是什么意思呢? 谎言还能"清白"、"无罪"、"天真"或"单纯"吗? 回答是: a white lie 指"不怀恶意的谎言"。例如,姐姐会对妹妹和妹妹的男朋友说:"你们俩去看电影吧。今天晚上我还有许多事情要做。谢谢。"她知道他们两个人想单独去;邀请她不过出于礼貌,所以她以有事要做为借口。这就是 white lie,说这个谎毫无恶意,也没有骗人的意思。

多数西方人对汉语中的"红白喜事"里的"白"字感到费解。最好根本不把"红"、"白"这两种颜色译出,只说 weddings and funerals(喜事和丧事;婚礼和葬礼),因为西方人举行婚礼时,新娘总穿白色服装。把白色与丧事联系起来,会引起反感;而把 funerals(丧事)说成是 happy occasions(喜事),会使西方人感到吃惊,尽管这种说法反映了中国人对待死亡的达观态度。

应当指出,在汉译英时,应注意有"白"字的汉语词语。在某些场合汉语中的"白"字指的是颜色,但在英语对应词中并无 white 一词:"白菜"(Chinese cabbage),"白熊"(polar bear),"白蚁"(termite)。在另一些场合,"白"字与颜色毫无关系,表示"徒劳、(in

195

vain), 如:"白费事"(all in vain, a waste of time and energy), "白送"(give away, free of charge, for nothing)。此外, "白"字还可以表示"单纯的, 不掺杂的"(plain, unadulterated), 如:"白开水"(boiled water), "白肉"(plain boiled pork)。在某些场合甚至很难概括出某种涵义。如:"坦白"(to confess, to make a clean breast of something), "白痴"(idiot), "白话"(vernacular)等等。应当记住的是:"白"字并不总是 white。

black(黑色):在英语和汉语中都有不少词语表明 black(黑)与"不好"、"坏的"、"邪恶的"特征相联系。如:blacklist(黑名单), black market(黑市), black-hearted(黑心的)等。

有趣的是, 在商业英语中 in the black 有好的意思, 即"经营一项企业盈利"。如:Since he was made manager, the company has been running *in the black*. (自从他当了经理以后, 公司一直盈利。)be in the *black*(盈利)的反义词是 be in the *red*(亏损, 负债), 这两个术语都来自记账时所用墨水的颜色。in the red 显然已被汉语借用, 即"赤字"。

blue(蓝色):在英语中蓝色通常表示不快。除上述 in a *blue* mood 或 having the *blues* 表示"情绪低沉"、"忧郁"、"沮丧"、"烦闷"外, 在 a *blue* Monday(倒霉的星期一)中, blue 也表示类似的意思——过了愉快、幸福的周末, 星期一又要上班或上学了, 所以情绪不佳。如:*It was blue Monday* and he just didn't feel like going back to work. (又是倒霉的星期一, 该上班了, 他可真不愿意。)

蓝色还常用来表示社会地位高、有权势或出身于贵族或王族。He's a real *blue blood*. (他是真正的贵族。)在美国英语中 blue book(蓝皮书)是刊载知名人士, 尤其是政府高级官员的名字的书。

green(绿色):除了前面提到的 *green* with envy, 英语中还有 *green*-eyed monster 和 *green*-eyed, 都表示"嫉妒"。可是, 常用来表示"嫉妒"的汉语词却是"眼红"(或"害了红眼病"), 英语直译为 *red*-eyed, 恰恰与英语 *green*-eyed 相反。有趣的是, 过去汉语有

196

"戴绿帽子"(to wear a green hat)或"戴绿头巾"(wear a green head band)的说法,如说"某人戴了绿帽子",即指某人之妻与他人私通。

英语中还常用绿色表示没有经验、缺乏训练、知识浅薄等。如:You are expecting too much of him. He's still *green*, you know.(你对他要求太高。他还没经验嘛。)greenhorn 则表示"没有经验的人"或"新到一个地方不了解当地习惯的人",这一词语经常用于移民并带有轻微的贬义色彩。

yellow(黄色):汉语中有"黄色电影"、"黄色书刊"、"黄色音乐"等说法,译成英语怎么说呢? 不能译为 yellow movies, yellow books, yellow music,这种词语没人懂,因为英语中没有这样的说法。把"黄色"译成英语可用 pornographic(色情的), trashy(无聊的, 低级的), obscene(淫秽的, 猥亵的), filthy(淫猥的)或 vulgar(庸俗的;下流的),所以"黄色电影"可译为 pornographic pictures, obscene movies, "黄色书刊"可译为 filthy books, "黄色音乐"可译为 vulgar music。

但 yellow(黄色)这个词却用于英语的 *yellow* journalism 这一短语中,指不择手段地夸张、渲染以招揽或影响读者的黄色新闻编辑作风,如突出社会丑闻,把普通新闻写得耸人听闻,有时甚至歪曲事实以引起轰动等。

许多美国商店和家里都有一本厚厚的 Yellow Pages(黄页电话查号簿),这是按不同的商店、企业、事业、机关分类的电话簿。如按所有的食品商店、电子器材商店、娱乐场所, 航空公司及医院等分类,列出电话号码。这是一本很有用的书,全书用黄纸印刷,所以称 Yellow Pages,与汉语中的"黄色书"(filthy books)意思完全不同。

其他颜色也可以引起某种联想,这里就不谈了。

应当指出,不同颜色在不同语言中表达的方式并不一样。多年来一直有人在研究这一问题,看来一切语言都有表示黑色和白色的词,大多数语言有表示红色的词,但也不是所有的语言都有。

其次，最普遍的可能是黄色和绿色，然后是蓝色和褐色。有些语言表示颜色名称似乎是相同的，但显示在色谱上相邻颜色的划分却有所不同。汉语和英语中的主要颜色是相同的或相近的，但也有区别。例如：

青[qing]：可以指绿色(green)，如"青椒"(green pepper)；可以指蓝色，如"青天"(blue sky)；也可以指黑色，如"青布"(black cloth)。

黄[huang]：一般是指黄色，但也可以指褐色，如"黄酱"(soy bean paste)；可以指金色，如"黄金"(gold)。

有趣的是，在不同的语言中对同一物体或现象却用不同颜色来加以描述。英国人喝的 black tea 在汉语中不叫"黑茶"而叫"红茶"。美国人谈到皮肉受伤时说 be bruised black and blue，而中国人则说"被打得青一块，紫一块"(直译为：be beaten blue and purple，当然应译为地道的英语 be beaten black and blue)。

在结束本章时，讲一件事：一位美国教授到中国来讲学，所讲题目之一是《国际关系中理解不同文化的重要性》。这个报告很有意思。他提到许多因文化不同而发生的奇闻轶事，可是他却不断用自己杜撰的术语 cultural red flags(文化红旗)，意思是在某种文化中应回避和特别注意的事物。red flag(红旗)一词就像 red traffic light(交通信号灯中的红灯)一样——人们一看到就要站住，不再往前走。可是在中国和别的社会主义国家里，"红旗"是一个有积极意义的褒义词。当别人告诉他时，他的窘态就可想而知了——他恰好违背了自己订的戒律。

# 第八章

## 典　故

　　几乎所有的人在说话和写作时都引用历史、传说、文学或宗教中的人物或事件。这些人物或事件就是典故。运用典故不仅可润饰语言，使之丰富多采，生动清晰，而且使人们更易于沟通思想。汉语中的"你这个人真阿Q"和"她是林黛玉式的人物"这样的话的含义十分明显，无需多加解释。像"原来是空城计呀?"和"真没意思，让我们来跑龙套"这样的句子把说话人的感情表现得多么充分!

　　在汉语和英语中都有大量的口头流传和文字记载下来的典故，反映操这两种语言的人民丰富的文化遗产。不过，这些典故往往不易理解，也就难于欣赏。没有读过鲁迅的小说《阿Q正传》(*The True Story of Ah Q*)就不可能理解上面提到阿Q的那句话，仅仅知道《红楼梦》(*Dream of Red Mansions* 或 *Dream of the Red Chamber*)的大致情节，也不会懂得涉及林黛玉的那句话。英语中的典故也是这样。

　　许多英语典故涉及的人物和事件来自英国文学宝库，尤其是莎士比亚的作品。讲英语的人每天都在引用出自莎士比亚作品的典故，但往往是不自觉的。尽管莎士比亚的戏剧写于三百多年以前，但是他的剧本中的许多台词流传至今。有些话已经成了日常英语口语的一部分。例如：forgive and forget(不念旧恶，不记仇)，that's all Greek to me(我对此一窍不通)，all's well that ends well

(结果好就一切都好),all is not gold that glitters(发亮的东西不一定是金子——好看的东西不一定都有用),discretion is the better part of valour(小心即大勇;考虑周到胜过勇敢——此语常作为胆怯者解嘲的借口)等。

有这样一个故事:一个上了年纪的英国人,从未看过莎士比亚的剧本。有一次,别人请他去看《汉姆莱特》(*Hamlet*)。事后,人家问他:"您觉得怎么样?"他摇摇头说:"哎,不就是一大堆引文嘛!"他根本没有想到,这些"引文"来自《汉姆莱特》这个剧本,莎士比亚正是这些格言的作者。莎士比亚对人类的洞察力、对社会问题的敏感性和他运用语言表达思想的天赋在英语方面和全世界讲英语的民族的思想上产生深远的影响。

莎士比亚戏剧中的许多人物已成为具有类似特征的人的代名词。这很像汉语中说某人是猪八戒,就是说他很像《西游记》里那个粗疏鲁莽、贪图享乐、性情乖僻,有时又满可爱的猪八戒。在英语中,如果把一个人叫做罗密欧,就是说他像莎士比亚戏剧《罗密欧与朱丽叶》中英俊、多情、潇洒、对女人颇有一套的青年。

莎士比亚戏剧和以后英美文学中的许多其他的人物或名称也已家喻户晓:

a Cleopatra(克娄巴特拉),指绝代佳人——这是莎士比亚戏剧《安东尼和克娄巴特拉》中的人物。

a Shylock(夏洛克),指贪婪、残忍、追求钱财、不择手段的守财奴——这是另一个莎士比亚戏剧《威尼斯商人》中的人物。

a Dr. Jekyll and Mr. Hyde(吉基尔医生和海德先生),指有双重性格的人;一方面善良、温和(吉基尔医生),另一方面凶恶、残暴(海德先生)——这是史蒂文生的小说《吉基尔医生和海德先生传》中的人物。

a Frankenstein(弗兰金斯坦;人们常说"制造一个弗兰金斯坦"),指杀伤原制造者的怪物或东西,也指制造这种东西的人以及可怕的怪物或人——这是玛丽·雪莱的小说《弗兰金斯坦》中的人物。这本书的主人公是医学院的学生。他把尸体中的骨头取来,制造了一个似人的怪物,最后自己被这个怪物杀害。

a Sherlock Holmes(歇洛克·福尔摩斯),指有非凡才能的侦探或敏锐精明的人,这种人善于通过仔细观察、科学分析和逻辑推理,进行追捕或解决疑难问题——歇洛克·福尔摩斯是阿瑟·柯南道尔著名侦探小说中的主人公。

an Uncle Tom(汤姆叔叔),指逆来顺受的人,尤其是黑人,这种人情愿忍受侮辱和痛苦,在思想上和行动上绝不反抗——这个词有贬义,来自哈利特·斯托的小说《汤姆叔叔的小屋》中的主人公。

a Horatio Alger story(霍雷肖·阿尔杰式的故事),指一种神话般的"飞黄腾达"的经历,往往描写穷小子艰苦奋斗往上爬,最后功成业就,成为富裕的社会名流的故事——因霍雷肖·阿尔杰写的小说情节几乎全部如此而得名。他的最著名的作品是《衣衫褴褛的狄克》(*Ragged Dick*)系列小说和《衣衫褴褛的汤姆》(*Tattered Tom*)系列小说。

a catch-22 situation (第二十二条军规式的处境),指不可摆脱的困境:各种因素相互依存,A 决定于 B,而 B 又决定于 A,所以是一种无出路的、连锁性绝境——这一用语出自美国作家约瑟夫·海勒写的《第二十二条军规》。

在英美语言和著作中典故的另一个来源就是传说和神话。实际上,整个西方文学、艺术都深受希腊、罗马神话的影响,其次还受斯堪的纳维亚神话的影响:

地理名称:

Europe (欧洲)——来自欧罗巴(Europa)公主的名字。在希腊神话中,她被化作白牛的主神宙斯劫往克里特岛。

Atlantic Ocean(大西洋)——来自神话中阿特兰梯斯(Atlantis)岛的名字,该岛位于现在的大西洋。

Paris(巴黎)——来自希腊神话特洛伊王子帕利斯(Paris)的名字。他拐走美丽的海伦(Helen)引起特洛伊战争。

一星期各天的名称:

Tuesday(星期二)——来自古斯堪的纳维亚英勇战神铁尔(Tyr)的名字。

Wednesday(星期三)——来自盎格鲁·撒克逊神话中最有威力的神伍敦(Woden)的名字。

Thursday(星期四)——来自古斯堪的纳维亚雷神索尔(Thor)的名字。

Friday(星期五)——来自于音乐女神弗丽亚(Freya)的名字。

Saturday(星期六)——来自罗马农业之神萨托恩(Saturn)的名字。

科学名称和术语：

Uranium(铀)——来自罗马神话中天神尤拉纳斯(Uranus)的名字。

Mercury(水银)——来自罗马神话中诸神的使者、商业与科学之神墨丘利(Mercury)的名字。

Mars(火星)——来自罗马神话中的战神玛尔斯(Mars)的名字。

Jupiter(木星)——来自罗马神话中主神朱庇特(Jupiter)的名字。

有些神话故事人人皆知，有些讲英语的青年可以当场背出。有些神话故事在不讲英语的国家流传甚广。如特洛伊木马的故事可在全世界许多国家的教科书和著作中找到，常被用来告诫人们要提高警惕，谨防内部敌人，不要在可疑的情况下随便接收貌似无害的礼物。希腊神话中普罗米修斯的故事也许知道的人少一些，但他对人类的爱，他授予人类的火，他对主神宙斯的蔑视，在威胁和折磨下坚韧不拔的意志，在各国不同语言的散文和诗歌中都受到高度赞扬。普罗米修斯在全世界成为热爱人类、反抗压迫的象征。

希腊的荷马史诗《奥德赛》中的主人公奥德修斯(Odysseus)的故事也在许多国家传颂。奥德修斯经历的艰辛、考验，同形形色色的敌人(有的是人类，有的是鬼怪，有的凶恶残暴，有的温柔迷人)进行的斗争，以及许多奇遇，无论用何种语言来描写都会引人入胜，十分有趣。从某些方面来说，《奥德赛》很像中国的《西游记》。书中许多人物和事件已成英语中的典故。例如，奥德修斯遇到的独眼巨人赛克罗波斯(Cyclops)。还有诱惑男人后把他们变成野兽的美丽女妖赛丝(Circe)等。

英语中其他来自神话典故的普通词语还有：

a Herculean task(艰巨的任务)——指需要巨大的体力或智力才能完成的任务。海格立斯是希腊神话中的身材魁梧、力大无穷的英雄。

他曾被罚去完成 12 项极为艰巨的任务,成功后,被封为神。如:It was a *Herculean task*, but he managed to do it. (那是非常艰巨的任务,但他终于完成了。)

Achilles heel(唯一致命的弱点)——指一个人(或组织、国家等)的弱点。故事是这样的:在荷马的另一个叙事诗《伊利亚特》中有一位希腊英雄阿基里斯(Achilles),出生后被他的母亲倒提着在冥河中浸过,以便使之刀枪不入。阿基里斯全身浸入水中,唯独脚跟抓在他母亲手里未湿,所以脚跟成了唯一弱点;以后阿基里斯在战斗中恰恰因脚跟受伤而死。如:He would be an excellent candidate for the position. He has energy, knowledge and experi- ence. But he's got *an Achilles heel*—his terrible temper. Three months ago he beat up a colleague in an argument. (他是这个职位的理想候选人:他精力充沛,有知识,有经验。但他有个致命的弱点——脾气很坏。三个月前,他和一个同事争论,把人家打了一顿。)

a Pandora's box(潘朵拉之盒——灾难、麻烦、祸害的根源)——指看上去有用却引起祸害的礼物或其他物品。在希腊神话中第一个妇女潘朵拉因受惩罚,被众神谪下凡间,宙斯(罗马神话中的朱庇特)给她一个盒子,让她带给娶她的男人。当盒子最后打开时,所有的罪恶、不幸、灾难等都跑了出来,从此给人类带来无穷的祸害。如:The project, which seemed so promising, turned out to be *a Pandora's box*. (那个项目看起来好像很有希望,结果招来许多灾祸。)

A Damocles sword (the Sword of Damolces, 即将临头或无时不在的危险——达摩克里斯(Damocles)是赛拉丘斯(Syracuse)暴君狄俄尼索斯(Dionysius)的廷臣。达摩克里斯贪图钱财,追求享乐,羡慕主子的生活。有一次,他对狄俄尼索斯极力恭维一番,羡慕之情十分明显。狄俄尼索斯邀他赴宴,但在达摩克里斯头上用一根头发悬挂着一把剑。在宴会过程中达摩克里斯坐在剑下,恐惧万分。狄俄尼索斯意在告诉他,当国王并不享福,而是时刻都有生命危险。如:The terrorists had been caught and jailed. But the two leaders had escaped with machine guns and explosives. This fact hung like *the sword of Damocles* over the police commissioner's head. (那些恐怖分子已被捕入狱。但两个头头却携带机关枪、炸药逃脱了。这件事使警察局长仿佛头悬利剑,时刻坐立不安。)

宗教是典故的另一个来源。在英语国家里基督教是主要的宗教，许多典故来自基督教的《圣经》中的人物和事件。如：

a messiah(弥赛亚一救世主)——指被压迫人民的解放者或期望中的解放者。《圣经·旧约全书》中预言，有一天弥赛亚将要降生，把犹太人从压迫下解救出来。

like (a) Moses leading his people(像摩西那样领导/带领他的人民)——摩西是古代(公元前 13 或 14 世纪)以色列的先知和领袖，是《圣经·旧约全书》中最伟大的人物之一。他率领以色列人经过 40 年的艰苦跋涉，穿过了大沙漠，终于摆脱埃及人的奴役。

a Solomon(所罗门)——指聪明人。贤人所罗门是公元前 10 世纪左右的希伯来人的国王，以智慧著称。

David and Goliath(大卫和歌利亚)——大卫是个牧童，在与地中海东岸古代居民腓力斯巨人歌利亚交战中用弹弓将巨人射死，后来当了希伯来人的国王。后人用大卫和歌利亚来比喻弱小者与强大者(不论是两个人、两个企业，还是两个国家)之间的斗争——结果弱小者取胜。

a Judas(犹大)——指叛徒(尤指伪装亲善的背叛者)。犹大是耶稣的 12 个门徒之一。据记载，犹大为了 30 块银币把耶稣出卖给犹太教祭司。

thirty pieces of silver (30 块银币)——因叛卖获得的钱财或其他报酬。(见上条)

a kiss of death(表面上友好实际上坑害人的行为)——此语来自犹大出卖耶稣时吻了耶稣。

英语中有些典故来自体育项目，不会讲英语的人如果不知道有关体育项目就不懂。特别是美国英语，其中有些典故与美国很流行的棒球和橄榄球运动有关。在许多别的国家这两种球类运动还不十分普遍：

baseball(棒球)

to not get to first base(没有取得初步成就)——原指棒球击球手没有跑到第一垒，转义为一开始或很快就失败了。如：She attracted him at first sight and he made elaborate plans to court her, but he didn't even *get to first base*.(他一眼就看上了她，于是就盘算着怎样去追她，结果

第一招就不灵。)

to have two strikes against one(三击中已有两击不中)——原指棒球击球手已击两球不中,如第三击再不中,就要出局。转义为"处境不利"、"形势不妙"。如: When he applied for the job, he already *had two strikes against him*: he didn't have a college diploma like the other applicants, and he was ten minutes late for his interview. (他在争取这项工作时,处于十分不利的地位。第一,他不像其他应聘者那样有大学文凭;第二,他去面谈时迟到了 10 分钟。)

### American football(橄榄球)

to carry the ball(负主要责任)——原指橄榄球运动员执球,转义为对完成某项任务负主要责任。如: The negotiations are the key to the undertaking, we'd better ask Mumford *to carry the ball*. (这个项目的关键是谈判,我们最好让曼福特负责去做。)

an armchair quarterback(坐在扶手椅上的指挥者)——quarterback 原指橄榄球赛指挥进攻的四分卫,加了 armchair 一词,往往指局外人大谈应如何做某事而未身体力行也不用负任何责任。如: It's easy to be *an armchair quarterback* but your idea wouldn't have worked at all! (坐着说说倒很容易,你的主意根本行不通!)

### 来自其他运动项目的常用说法有:

### boxing(拳击)

to be down and out(被困难压倒,完全失败)——原指在拳击运动中被击倒而不能继续比赛,转义为虽经过努力挣扎,但已处于绝望境地而彻底垮台。如:He made one last effort, but it didn't work. There was nothing left to do but close shop—he *was down and out*. (他作了最后的努力,但无济于事,只好让商店倒闭——他彻底垮了。)

to hit below the belt(用不正当的手段打击别人)——原指拳击比赛时打对方下身的犯规行为,转义为在比赛或与人打交道时,用不正当的手段去伤害对方。如:How could you do a thing like that? That's *hitting below the belt*. (你怎么能这样干呢? 这不大像话吧!) card games(纸牌)

play one's trump card(s) (打出王牌;使出绝招或最后一招)——原

205

指打桥牌时出王牌,转义为采取自认为对付敌手不会失败的行动。如:
Just when his rivals started to rub their hands with glee, he *played his trump card*. (正当他的对手得意洋洋的时候,他使出了绝招。)

squeeze play(逼对方失败或受损失的行动)——原指打桥牌时逼对方出某张牌,转义为迫使对方失败或付出代价的行动。如: He was caught in a *squeeze play*; if he agreed to the demands, he would lose a fortune; if he didn't agree, he would have to close down his shop. (他处于进退两难的境地:要是答应对方的要求,就得损失一大笔钱;要是不答应,他的店就得关门。)

fishing(钓鱼)

to swallow the bait, hook, line and sinker(上钩,上当)——原指钓鱼时鱼吞鱼饵、鱼钩、鱼线和坠子,转义为稍微给点甜头就完全上钩了。如: They knew he liked to collect art goods, so when they promised him a Ming dynasty drawing, he *swallowed the bait*, *hook*, *line and sinker*. (他们知道他喜欢收藏文物,所以他们答应给他一幅明时代古画时,他就上钩了。)

引用某社会近代或当代的人物、事件作为典故最难理解。一个人除非十分熟悉美国近况或进展,否则对下列名称会感到不知所云。

a Rambo(兰博)——兰博是 80 年代中期美国电影中的一个著名人物。他是在侵越战争中为美军卖过命的汉子,足智多谋、沉默寡言,性情孤僻,行为有点古怪。在电影中,他历尽艰险并经常使用暴力,又奇迹般地死里逃生,他用射击、刀砍、轰炸及火烧杀出一条活路,虽然这些情节令人难以置信,而且他的某些暴力行动也使人反感,他却是许多美国男孩和青年心目中的当代英雄。

as American as apple pie(像苹果馅饼一样是典型的美国式的)——苹果馅饼是美国人喜欢的甜食之一,吃时常配有冰淇淋。有人说苹果馅饼是美国人发明的,也有人说它是在美国最先流行的。这一短语用来强调某种东西是真正美国式的。

a Pepsodent smile(广告式微笑)——露出洁白牙齿的微笑。此语出自 Pepsodent 牙膏的广告。pepsodent 是美国较著名的牌子之一。

206

an Ivy Leaguer(名牌大学学生)——指在八所名牌大学学习的富家子女。这八所是：哈佛大学(Harvard)，耶鲁大学(Yale)，普林斯顿大学(Princeton)，哥伦比亚大学(Columbia)，宾夕法尼亚大学(Pennsyvania)、科耐尔大学(Cornell)，达特茅斯大学(Dartmouth)，布朗大学(Brown)。

That's something for Ripley(那简直是里普利的奇闻)——美国有许多家报纸刊登里普利写的"信不信由你"这一专栏，所报导的都是一些稀奇古怪或异乎寻常的事，却都是真实的，都是经过核实的。但因为这些事太古怪，非同一般，人们觉得难以相信。这一短语一般指令人难以置信而又很可能是真实的事。

汉语中的典故同样来自文学、历史、传说、神话、体育等。

文学典故多出自《红楼梦》、《水浒》、《三国演义》、《西游记》中的人物和事件。如："像刘姥姥进了大观园"，"智多星"，"三顾茅庐"、"万事俱备，只欠东风"，"猪八戒倒打一耙"等。

中国有记载的历史达两千多年，历史典故很多。如："四面楚歌"，"身在曹营心在汉"，"围魏救赵"，"完璧归赵"等。

有些典故来自中国寓言。如："画蛇添足"，"守株待兔"，"拔苗助长"，"刻舟求剑"，"对牛弹琴"，"黔驴技穷"等，在说话和写作时都常用到。

有些典故来自民间传说。如："过着牛郎织女的生活"，"八仙过海，各显神通"等。

与佛教和道教有关的典故有："临时抱佛脚"，"做一天和尚撞一天钟"，"道高一尺，魔高一丈"，"放下屠刀，立地成佛"等。

来自体育或文娱项目的典故中，有些与中国象棋有关，如："马后炮"，"舍车马，保将帅"。有些与音乐有关。如："异曲同工"，"一唱一和"等。

有些典故来自中国戏剧。如："亮相"，"跑龙套"，"唱红脸"，"唱白脸"，"粉墨登场"等。

显然，大部分外国人遇到汉语中的典故时都会感到费解。我们建议翻译人员或直接与外宾交谈的人碰到这类典故时，只需说

207

一个意思大体相似的英语对应词或简短的解释,不要详细介绍典故背景,以免谈话者分心,影响讨论的主要内容。如遇到下列话语时可以这样处理,如:

　　将他一军——to put someone in check(意义相同,出典相似)

　　白骨精——the White Boned Demon, an evil spirit who often took the guise of a charming young woman in the novel *Pilgrimage to the West*.(比较详细的解释)

　　此地无银三百两——a saying that means a guilty person gives himself away by conspicuously protesting his innocence.(只释意,不提原文典故)

# 第九章

## 委 婉 语

看来在所有的文化中，人们对某些概念或事物总想避免直接提到它，尽管在他们所用的语言里有这些词语。要提到某种概念或事物时，就用另一个听起来比较委婉的词语来替代。

人们普遍忌讳用的词之一就是 death(死亡)。不论在某种特定的语言中表示"死亡"这个概念的原词是什么(如英语中的 die 和汉语中的"死")，人们总会用许多不那么刺耳的说法来代替它。

下面是英汉两种语言用来表示"死亡"这一概念的一些词语：

英语中表示"死亡"的委婉语：go (e.g. *He's gone*), depart, depart from the world for ever, decease, pass away, breathe one's last, go the way of all flesh, pay one's debt to nature, go to a better world, be in (go to) Heaven, be with God, etc.

汉语中表示"死亡"的委婉语："去世"，"逝世"，"故去"，"病故"，"寿终"，"亡故"，"牺牲"，"作古"，"谢世"，"弃世"，"与世长辞"，"心脏停止跳动"，"去见马克思"等。

上列词语并非是"死亡"一词的全部委婉说法，连比较通常用的词语也没有列全。还有一些比较不常用的英语词语，如莎士比亚用过 shuffle off this mortal coil(摆脱人世的纷扰；解脱；死)马克·吐温在《汤姆·索亚历险记》(*The Adventures of Tom Sawyer*)中也曾用 release(解脱)来表示"死亡"：It seemed to him that life was but a trouble, at best, and he more than half envied Jimmy

Hodges, so lately *released*.（在他看来，人活着至多不过是一件麻烦事，他非常羡慕刚刚去世的吉姆·霍吉斯。）

所有上述这些短语或说法都对死者有褒义或至少是不带感情色彩。其中有一些反映了人们对待死亡及来世的不同态度，例如：go to a better world(到一个更美好的世界去)，be with God(与上帝同在)。有的是说话人用来指自己的，如："反正我过不了几年就去见马克思了。"(In a few years I'll be seeing Marx anyway.)

然而，英语中还有一些极为随便的说法或俚语，如 kick the bucket(翘辫子)，be done for(完蛋)。类似的汉语有："丧命"，"毙命"，"一命呜呼"，"呼呼哀哉"。很显然，这些并不是褒义词，而且也不能算作委婉语。但不管有什么样的区别，所有上述词语都是"死"这一概念的代名词。

上列实例说明委婉语的基本特征，就是用一种令人愉快的、委婉有礼的、听起来不刺耳的词语来代替令人不快的、粗鲁无礼的、听起来刺耳的词语。

除表示"死亡"的词语外，也往往使用比较委婉说法来表示许多别的概念。这一方面可分许多类，下面举一些例子：

在提到人体的缺点、生理缺陷、年老、人体的某些功能(如大小便)、性行为等方面时，往往用委婉的说法。例如，用 plain(平平，一般)表示人长得丑，代替 ugly；用 heavyset, on the heavy side(身体发福)表示男人身体太胖，代替 fat；用 slender(苗条，纤细)表示女人太瘦，代替 skinny；用 physically handicapped(生理上有缺陷的)指瘸子或其他残疾人，代替 crippled；用 senior citizens(年长的公民；senior 一词可以有两种理解，即可指年龄，也可指地位)表示老人，代替 elderly people；用 advanced in age, elderly(上了年纪)指老迈，代替 old 等。

在这里要特别提一下有关人体功能方面的委婉语，如果不知道怎么说，就会弄得很尴尬。英语和许多别的语言一样，在这方面也有各种词语表示委婉的说法。如"去上厕所"(go to the toilet;

210

go to the men's (ladies') room, rest room, washroom, lavatory, the john)一般无须解释。非说明不可时，可以说 to wash one's hands, to relieve oneself 或 because nature calls(幽默语)。另外，男人可以说 to see a man about a horse(幽默语)，妇女可以说 to powder her nose, to freshen up 等。如果某人因饮食不调、肠胃不适，医生想知道他大便是否正常时，可以问：How are your bowel movements? 医生要他检查一下大便时可以说：We need a stool specimen. 中国人在国外学习或在国内陪外宾去看病，如果不会说这些比较委婉的话，表达上述概念，就会弄得很窘。

这里提一下美国委婉语中的某些倾向。美国近年来在社会生活和事务方面委婉说法用得越来越多。如有些职业或工作不再叫 jobs(指一般性的工作)，而称 professions(多指从事脑力劳动或受过专门训练的职业)。有些职业的名称很容易令人误解；突出的例子是 sanitary engineer(卫生工程师)指清除垃圾的清洁工。

在经济萧条时期，找个从事脑力劳动或受过专门训练的职业不容易，工资最低的工作，包括体力劳动的活儿，也难找到。找不到工作就要"失业"(become unemployed)，或者用新出现的、比较微妙的词儿"赋闲"(involuntarily leisured)。长期"赋闲"也很难受，尤其是穷人。尽管 poor(穷人)这个词有被淘汰的危险，近二十年来已经有好几个词用来代替 poor，至少在知识界和"官方文件"中是这样的。有个不幸的人说：

At first I was *poor*, then I became *needy*, later I was *underprivileged*, now I'm *disadvantaged*. I still don't have a cent to my name, but I sure have a great vocabulary. (起初我"穷困"，过后我"拮据"，后来我"受到不公正的待遇"，现在我"机遇不佳"，我虽仍不名一文，但词汇却学了一大堆。)

这段话是一个没受过多少教育的穷人说的，其中 poor, needy, underprivileged, disadvantaged 实际上都是"贫困"、"穷困"、"贫穷"的不同说法，也都是负责调查贫民生活及发放救济金情况的人所用的,但一次比一次委婉。不过,穷人也不愿别人直接称他们为"贫民"或"穷光蛋"。措词尽管不同,穷人的处境未变,仍然一文不名,只是学到了几个词儿而已。这段话有自我嘲笑之意。

教育界新出现的委婉语也不少。有人不称教师为 teacher, 而称 educator。学生仍然叫 students, 但对学生的评价则需要仔细考虑措辞, 用"积极用语"来代替"消极用语"。谈到学习成绩差的学生(below average student)时可以说:She/He is working at her/his own level. (她/他在根据自己的水平学习。)这样说就不会伤害别人的自尊心。说 Can do better work with help(有别人帮助可以学得更好些)比直接说学生 slow(迟钝)或 stupid(笨)不会得罪人。当然不要说一个青年 stupid(笨)或 lazy(懒), 这样说学生和家长都很难接受。所以懒学生就叫 underachiever(未能充分发挥潜力的学生), 这个词听起来不刺耳, 但也没有说明这个学生成绩如何, 这个学生可能勉强及格, 也可能不及格。再举几个例子, 如:depends on others to do his/her work = cheats in class(靠别人做作业 = 堂上考试作弊);has a tendency to stretch the truth = sometimes lies(有夸大事实的倾向 = 有时说谎);takes other people's things without permission = steals(未经许可而拿别人的东西 = 偷别人的东西)。

使用委婉语的目的在于减少某些词语或概念所引起的不快, 所以一些企业、组织及政府的公告和出版物常使用委婉语。例如, 在纽约, 地铁有一段失火, 影响车辆正常运行, 当时就是这样宣布的:We have a fire situation. 直译是:"我们现在出现了失火的局面。"美国总统里根在竞选时曾向美国公众许诺 cut taxes(减税), 而当他成为总统, 要亲自处理国家财政问题时, 却呼吁 revenue enhancements("扩充财源"——增加财政收入), 避免谈 tax increases(增税)。在劳资关系中出现工潮时, 在谈到如何对付罢工时, 不说 strikes(罢工), 而说 industrial action(直译是:"工业行动")。在另一方面, 1983 年下半年, 为防止传染病蔓延, 美国政府解释用煤气杀死宾夕法尼亚州的鸡这一计划时说 depopulated the birds(减

212

少家禽的头数)。据联邦新闻官员说,选用 depopulated 一词是因为要"避免用 slaughter(屠杀)一词"。显然,人们认为用 kill(杀)一词也太生硬了。

在国际关系中,"美化"词语的作法也很普遍。里根政府 1986 年决定向利比亚展开"一场小小的心理战"(美国国务院舒尔茨用语)时,政府编造了关于利比亚领导人卡扎菲"计划采取新的恐怖主义行动,美国准备还击"之类的新闻。真相大白之后,公众大哗。白宫官员赶忙出来解释,说他们不是故意欺骗公众。他们声称,政府所做的无非是组织一次"反信息"战役——用这种说法来说服公众接受政府的行为当然是软弱无力的。他们如此费尽心机美化这种勾当,引起国务院发言人伯纳德·卡尔伯的不满,他宣布因"小小的意见分歧"而辞职,使白宫陷于困境。

1983 年,美国派武装部队入侵格林纳达。美国总统里根对新闻记者"经常使用 invasion(入侵)一词"十分恼火。他说,"这是 rescue mission(营救使命)"。实际上是里根自己首先称之为 invasion(入侵)的。

格林纳达是第三世界国家。这些国家大部分很穷。这些国家起先叫 underdeveloped nations(不发达国家),后来又改为 developing nations(发展中国家),近来常用的是 emerging nations(新兴国家)。而联合国称这些国家为 LDCs,即 less-developed countries(欠发达国家)。

军界特别喜欢使用委婉语,就军人所从事的业务来看,这样做并不奇怪。对他们来说,只有 advances(前进),没有 retreats(撤退);只谈 victories(胜利),不谈 defeats(失败)。在这一方面,近年来兼任美国武装部队总司令的杰米·卡特和罗纳德·里根两位总统就是这么干的。1980 年美国派直升飞机去营救美国在伊朗的人质失败,卡特称之为 incomplete success(不圆满的胜利)。原被称为 MX 的美国试验导弹,居然被里根正式命名为 Peacekeeper(和平保卫者)。下级军官有时把美国士兵屠杀越南人叫做 wasting

213

the enemy(消耗敌人)或 pacification(绥靖行动)。这使人们想到第二次世界大战时纳粹德国处置战俘的情况。当时,有些战俘身上带的文件上写着 Rückkehr unerwünscht（return unwanted—勿回）;有些写着 Sonderbehandlung（special treatment—特殊待遇）。两词同义——都是 death(处死)。如果己方有伤亡,通常要把所受的损失写得轻一些,一般用 light casualties(略有伤亡)这个词来表达战斗人员损失。如果所在部队误伤己方人员,措辞就更需巧妙;多年来造出不少巧妙的词语,但很少比下列说法更绝的了——美国炮兵轰击了美国部队后,报道说:accidental delivery of ordnance(误送弹药)。

现在,对敌人的突然袭击大都称为 pre-emptive strikes(先发制人的攻击)。故名思义,pre-empt(先发制人)是说在他人采取行动之前率先采取行动。"先发制人的攻击"给人的印象是,必须攻击敌人以便制止敌人的进攻,因此似乎在道义上是无可责备的,而 surprise attack(突然袭击)意味着鬼鬼祟祟的行动,是不道德的。近来出现了更新的说法,叫做 surgical strike(外科手术性的攻击),给军事行动以人道主义的色彩。外科手术一般用于摘除人体恶性病变部分、整形或医治外伤等,所以"外科手术性攻击"给人的印象是,这是一次为消除邪恶而必须采取的军事行动。

# 第十章

## 禁 忌 语

我们在前一章里谈到,因某些词语和概念令人不快,最好不用,而换一种婉转的说法——这就是委婉语。有些词语因传统习惯或社会风俗不同,会引起对方强烈反感,也应避免使用——这就是禁忌语。在语言方面犯忌和在文化方面犯忌一样,都会显得唐突无礼,令人生厌。在公开场合使用某词语或提及某事会使人吃惊或引起强烈不满,如有人经常触犯当地社会禁忌,就会被该社会所排斥,成为不受欢迎的人。然而,各国人民所忌讳的行为和词语并不一致,所以,学习外语的人对此应有所了解,这是很重要的。

英语和汉语中有些忌讳是一致的,例如,在讲究礼貌的场合谈话时都不提大小便。非用英语说不可时,就得用委婉语。在汉语中,虽说也忌讳,却不像英语那样严格,有时,在公开正式的场合,发言或交谈时,也会听到"吃喝拉撒睡"之类的说法。

在英汉两种语言中,都忌讳直接提到人体某些器官和性行为等。可是,60年代美国出现的"性解放"之风使这种情况有所改变。近年来,在英语国家对此采取更加随便、直率的态度。因此,在书刊中 to make love, to have sex with 之类表示"与……发生关系"的字样并不罕见。不过,即使是这些词语,也已是稍加"美化"了的。然而,所谓"具有四个字母的词语"(four-letter words),如 fuck, tits 等,在大部分谈话中仍被认为是不得体的,尤其是在都有男女的场合,就更显得不雅了。

在许多语言里都忌讳诅咒、骂人的话。英语和汉语都是这样的,但还要说明一下:第一,有些骂人的话过于粗鄙、难听,所以受到社会更严格的限制。英语听 Jesus Christ, Holy Mary, son of a bitch 就是这种话;而 Damn, Damn it, Hell 这样的话在语气上就稍微轻一些。请注意,在英语中,大部分诅咒、骂人的话与基督教的词语和名称有关。在汉语中这种固定的咒骂或骂人的话似乎少些,最常用的是"他妈的",但听的人不会引起很强烈的反感,因为有时它已转化为无教养的人的口头语。第二,诅咒、骂人的话受到年龄、性别、职业的限制。孩子骂人马上会受到大人责备。妇女骂人会被人认为粗俗失礼。教师骂人被认为有失体统。第三,这种话也受环境和场合的限制。在当众发言、课堂教学或和有一定社会地位的人在一起时,人们就不大会说诅咒、骂人的话。在家里、在劳动场合、在办公室、在公共汽车上或市场上,说的人就比较多。

应当指出,人们对诅咒、骂人的话反应并不始终如一。有些这样的话听得多了,也就不那么刺耳。现在人们常听到年轻人用骂人话。不过,对非本族人还是少讲粗话为妙。

现在谈一下英语和汉语在禁忌方面的不同处,先讲一个有趣的故事:

一位50来岁的美国妇女在中国任教。有一位年轻的中国同事请她到自己家里来吃饭。一进门,女主人就把4岁的女儿介绍给客人。小姑娘用英语说:"阿姨好!"她妈妈跟她说过,见了成年妇女要这样问好。

"不对,不能叫阿姨,"妈妈连忙纠正说,"要叫奶奶。"

"不要叫奶奶。就叫我阿姨好了。"

"那太没有礼貌了。您比我年纪大多了。"

美国妇女脸红了,笑笑说:"就叫我阿姨吧。我喜欢这样。"

为什么美国妇女在这种场合会感到尴尬呢?因为中国人和美国人对待年龄问题的态度不同。

对大多数英国人和美国人来说,打听陌生人或不大熟悉的人

216

的年龄是不得体的。此外,收入多少、是否已婚、政治倾向、宗教信仰等,除非对方表示不介意,这些情况也不宜过问,否则就是失礼。因此,同讲英语的外国人谈话时,应避免提下列问题,尽管中国人不认为这样做有什么不妥。

How old are you? (你多大年纪?)

What's your age? (你多大年纪?)

How much do you make? (你挣多少钱?)

What's your income? (你的收入是多少?)

How much did that dress cost you? (你的连衣裙花多少钱买的?)

How much did you pay for that car? (你的汽车是多少钱买的?)

Are you married or single? (你结婚了吗?)

How come you're still single? (你怎么还没结婚呢?)

So you're divorced. What was the reason? Couldn't you two get along? (噢,你离婚了。什么原因呢? 两人合不来吗?)

Are you a Republican or a Democrat? (你是共和党人还是民主党人?)

Why did you vote for—(你为什么投……的票?)

Do you go to church? (你信教吗?)

What's your religion? (你信什么教?)

Are you Catholic? (你信天主教吗?)

如必须了解这类情况,可以在提问前说明理由。例如,在旅馆里、在医院里或者在填写表格的时候,可以这样说:

"为了登记,我要了解一些情况,您能告诉我您的——(年龄、是否已婚等)吗?"

"这些人想了解您的情况,您能告诉我——吗?"

有时,我们想了解别人的情况,并非出于好奇,也不是为了登记注册,而是想知道怎样对待他,怎样和他相处,这时应处理得比较得体,可以先谈谈自己的情况,然后再引对方谈出他的情况,这样做往往会得到预期的结果。如采用以下方式:

"我结婚了,我们有一个孩子,是女儿。全家相处得很融洽,可我觉得跟妻子和女儿在一起的时间太少,有时真不知道该怎么办……"

对方可能会接下去说:"我也有同样的问题。我的孩子们常抱怨说……"

这样就可以知道他已经结婚,有孩子。

如果想知道别人的政治观点,可以用一种比较随便的态度一般地谈起来:

"最近报上有不少关于美国总统选举的报道,我觉得很有意思,可有时又有点搞不清楚,特别是我听说美国人不大关心政治。我也许想错了。美国人对这种事是怎么看的?多数美国人都参加政党吗?"

对方多半会回答这样的问题,或发表一些意见,在此过程中可能谈到自己:

"嗯,不一定。他们在登记的时候可能注明自己是民主党人或共和党人,但并不认为自己属于那个党。实际上,在选举时,他们投谁的票都行。比如说,我一般认为自己是民主党人,但在上届选举中,我投了共和党人的票,因为……"

这样就了解到所想知道的情况了。

讲英语的人很重视 privacy,所以不愿别人过问个人的事。privacy 这个词含有"秘密"、"隐私"、"私下"、"隐退"、"独处"、"不愿别人干涉"、"不希望别人过问"等义。"个人的事"包括"个人事务"(private business)、"私事"(private affairs)、"个人所关切的事"(private concerns)等。在英语中有句谚语:A man's home is his castle. (一个人的家就是他的城堡。)意思是:一个人的家是神圣不可侵犯的,未经许可,不得入内。个人的事也是这样,不必让别人知道,更不愿别人干预。一提上列问题就会被认为是在打听别人的私事,即用另一种方式侵犯了别人的"城堡"。

许多中国人对西方人所理解的 privacy 的全部概念非常陌生,汉语中也没有与 privacy 相当的词语。部分原因可能是:中国人各家住得很近。千百年来,中国农村居民往往几十户、几百户住在一个村庄,挤在一小块地方生活。在中国北方大小城镇的"四合院"

或"大杂院"里,人们住得近,,接触多,个人生活或私事很难不被人知道或干预。这种情况和西方很不一样。在西方国家,直到不久以前,典型的家庭还是独门独户,住宅周围有相当大的院子或花园。另一个原因可能是:中国人民之间长期以来有团结友爱精神,住得近,人与人之间接触的机会多,就会互相帮助,互相关心,个人的事也就是一家的事、邻居的事,甚至是更大的集体的事。这种情况与西方重视 privacy 的条件完全不同。

还有一个问题与此有关:英语中有些表达方式是故意含糊其辞。如果人家说:I'm going out.(我要出去。)那就不要再问他到哪儿去。如果他(她)说:I have an appointment.(我有个约会。)再问跟谁约会,是什么约会,就不合适。同样,如果一位妇女说她头疼,别人也不必过于担心,不要问:到底怎么不舒服,要不要吃点什么药之类。她真不舒服,多半会跟你说的。应该明白,当人们不愿意做什么事、不参加某种活动或拒绝别人的邀请时,往往用上列说法来推托,以免别人再问什么话。

英语中的禁忌语近来有所发展,已包括那些鄙视社会上某些人的词汇和用语。人们尤其注意那些被称为性别歧视语言和种族歧视语言,对此比较敏感。现就这两方面略加说明。

目前,性别歧视语言主要指轻视妇女的语言。在某些社会中,妇女用的语言和男人用的语言有区别。在另一些社会中,语言有高级、低级之分,妇女只能用低级语言。美国妇女首先研究英语中的性别歧视现象。她们发现:语言可以影响人们对妇女的态度,而英语是以男子为中心的语言,偏袒男性,贬低女性。比如说,不论说话还是写文章,提到性别不明的人时,一律用 he 而不用 she。主持会议的人,即使是妇女,都叫 chairman,以致出现 Madam chairman 这样的称呼。在"世界的历史是人类的历史"这句话里,"人类"一词用 mankind,不用 womankind。表示在两性关系上行为不检的妇女的贬义词远较表示乱搞男女关系的男子的贬义词为多。同样,prostitute(妓女)的同义词也远比 whoremonger(嫖客)的同义词多。这些现象表明,在男女关系方面,人们对男子比较宽容。如果男孩子或男人有女相,就称之为略带贬义的 sissy(女孩子气的男孩子,女人气的男人);如果女孩子或姑娘的行为举止像男孩子或小伙子,就称之为带有褒义的 tomboy(男孩子,小伙子似的顽皮姑娘)。

汉语中也有歧视妇女现象。从前,人们认为妇女愚昧无知、地位低下,比如"妇人之见"、"男子汉不同妇人一般见识"之类的话就反映了人们瞧不起妇女的态度。丈夫把妻子叫做"家里的"、"内人"等,表明妻子无非是在家里干点家务活儿的人而已。此外,妻子的命运和社会地位完全取决于丈夫。俗话说:"夫唱妇随",就反映了这种依附关系。

汉字的写法有明显的歧视妇女现象。许多汉语贬义字都有"女"字偏旁(或部首),数目多得惊人。这里只举几个例子,如:"奸"、"婪"、"嫉"、"媚"等。连指女性的"阴"字也常用来构成贬义词。如:"阴毒","阴森","阴谋"等。

近几十年来,中国妇女的地位提高了,在汉语中对妇女的称谓也有相应的变化。像"家里的"、"内人"这样的称谓不大用了。已婚妇女仍用原来的姓,不用丈夫的姓,也不像在旧社会那样,被人称为"刘太太"、"张太太"。妇女和男人一样称"同志",既表示男女平等,又含有志同道合等积极意义。使用公然嘲笑或轻视妇女的词语或说法会招致不满或受到批评。

种族主义认为,有些人种天生低劣,素质不如其他人种(见 Light 和 Keller 于 1985 年发表的著作)。种族歧视语言就是显示对某些种族带有偏见的词语和说法。在英语中,不管有意无意,多数这类词语显示对黑人有种族偏见或无意中会使他们不快。上文提到,"白"表示"清白"、"纯洁"、"干净"、"慈善"等——这些都是有积极含义的褒义词。另一方面,"黑"则与"邪恶"、"罪孽"、"肮脏"等有关,如:blackguard(恶棍),blacklist(黑名单),black mark(污点)等。全家引以为耻的"败家子"叫 black sheep,不叫 white sheep。无恶意的谎言叫 white lie, 不像 ordinary lie(一般的谎言)或 black lie(用心险恶的谎言)那么坏。难怪有些黑人抱怨说,连语义学也使"黑"字显得又丑又贱。此外,用 nigger, boy 之类的词来称呼成年黑人男子有明显的轻蔑意味。如今,除持种族歧视观点的人故意用以侮辱黑人外,这些词已很少有人使用了。

不过,在美国,不仅黑人有蔑称,某些其他国家或种族的人也有蔑称。如把意大利人叫做 dagos,把犹太人叫做 kikes,把波兰人叫做 polacks,把中国人叫做 chinks,把日本人叫做 japs 等。这些都是带有诬蔑性的名称,反映强烈的种族偏见。

人们有时会听到带有污辱性的有种族歧视意味的议论,或意在嘲笑某些种族愚昧无知、行为古怪的所谓"种族笑话"。有些笑话也许听起来滑稽可笑,但还是令人不快的。

汉语中也有种族歧视的痕迹。新中国成立后已大有变化,在此之前,轻视或贬低汉族以外的少数民族的词语不少,如"蛮人"一词实际上把某些少数民族看作野蛮人。又如"蒙古大夫"(指不称职的医生)这个带嘲弄意味的说法显然有贬低少数民族的意味。自本世纪中叶以来,宪法已明文规定各族人民一律平等这一政策。在汉语中,这类种族歧视的词语和说法大部分已经消失,但并不彻底。至今仍有人把外国人叫做"鬼子"或"洋鬼子",把外国人叫做"大鼻子"可能并无明显的贬义,但也不是尊敬之词。

在汉语中,许多贬义词有"黑"字。如:"黑心","黑帮","黑话"等。这当然不表明中国人对黑人怀有偏见,对白人有所偏爱。在中国,"白"字也常构成贬义词。如京剧中的奸臣或小人画"白脸","白脸"就转义为"坏蛋"(villain)。在社会主义的术语中,"白区"指反动派统治的地区,"白色恐怖"指反动派制造的恐怖。然而,在中国的懂汉语的黑人对带有"黑"字的贬义词很敏感,据说他们对此有怨言。人们应当了解他们的感情,尽管说话的人并无冒犯之意,在使用这些词语也应审慎从事。

虽说发生了上述变化,而且在某些方面已取得长足进展,但不论在汉语中还是在英语中,都仍有轻视妇女和歧视少数民族的痕迹。说话时一不小心,就会无意中得罪了对方,因而有必要及时了解语言在这一方面的变化;更要紧的是,应善于体会被歧视者的感情,切不可对此麻木不仁,掉以轻心。只要人们对社会不平等的非正义性有所了解,就可能避免说出歧视妇女或其他种族的话,不论有意还是无意。

# 第十一章

## 敬辞和谦辞

一天早晨，一位英国妇女在中国公园里遇见了一位上了年纪的中国人，看见他长长的白胡子，就走上前用汉语客气地问道："爷爷，你几岁啦？"老人诧异地看看她，转身对周围的人有点生气地说："您瞧，她问我几岁啦！几岁啦！"这位年轻的英国妇女根本没有想到自己的话会引起对方这样的反应。后来她才知道产生误会的原因：她用这句话问一个小孩的年龄是对的，对上了年纪的人应当问"您高寿？"或"您多大年纪啦？"

这个有趣的事说明，讲英语的人和中国人交谈时，要注意语言上和文化上的差异之一：跟长辈或上级说话时与同辈或下级说话时不一样，往往要使用某些尊称或敬辞。如果使用同样的词语，会认为用词不当而失礼，甚至显得高傲。另一方面，在跟长辈谈话或给长辈写信提到自己时，要用谦辞或卑辞，否则也会被人认为失礼。近二三十年来，这种情况虽有变化，但未消失；敬辞和谦辞仍在使用，但不像从前那样普遍。

讲英语人在用汉语交谈时，对敬辞和谦辞问题感到特别困难。因为在英语中敬辞和谦辞很少，目前一般还在用的就更少了。在英语中，同自己的上级说话或写信时也许需用比较尊敬的语气，但并不需要什么特殊的词语。不论对方年龄多大，级别或地位多高，"你"就是"你"，"我"就是"我"，没有像汉语中的"您"这样的称呼。

另一方面,中国人不习惯用平常的话语直截了当、不加修饰地与年长的人、客人或有地位的人说话。甚至同讲英语的人谈话时,也难于接受或遵守对方的习惯;中国人说话时,总是用"有礼貌的"或"客气的"词语,有时用尊称或敬辞,有时则用谦辞。

下面是两份请帖,试比较一下,就可以看出两者的区别:

Will you please honor me by coming to my humble home for a simple meal this Sunday evening? We will be very pleased if you can come at 6 o'clock...

(兹定于星期日下午 6 时在寒舍举行便宴,敬请光临。)

Frank, we'd like you and your wife to come over for dinner this Friday evening. Six-thirty at our place. Can you make it? (福兰克,请你跟你爱人星期五晚上来吃饭。6 点半在我们家。你能来吗?)

前一个请帖措词客气,文雅有礼,后一个请帖简明扼要,直截了当。

这不是说英文请帖都是这样随便,有的是相当正式的。例如:

Dr and Mrs. John Q. Smith

request the pleasure of the company of

Mr. and Mrs. Wang Xiaotang

at a reception

in honor of the arrival of the——delegation

4:30 p.m., October 6

Pacific Room, Continental Hotel

R.S.V.P.

约翰·Q·史密斯博士及夫人

敬请王晓唐伉俪

莅临欢迎某代表团招待会

10 月 6 日下午 4 时 30 分

大陆饭店,太平洋厅

请敬赐复。

这份请帖没有用 you 和 we 而用了主人和客人的名字,所以语气显得庄重,而且这类请帖也有固定的格式。

下面有一些汉语中常用的敬辞和谦辞。右附英语中的相应称呼或说法,以便比较:

(对客人、长辈、上级说话或写信时)

| | |
|---|---|
| 您,您老人家 | You |
| 先生,伯父,叔叔,大婶, | You (*or* the person's name) |
| 局长,经理,师傅,老师等 | Mr. (Mrs.)— |
| 敝人 | I, me |
| 贵姓,尊姓大名 | Your name? Could I have your name? |

(对家庭成员或亲戚说话或写信时)

| | |
|---|---|
| 令尊,令兄 | your father, your brother |
| 家严,家慈 | my father, my mother |
| 师母,伯母,嫂子 | Your wife, Mrs — |
| 舍亲,舍侄 | my relative, my nephew |
| 令郎,令爱 | your son, your daughter |
| 我那个丫头(多用于农村) | my daughter |
| 我们那个小子(多用于农村) | our son |

(称呼对方或自己的住处、工作单位、所属组织等时)

| | |
|---|---|
| 府上 | your home, the place you're from |
| 贵校(店) | your school (shop) |
| 敝厂(所) | this (our) factory (institute) |
| 敝处 | my home, my place |

我们看到,在汉语中用"贵"、"令"等字表示"尊敬"或"敬重",用"家"、"舍"、"敝"等字表示"谦虚,实际上,过去教尺牍的老师让学生记住一个口诀:"家大舍小令他人。"意思是:在写信时,称自己家里辈分或年龄比自己大的亲属时,在称呼前面要加一个"家"字。对自己家里辈分和年龄比自己小的人,在称呼前面要加一个"舍"

字。称呼他人时不论尊卑长幼,一律加一个"令"字。英语中没有与这些汉字对应的词语。把上列汉语称呼译成英语时,最好把任何修饰语都省掉。如把表示处所的词直接译成 home, shop, school, organization 等。如果把"请光临寒舍"译为 Please come to my humble home 或把"我们希望到贵处访问"译为 We would like to visit your honorable organization,听起来就很不自然。

最近二三十年人与人之间关系渐渐趋于平等,在我们的日常生活中也不大使用过于拘谨的、礼节性的套语,许多显得很庄重、很客气的尊称和敬辞已经淘汰。有些敬辞或套语还有人用,但主要是上年纪的、受过教育的人。下面举出一些例子,右附的英语译文或释义,在语义上不一定完全对应,但比较合乎英语习惯:

久仰,久仰大名　　　　　　　I've heard a lot about you.

Your name is well-known here (to us).

欢迎光临　　　　　　　　　　Welcome. Welcome to... (name of place)

欢迎指导　　　　　　　　　　Welcome. (To a person on a professional or business visit)

We're very pleased to have you come and visit us.

您有何高见?　　　　　　　　What's your opinion?

We'd like to have your opinion.

请提宝贵意见　　　　　　　　Please give us your comments or suggestions.

Could you give us your comments or suggestions?

拜读了大作　　　　　　　　　I've read your book (article, report, work, etc.)

拙作　　　　　　　　　　　　My book (painting, literary work, research paper, etc.)

敬请指正(这是把自己写的　　　(literally: I respectfully request that

226

| | |
|---|---|
| 书或其他作品赠送他人时 | you point out the mistakes.） |
| 常用的客气话。） | |
| 敬请光临 | You're invited to come... |
| ……惠存 | To（for）...（name of receiver of gift） |
| ……敬赠 | From...（name of giver） |
| 请教 | to ask for advice |

有一句至今还常用的客气话"不敢当"应该特别提一下。用什么英语来表达"不敢当"的意思，要看场合：如果对方说 Kindly give us（me）your advice（请您指教）这样的客气话，可以回答 I'll be glad to（我很高兴）或 Thank you（谢谢），也可以说 I'm honored, but I'm not sure I'm the right person（很荣幸，不过我是否胜任，可没把握）。如果对方恭维说 You're one of the top scholars（authorities）in the field（您是这方面的权威），可以回答 Not really（不是的，不敢当）或 It's such a small field（从事这种研究的人本来就很少，谈不上什么权威不权威）。如果发言后有人赞扬说 That was a magnificent speech. I found it very stimulating.（你的发言真精彩，我听了很受启发。），可以回答 That's very kind of you to say so 或只说 Thank you，表示对别人说这句话的谢意。可见英语与汉语在体现"不敢当"这个词儿的意义时，方式不同：英语的 Thank you 表示接受赞扬，而汉语的"不敢当"表示对赞扬受之有愧。

在别人称赞时，中国人常说："哪里！哪里！"用英语表达它的意义，主要也看上下文和说话的场合而定，这里不再详述。

政府各机关之间或同一机关各部门之间来往的文件所用语体可称"公文语体"。英语和汉语中都有类似说法来区别上级和下级、领导和被领导之间的关系。英语中有 hand down a directive, issue orders, submit a report 等。汉语中有"发布命令"、"下达指示"、"呈报"、"呈递"、"呈请"等。英语中这种词语可能比较少，但

227

整个行文语气会使人感到生硬、不自然；下级给上级的文件中，有时充满"谦"的语气。上级给下级的文件中有时又有居高临下，咄咄逼人的语气。

# 第十二章

## 文体的区别

为什么中国学生的英语作文读起来很像从汉语翻译过去的?为什么很容易看出一篇文章是中国人写的还是讲英语的人写的?

是否因为多数中国学生还没有掌握英语?

是否因为中国人和西方人的思想方法两样?

是否因为汉英文体不同?

这三方面的原因大概都有。如果学生的英语水平高些,可能写得更像讲英语的人写的东西。西方人和中国人看问题的方法在很多方面确实不同。英语和汉语的文体也确有差别。

本章讨论最后一个问题——文体的区别。具体地说,主要探讨反映文化差异的文体区别。

首先应该指出,用汉语和英语写作有相同之处:深刻地了解主题,周密地考虑内容,慎重地选择材料,真诚而简洁地表达思想。下面两句话——出处不详——不仅适用于英语,而且很可能适用于一切语言:

善于写作的人,不管用何种文字……应像普通人那样说话,而像聪明人那样思索。

任何艺术风格应像衣着一样尽量不引人注意。

现在谈谈不同之点。

1. 汉语文体中的叙述和描写与英语文体比,往往显得有些矫揉造作。这一段摘自一个学生的英语作文,其中就有这种缺点:

I walked joyfully along the path that was lit up by the golden rays of the morning sun. Beautiful flowers of many colors were blooming. How fragrant they smelled! Little birds were singing in the trees, as if greeting me "Good morning! Good morning!" My heart was bursting with happiness...

（我在小路上愉快地散步。朝阳金色的光芒把小路照亮。绚丽多彩的鲜花正在盛开。这些花儿多么芬芳！小鸟在枝头歌唱，好像在对我打招呼"早晨好！早晨好！……我心花怒放……"）

在这一方面，中国学生的普遍缺点在于形容词用得过多。在好文章里当然要有形容词，形容词可使文章生色，人物栩栩如生，情景跃然纸上。但如使用不当，则效果相反——读者很快失去兴趣，感到厌烦。据说美国著名律师和政治家丹尼尔·韦伯斯特有过这样一段经历。他年轻时发表演说，文胜于质，言过其实。后来认识到，只有简洁明快的演说和文章才能给人以深刻印象。一番话是否有力量全在于内容。韦伯斯特的语体文风变了，他把注意力集中在思想内容上，研究怎样把思想内容表达得鲜明有力。他尽量少用形容词，非用不可时，通常也选最简单、最确切的词语。他的演说变得像宝剑一样尖锐锋利。时至今日，人们对他那雄辩的口才记忆犹新。

形容词用得过多不好，使用不当也不好。这不仅是学习外语的学生的写作特点，也是初出茅庐的作者的通病。他们往往借助大量形容词和副词来装点自己的作品。像 great, marvelous, wonderful, very 之类的修饰词用得太滥，早已毫无意味，显得苍白无力。有些形容词经过仔细推敲后选用，还可能起一些作用，但效果未必理想。作者试图美化文字，未能使内容富有生机。词藻华丽、内容贫乏的文章，有什么吸引力呢？

研究一下英国优秀作品就可以看出，真正的艺术家遣词造句都是十分精确的，他们选用的动词特别耐人寻味。请看莎士比亚戏剧中的几个句子：

A poor player/That *struts* and frets his hour upon the stage /And then is heard no more. (一个在舞台上指手画脚的拙劣的伶人，登场片刻就在

无声无息中悄然退下。)

But *screw* your courage to the sticking-place,/And we'll not fail.（只要你鼓足你的勇气，我们决不会失败。）

Daffodils /That come before the swallow *dares*, and take the winds of March with beauty.（在燕子尚未归来之前就已经大胆开放的水仙花，在 3 月的和风中丰姿绰约地招展着。）

下面是《汉姆莱特》中奥菲丽亚的一句话：

Now see that noble and most sovereign reason,/Like *sweet* bells *jangled*, out of tune and harsh.（现在却眼看着他的高贵无上的理智，像一串美妙的银铃声失去了谐和的音调。）

在选用令人喜爱的 sweet（美妙的,悦耳的）之后,出人意料地接用 jangled(发出不和谐的刺耳声)——难道还能找出更好的词来体现同一个人充满理智而又精神失常的不协调的情况吗？难道还能找出更好的词来反映奥菲丽亚的精神痛苦吗？

当然不是人人都能像莎士比亚那样善于遣词造句,大多数中国人也不会用英语写诗编剧,何况诗歌更应语句简洁,用词精当。但诗歌的选词的基本原则同样适用于散文。请看托马斯·佩因（1731～1809）在《危机》一文中的一段：

These are the times that try men's souls. The summer soldier and the sunshine patriot will, in this crisis, shrink from the service of their country, but he that stands it now, deserves the love and thanks of man and woman. Tyranny, like hell, is not easily conquered; yet we have this consolation with us, that the harder the conflict, the more glorious the triumph. What we obtain too cheap, we esteem too lightly: it is dearness only that gives everything its value. Heaven knows how to put a proper price upon its goods; and it would be strange indeed if so celestial an article as freedom should not be highly rated.

（这是触及人们灵魂的时刻,在这次危机中,那些和平兴盛时期的士兵和处于安逸顺遂环境中的爱国者将退缩不前,不为祖国效力;那些经得住考验的人将赢得人们的爱戴和感激。暴政犹如地狱,难以征服;斗争越艰苦,胜利越光荣。从这一点,我们可以得到安慰,轻易获得的东西从不被珍惜;付出代价后才感到珍贵。凡物必有其合理的价值,所以,自由这样神圣,若不付出一定代价,那倒不可思议了。)

2. 看来,中国人和讲英语的人对固定词组的看法有所不同。在用英语写作时,人们不主张多用所谓"陈词滥调"或"老一套的说法"。然而,用汉语写作时则讲究用四字成语。讲英语的人认为下面这个句子写得不好: He slept like a log and woke up at the crack of dawn, fresh as a daisy. (他酣睡一夜,破晓醒来,感到精神焕发。)

这句话的毛病倒不在于写得不生动,而在于连用了三个老一套说法:sleep like a log, at the crack of dawn, fresh as a daisy。这些老一套的固定说法,色彩鲜艳,富于表现力,原来也很引人注目,但用得太滥,就失去了魅力和新鲜感。在英语中这种例子很多,如:last but not least (最后但不是最不重要的[一点])it goes without saying (不用说),by leaps and bounds (飞跃地,极迅速地,大踏步地),in our day and age (在我们的时代),as busy as a bee (像蜜蜂一样忙),happy as a lark (像云雀一样高兴)等。

汉语则不然。许多成语虽经反复使用,在文章中仍不断出现。在一篇论文中总是少不了的,举个例子来说,在评论一篇论文或发言时,几乎免不了要用这样的说法:"一气呵成","别具一格","引人入胜","慷慨激昂","栩栩如生","言简意赅","咬文嚼字","油腔滑调","强词夺理","牵强附会",等等。在文章中适当运用这些四字成语进行润饰,可起"画龙点睛"作用,使文字更加生色。当然,即使用汉语写文章,也应尽量避免过多地使用这类成语。

3. 在说理性文章(如政论文、社论或讨论社会问题的论文等)中讲英语的人写起来和中国人不同,在语气上和措辞上不那么强硬或富有战斗性。其指导思想是: to let the facts speak for themselves (让事实本身说话)。换句话说,事实本身应该能说服读者。因此,这类文章中很少使用下列短语:we must(我们必须),we should not(我们不该),it is wrong to...(……是错误的),it is ab-

232

surd（是荒谬的），cannot be denied（不可否认），resolutely demand（坚决要求）等。一般地说，在语气上比较有节制，措辞比较温和。当然，现代中国的政论性文章也首先注重事实，但仍比较强调战斗性，强调立场鲜明。应该认识到这种不同的态度，这是十分重要的。经验证明，一篇用汉语写的措辞强硬的政论文或社论，译成英语后往往不能达到预期效果。直率生硬的语气和措辞有时使人不快，怀疑作者自知理亏，不能摆事实，讲道理，只好使用激烈的言辞。

优秀的英语论文一般列出令人信服的事实，作者不作结论，结论让读者自己来下。必要时至多简单地提一笔。讲英语的人不喜欢别人"强加某种观点"，也不愿意别人叫他们该怎样思考问题。

美国安妮特·鲁宾斯坦博士在她的著作中提到她在教美国文学选读课纳·霍桑的作品时，班上中国学生的情况：

> 他们（指中国学生）批评霍桑在小说结尾处观点不明朗，结论不明确。他们说，读者看完中国作家写的小说，就完全知道作者的观点。我说，在美国，我们认为，作者最好启发读者进行独立思考。但是他们问道：那怎样知道是非曲直呢？

虽然不是所有中国人都这样看的，但却有相当一部分人持有这种观点。

除上述三点外，还有别的区别。在文体方面汉语和英语的差别足够写一本专著来详加论述。本章只能提醒读者注意这一现象，并略加说明，希望有兴趣的读者就这一问题作进一步探讨。

下面谈一谈中国式的英语问题。此事原与文体无关，为方便起见，在这里提一下。中国式的英语是受汉语干扰或影响而说出或写出的英语。有些英语句子是从汉语句子逐字翻译而来的。在语法上，中国式英语可能不错，但遣词造句和表达方式与标准英语的习惯用法不符，虽可能不妨碍理解原意，但不宜用。

下面是学生的作文及对话中的一些错误例子：

1．* His body is very healthy.

2. * We are difficult to finish all this tonight.

3. * His sick conditon is much better. He is no longer dangerous.

4. * We must spend bitter work to master knowledge.

5. * He only said a few sentences. He made us very disappointed.

6. * Recently she doesn't study well. All day she talks love.

第1句是汉语"他身体很好(健康)"这句话的直译文。不过人们用英语时,只说 He's very healthy. 加上 body 这个词听起来很别扭。

第2句也是按汉语句子的意思直译的。问题在于 difficult 一词用得不对。正确的说法是:It'll be difficult for us to finish all this tonight.(今天晚上我们很难把这件事做完。)

第3句有两个错误。我们可以用汉语说"病情好转",而讲英语的人一般说 His condition is much better. 或只说 He's much better. 说某人 be dangerous, 实际上是说他在某一方面构成对别人的威胁。这个词用错,句子的意思就完全变了。原意当然是病情已不严重,脱离危险了。

在第4句中 bitter work 的字面意义是"痛苦的工作",汉语句子的原意是"刻苦学习";spend 也不对,不能说 spend work。学生要说的显然是 spend a lot of time on...(在……方面花大量时间)。在一定的上下文中可以用 to master knowledge 来表示"掌握知识",不过许多中国学生以为 master 就是"掌握",几乎在任何场合都把"掌握"译成 master。如把这句话改成 We must work hard and try to learn as much as possible 就好多了。

第5句用下列两种方式表达较好:(1) We were quite disappointed that he said only a few words. (2) He only made a few comments (remarks). We were quite disappointed. (It was quite a disappointment.) 在英语中 say a few sentences 不错,也有人这样说,不过 say a few words 用得更加广泛。make someone disappointed 勉强可用,不算错,但很少用。

234

在第 6 句中,前一句有语法错误,如改为 She hasn't been studying well recently, 在语法上就对了。不过,这个学生想说的是,她没有"好好学习"。"好好学习"的意思是"努力学习"(studying hard), 不是"学习得好"(studying well)。在后一句中把"谈恋爱"译成 talk love 是照汉语字面上逐词直译的。汉语中的"谈恋爱"不是英语中的 talk love。在特定的场合和上下文中,可以说 talk love, 比如男女两个人交谈, 一个人用略带诙谐的口气说: Enough of such things. Let's talk about something more interesting. Let's talk about love. (不谈这些事了。谈点有意思的事儿。谈谈爱情吧。)即使如此,这种说法也很少见。因此,这两个句子的意思用 She hasn't been studying hard because she spends most of her time with her boyfriend 来表达比较好。

另一种常见的中国式英语与汉语中"吃饭"、"读书"、"唱歌"、"跳舞"、"付钱"之类的动宾词组有关。学生遇到这种动宾结构时,差不多一定要把宾语说出来或写出来。英语则不然,动词本身含有宾语所表示的意思,不言自明,一般可省略。中国学生没有意识到这一点,经常造出下列听起来很不顺耳的句子:

    * Let's go and eat our meals.

    * They're reading books.

    * He's going to sing songs at the concert.

    * We danced some dances last night.

    * Have you paid the money?

这些句子若改成下述说法就自然了:

    Let's go and eat.

    They're reading.

    He's going to sing at the concert.

    We danced last night.

    Have you paid yet?

有些中国式英语的说法与人体部位有关。汉语中说"腰痛",英语中不说 waistache, 而说 backache。例如:Oh, my aching back!

如果发生了什么滑稽可笑的事,中国人会"捧腹大笑",而讲英语的人则说 hold one's sides with laughter, 不说 hold their stomachs or bellies。有趣的是,stomachache 既指"胃痛",也指"肚子痛",在英语中两者并无区别。中国人往往会去找"胃痛"的英语对应词。再说说人体的其他部位。汉语中有"双目失明"的说法,但把它译成 His two eyes are blind 就很可笑。讲英语的人会问 How can one be blind except in the eyes?(一个人除了眼睛还有哪儿会瞎呢?)blind(瞎)只能指"眼睛瞎"。可以说:He's blind, He's completely blind 或 He's lost his eyesight。

有些汉语语句中带有修饰语显得很自然,完全合乎汉语习惯,但这个修饰语译成英语,效果适得其反。一位在某专业方面有地位的人到某机关、团体或公司去访问,人家往往会对他说"请提宝贵意见"。如果这句话译成 Please give us your valuable opinions,访问者就会感到为难,大概会想:How do I or they know whether my opinions are valuable or not?(我或者他们怎么知道我的意见是否宝贵呢?)在这种场合如果提了意见,就不够谦虚,等于说 Yes, my opinions are valuable, here they are.(好,下面就是我的宝贵意见……。)因此,为了避嫌,他(她)干脆什么意见也不提了。其实,在这句话里汉语的"宝贵"二字表示 your opinions will be appreciated(您提的意见我们会尊重并加以认真考虑的)。

同样,"毫无根据的捏造"这一说法在汉语里完全说得通。"毫无根据"四字有加强语气的作用,并非表示有限定意义的修饰语。但这个汉语短语不能译成 groundless lies 或 groundless fabrication。在英国人或美国人的心目中 lies(谎言)或 fabrication(捏造)本身就是 groundless(毫无根据的),如果能说 groundless lies, 那就意味着能说 well-grounded lies (fabrication) 这样荒谬的话。因此 groundless 不但是多余的,而且是不合逻辑的——正如中国谚语所说的,那是"画蛇添足"(adding feet to the serpent)。

不少常用的汉语说法译成英语时要仔细斟酌。如:"不切实际的幻想"(impractical illusions——难道有合乎实际的幻想吗?)"残酷的迫害"(cruel persecution ——难道有不残酷的迫害吗?)等。

在处理这种汉语说法时,要考虑英语中是否保留修饰语,如果修饰语不起强调作用,反而歪曲了原意,则应将修饰语略去。在翻译时省略或变通不仅是允许的,而且是必要的。

下面再谈一下文章的标题问题。标题通常要求简短并能概括文章的内容。用英语写的文章的标题和用汉语写的文章的标题有些区别,尤其是在学术性刊物上发表的文献或论文的标题。这里指出一种比较明显的差别。

英语文章的标题一般比较直截了当,不加修饰。请看几个实有的标题:

*Science and Linguistics*《科学与语言学》

*Filmmaking in Contemporary America*《当代美国的电影业》

*Women US . Men in the Work Force*《论职工队伍中的妇女和男人的优缺点比较》

*Art History in a New World*《新世界的艺术史》

*The Farm Revolution Picks up Speed*《农业革命迅速发展》

汉语文章的标题除说明文章内容外,往往有表示作者自谦的字眼。例如:《浅谈……》,《试论……》,《……初步分析》,《……初探》,《……之我见》,《……刍议》等。这类标题在不大知名的作者的文章中尤为常见。他们不想让别人认为自己是所论问题的权威。此外,如果日后发现文章的某些论点或某些部分有错误,作者可以说,这篇文章本来就像标题所表明的那样,是"初步分析"、"浅论"、"初探"。这样一来,标题本身给作者提供了为这些错误开脱的借口。不幸的是一些思路不清、不负责任的作者在这种标题下就逃之夭夭了。

人们在掌握一种外语前,在用这种外语说话和写作时,必然会受本族语的影响。同样,在学会用英语思维前,在表达思想时,也往往会逐字把汉语译成英语。学生的英语越不熟练,英语的水平越低,这种情况就越明显,所以在英语学习的某一阶段或某些阶段,学生难免会用一定数量的中国式英语来说话和写作。要想用地道的英语表达思想,除需要在词汇、短语、表达方式等方面具有相当相当坚实的基础外,还需要知道怎样才能使自己的言语得体,合乎社会习惯。学生要把所有这些知识同他想表达的汉语意思联系起来,然后从各种说法中选出意义最相近的对应词语。请注意,在意义上、语气上、涵义上、文体上和联想上的对应才是真正的对应。

238

# 第十三章

## 英语的各种变体

据说有这样一件事:有一个欧洲国家的女王前往美国访问,到达芝加哥时,人们以接待君主的隆重的礼仪表示欢迎,一切顺利。访问圆满结束,女王一行即将离开该市,芝加哥市长当然在场,在举行欢送仪式时,市长致颂辞,与会者倾听,市长热情洋溢,为表示友好,他说:The next time you come, bring the *kids* along. (下次来时把孩子带上)

会场上的气氛突然发生惊人的变化。有些人目瞪口呆,感到此语难以置信。有人发出嗤笑声。即使有王族在场,人们也忍不住要笑。负责礼宾的人员个个面红耳赤。美国人感到困窘,女王随行人员则颇为气愤。

怎么会发生这样举座震惊的场面呢? 怎么会有人感到难以置信,有人感到好笑,有人会生气或发窘呢? 答案是:市长用了 kids 一词。不能称君王的子女为 kids(孩子),应称 princes(王子)或 princesses(公主)。市长说的这句话相当于在中国对地位高的人说:"下次您老人家光临,带上您的丫头和小子。"

据说确有其事,但笔者无法核实。此事可以说明:同样的话在不同的场合表示不同的意义或产生不同的效果。语言学家指出,语言在不同社会中有不同的功能;即使在同一社会中,人们也使用同一语言的不同语体或变体。

本章主要讨论美国英语变体概况,对讲英语的中国人来说可能有用。我们主要探讨地区差别、交际方式(口语或书面语)的差别和社会差别。

## 地区差别

一种语言的语音、语调、节奏、词语和习语的选择及用法等方面都会体现出地区差别,有时,甚至在句法上也有地区差别,但不常见。汉语和英语(英国英语,美国英语、加拿大英语及澳大利亚英语)一样,也有地区差别。如山西话、四川话和东北话在发音上就不一样。山西人说"山西"的"山"字,n音不清晰,发音有点像法语的鼻音n。四川人把"解放军"一词中的"解"(jie)字读作 gai,声调也有所不同,东北人则把"人"(ren)字读作 yin 等。再举几个有地方特色的词语和说法为例:"滚水"(gun fu"开水"——晋中方言),"打牙祭"(表示"吃顿好饭"——四川方言),"老鼻子"(表示"多得很"——东北方言),"贼"(表示"很"、"非常",如"那灯贼亮贼亮的"——东北方言)等。此外,上海话和广东话的差别更大,外地人简直听不懂。

美国英语的地区差别没有这么大,但也值得一提。新英格兰人(指美国东北部几州的人)说某些词时,发音和英国人一样。南方人(美国东南部十几州的人)说话有些拖音,说得也比较慢些,元音也较长。在南方各州,人们说某些物品的名称时,也与别的地区不同,例如,他们把 bag(口袋)叫 poke,把 purse(钱包)叫 pocket-book 等。

对习惯于听规范英语的中国人来说,英语的地区差别可能是个问题,不好解决。只有经常反复听各种有地区差别的英语,猜测其含义,才能渐渐听懂。幸而多数来华的英美人士没有多少口音方面的问题,他们通常都说比较标准的英语。

因篇幅有限,不能就语言的地区差别问题作进一步阐述。仅在此处提一下,望能引起读者的注意。

240

## 交际方式的差别
### ——英语口语和书面语的差别

人们有时说：He talks (speaks) like a book. 这句话的意思可能是"他说字儿话"，"他咬文嚼字"或"他讲起话来像背书"等。用汉语也可以说："他说话文绉绉的。"这种话说明此人在某种场合说的话与多数人有所不同，不符合一般人说话的习惯。同时也表明，语言(不论英语，汉语，还是其他语言)本身有差别，口语形式与书面语形式并不完全相同。在中国，读书人都知道有"之乎者也"的文言文与通俗口语不同，也与现代汉语白话文不同。尽管像"何许人也"、"公之于众"、"绳之以法"之类的说法仍在现代文章中出现，但在日常口语中肯定不适用。

英语也是这样，但正式的书面英语和口头英语的区别不像文言文与日常说的普通话之间的区别那么大。请看下面两个例子，一段是论文，另一段引自非正式的谈话：

1. 阿尔文·托夫勒在《未来的冲击》一书中写道：

In the three short decades between now and the twenty-first century, millions of ordinary, psychologically normal people will face an abrupt collision with the future. Citizens of the world's richest and most technologically advanced nations, many of them will find it increasingly painful to keep up with the incessant demand for change that characterizes our time. For them, the future will have arrived too soon...

Western society for the past 300 years has been caught up in a fire storm of change. This storm, far from abating, now appears to be gathering force. Change sweeps through the highly industrialized countries with waves of ever accelerating speed and unprecedented impact. It spawns in its wake all sorts of curious social flora——from psychedelic churches and 'free universities' to science cities in the Arctic and wife-swap clubs in California. (Toffler, 1970)

（从现在起到 21 世纪的短短 30 年中,千百万心理正常的普通人将会突然发现,他们与未来格格不入。在世界上最富有、技术最先进的国家的公民当中,许多人会发现,他们跟不上作为当代特征的变革所提出的要求,因而日益感到烦恼。对他们来说,未来到得太快了……

300 年来,西方社会一直处在变革的风暴中。这场风暴不仅远未减退,而且愈加猛烈。这场变革的浪潮以空前未有的加速度和冲击力,席卷高度工业化的国家,随之产生了各种奇异的社会现象,从"幻觉教堂"和"自由大学"到北极的科学城和加利福尼亚州的换妻俱乐部。）

2. 下面是内科医生马修·杜蒙在美国一个大城市中劳动人民常去的一家酒馆里听到的一段对话:

Don: Cancer is from too many cigarettes.

John: John Wayne smoked five packs a day and they took a piece of his lung out.

Don: I just take a couple of drags from each butt.

Tom: I heard a guy who got cirrhosis of the liver and he never took a drink in his life.

Jack: Yeah, but most of it's from too much booze and no food.

Don: You get holes in your liver.

（唐: 癌是吸烟过多引起的。

约翰: 约翰·韦恩一天抽五包烟,他们动手术把他的肺切掉了一块。

唐: 每个烟头我只抽几口。

汤姆: 听说有个人得了肝硬化,可他一辈子没喝过酒。

杰克: 也许是,不过,大多数肝硬化都是因为玩命地喝,而吃得少。

唐: 那样喝,肝上不全是洞了!）

上面引的是几个失业工人的闲谈,他们经常到酒馆去打发时间,在这段话中,他们随便聊聊抽烟和喝酒对人们健康的影响。先从癌症谈起,转到肝硬化。只有两句话同前一个说话的人的话题有直接联系:约翰提到约翰·韦恩那句话,杰克那句简短的评论。就是这两句话也省略了一些与前一句话有关的词,然而,这个对话

242

的内容不难理解。语法学家会说 I heard a guy who got... 不合语法规范,应为这 I heard about a guy who got...。有些人会不喜欢 booze(烈性酒)、drags(吸口烟)及 butt(烟头)这类俚语。

托夫勒所写的一段文章则大不相同:句子较长,结构严密,所用词语书卷气较重,如:abrupt collision(突然相撞)、incessant demand(不断的要求)、abating(减退)、unprecedented impact(前所未有的冲击)等,而且用了很多比喻,如:fire storm of change(变革的风暴)、waves of ever accelerating speed(不断加速的浪潮)、spawns in its wake(随后繁殖)、social flora(社会植物群)。

书面语和口语的区别主要在于前者一般是事前有构思,后者或多或少是自发的。写作时有时间思考、推敲、斟酌词语、讲究修辞,使文章更有文采,更有感染力或说服力。作者有时间修饰、润色,必要时可以改写或全部重写。然而,在说话时,人们的话和思想是在谈话过程中出现的。事先没有构思,也未经推敲,在表达一个思想或说一个句子中间往往有犹豫不决、改变主意、省略或重复词语或句子的现象,一般多用简单、常说、容易想到的词语。通常想不到要"润色"就脱口而出了。

书面语和口语各有特点:前者是有准备、有计划的,后者则是无准备、无计划的,因此,书面英语结构严谨,时而有来源于拉丁语的大词,而且往往用修辞手段使文章更生动。口头英语有时条理不清,句子结构松散;有时"不合语法",常用不完全句和省略句,有不少口语词和俚语词。

以上所说书面语的特征主要是指正式的、标准的书面语的特征。书面英语和其他语言的书面语(包括汉语)一样,文体不止一种。不同文体有不同的特征或标准。官方文件或法律文件(如合同)的语言与烹饪书中告诉人如何做蛋糕的语言大不相同。哲学论文的语言措辞讲究,同一篇评论体育锦标赛双方实力的新闻稿不同。在语气上,一封推荐信与好友之间的叙家常的信大不一样。

常用英语写作的人应该注意并研究各种差异。关于这一问题的细节不在本书论述的范围之列,就不在这里详谈了。对此有兴趣的读者可参考修辞学(或文体学)方面的著作。

## 社会差别

语言学的研究表明,人们根据情况变换语体。语言不同,变体的数量也不一样。一种语言如果有两种变体,一般说来,一种是正式语体,另一种是非正式语体。有些语言学家用"文言"和"口语"或者"高雅"和"粗俗"来表达这种区别。如果要分两种以上的变体,那也是在正式语体与非正式语体之间所划分的不同层次。

英语、汉语和许多别的语言(如阿拉伯语,现代希腊语,德语等)都有这种区别。

在适当场合使用正确的变体十分重要。对一个 4 岁的孩子致意说:How do you do, Mr. Mullins!(您好,穆林斯先生!)或用汉语说"您好,毛毛先生!"固然很可笑。同样,头一回跟一位政府部长或跨国公司的董事长见面就说:Hi, Jim. How're things goin'?("嗨,吉姆,怎么样啊?)或用汉语说"嘿! 老兄,混得怎么样?"也很荒谬。

有时,甚至外语掌握得很好的人也会犯这类错误。例如,一位美国教授在一所中国大学教书,在谈到她的工资时,同一大学的一位英语水平很高的中国人用了 bucks("美元"的俚语)一词,她非常吃惊。同样,如果问一位中国教授:"您每月挣几张'大团结'?"也是很不得体的。

使用哪种语体取决于下列因素:

1. 环境或情景——在公共集会上、在正式招待会或宴会上,同在非正式聚会上、在街头偶而相遇时不同。

2. 话题或谈话内容——谈哲学问题和谈生小病不同;招聘人员面试的谈话和向邻居借点糖时不同,正式提意见和随便聊聊家常不同。

3. 谈话者——谈话者双方的情况如何，他们是什么关系：是素不相识的人还是熟人，是亲属还是朋友，是亲密的还是一般的，是上级还是下级，双方的社会地位如何，情况各不相同。

4. 谈话者的情绪——谈话者的情绪如何：是高兴还是悲伤，是兴奋还是冷淡，是紧张还是镇定，是激动还是平静，是愤怒还是沮丧等，谈话的人当时的感情也会影响所用的语言。

在选用不同语体时应考虑上列一切因素。

美国英语中有多少变体？美国人在不同情况下有多少种可供选择呢？

对于这个问题语言学家们有不同的看法。著名语言学家马丁·朱斯(Martin Joos)的研究成果在世界各国被人们广泛引用，我们在这里介绍一下。他把美国英语分为五种变体：演说体，正式体，商议体，随意体，亲昵体。说明如下：

演说体：这是经常对公众演说的人用的语体。句子结构严谨，修辞讲究，词语精确，往往使用来自拉丁语的"大"词。

正式体：这是听众太多无法交谈时常用的语体，如高等院校教师讲课或在学术会议上发言等。一般都是有准备的，但不像演说体那样精确周密。如用这种语体对一个人说话，那就表示双方之间有一定距离。可能是因为职务或社会地位不同——如下级对上级，也可能是因为带有个人情绪——如说话的人看不起对方，故意保持某种距离等。

商议体：这是商谈公事、业务或进行交易时用的语体，一般不用于亲密朋友之间。这种谈话往往比较自然，想到什么就说什么，不必过于斟酌词语。

随意体：这是谈话双方都不感到有社会因素形成的障碍时所用的语体。如在非正式场合朋友之间随意闲聊，出于自然，往往句子简短而不完整，省去助动词和代词，常用口语和俚语。

亲昵体：这是至亲或至交之间用的语体。话语亲切，无任何拘束，完全出于自然，谈话所涉及的内容往往只有参与者知道，所以外人有时会听不懂他们谈些什么。

可以说,这五种变体表示话语正式程度的五个层次。下面就同一内容各举一例。

演说体:Visitors should make their way at once to the upper floor by way of the staircase. (来宾请立即顺楼梯到楼上去。)

正式体:Visitors should go up the stairs at once.(来宾请立即上楼。)

商议体:Would you mind going upstairs right away, please? (请您马上上楼好吗?)

随意体:Time you all went upstairs, now. (现在你们都该上楼了。)

亲昵体:Up you go, chaps! (伙计们,上去!)

现举两段实例来做进一步说明。头一段引自美国黑人运动领袖马丁·路德·金 1963 年 8 月 28 日在华盛顿林肯纪念馆前争取公民权的集会上所作的著名演说:

Five score years ago, a great American, in whose symbolic shadow we stand today, signed the Emancipation Proclamation. This momentous decree came as a great beacon of light and hope to millions of Negro slaves who had been seared in the flames of withering injustice. It came as the joyous day-break to end the long night of captivity.

But one hundred years later, the Negro still is not free. One hundred years later, the life of the Negro is still sadly crippled by the manacle of seg-regation and the chain of discrimination. One hundred years later, the Ne-gro lives on a lonely island of poverty in the midst of a vast ocean of material prosperity. One hundred years later, the Negro is still languishing in the corner of American society and finds himself an exile in his own land. So we have come here today to dramatize a shameful condition...

(100 年前,一位伟大的美国人在《解放宣言》上签了字。今天,我们站在他有象征意义的阴影下举行集会。这项伟大的法令对于备受欺凌在苦难中受煎熬的千百万黑奴来说犹如指路明灯,给他们带来希望。它像欢乐的曙光一样,结束了不自由的漫漫长夜。

但是,100 年以后,黑人仍无自由。100 年以后,黑人的生活仍因种族隔离的镣铐和种族歧视的枷锁而困苦不堪,难以改善,100 年以后,黑

246

人仍住在物质繁荣的海洋中的贫困孤岛上。100 年以后,黑人仍然困居于美国社会的角落里焦虑困顿。在自己的国土上被排斥在外。因此我们今天在这里集会,以引起人们注意这一可耻的状况⋯⋯)

这个对 20 万人发表的讲话很像一篇正式的文章。其中用了许多在非正式的英语中不常见的词:withering (毁灭性的),seared (烧焦),captivity (监禁,束缚),manacle (手铐),languishing (焦虑的,渴望的);有相当书卷气的用语:in whose symbolic shadow (在其象征性的阴影下——指林肯塑像); 连用四次并列结构:one hundred years later (100 年以后), 但是, 最突出的特点是用了较多的比喻:a great beacon of light and hope (光明与希望的灯塔), the long night of captivity (被囚禁的长夜), the life... is crippled by...(生活因⋯⋯而困顿不堪),a vast ocean of material prosperity (物质繁荣的辽阔海洋),a lonely island of poverty (贫困的孤独岛屿), in the corner of American society (在美国社会的角落里)等。所有这些词语都说明这篇演说是经过充分准备、周密思考、精心加工的作品。

下面这一段有所不同。斯塔兹·特克尔用了 3 年时间访问各行各业的美国人,谈他们的工作,然后根据访问的谈话录音整理成《工作》(Working) 一书,访问记所用的语言完全是会话体——随意自如,无拘无束,天然质朴,发自内心。

下面是汤姆·帕特里克对斯塔兹·特克尔谈他在纽约当警察的经历:

I worked in Harlem and East Harlem for three years. There was ten, eleven cops and they were all black guys. I was the only white cop. When they saw me come into the office they started laughin. "What the fuck are they sendin' you here for? You're fuckin' dead." They told me to get a helmet and hide on the roof.

My father's a great man. I see what he went through and the shit and hard times. I don't see how he lived through it. I used to lay awake when he was drinkin' and listen to him talk all night. And I used to cry. He

talked about the shittin' war, all the money goin' to war. And the work-
ers' sons are the ones that night these wars, right? And people that got
nothin' to eat...I tell ya, if I didn't have an income comin' in...these
kids hangin' around here, Irish kids, Italian kids, twenty-five years old,
alcoholics winos. One guy died of exposure. He went out with my kid sister
and he's dead now.

（我在哈莱姆和东哈莱姆(均为美国纽约黑人聚居区)干了3年。那
儿有十来个警察，全是黑人，只有我是白人。他们见我去报到都笑起来。
"他们混蛋，把你派来干吗? 真他妈混账。你找死呀! 别让人把你宰了。"
他们叫我戴上安全帽躲在房顶上。

我爸爸真了不起。我现在明白了，他吃过多少苦，受过多大罪，我不
知道他怎么熬过来的。想当初，我躺在床上，听他一边喝酒，一连唠叨，
我听着听着，眼泪就出来了。他讲起那场该死的战争，花那么多钱去打
仗，可打仗的呢，还不是工人的子弟，对吧? 还有那些没饭吃的呢? ……
告诉你吧，我要是没收入……咳! 这帮小子整天泡在这儿，有爱尔兰
的，意大利的，有的都25岁啦，老喝酒，酒鬼。有个家伙冻死啦。他还跟
我妹妹出去玩过呢，可现在呢，死啦。）

这段话里没有复杂的长句，也没有书面词语。全段由简短的
句子组成。用的全是最普通的日常词语，其中也夹着俚语(winos)
和粗鲁不文明的词儿(shit, shitting, fuck, fucking)。言语直率，
简洁生动。

有人可能会问:随意或亲昵的英语是地道的英语吗? 中国人
和西方人谈话应该用这种英语吗? 应当给学英语的中国学生教这
种英语吗?

首先回答第一个问题:什么是地道的英语? 我们应考虑一下
语言学家的意见。大多数人认为，语体的好坏取决于使用语言的
场合。如果一个人说的话同大多数人在这种场合说的一致，那就
是地道的、合适的。反之，如果一个人所用的语体不是人们通常在
某种场合使用的，不论说得多么正确、规范，甚至按其他标准来说，
还很文雅，那也不算得体。比如说，有些英语教师可能不赞成上面

引用的警察访问记和在酒馆里的谈话中的某些词语,但不该认为这些话有"缺点"或"错误"。那些正是某些场合或人会话的特征,只不过按正规或书面英语的标准才被人认为是"错误"的。实际上,在酒馆、饭店、娱乐场所、商店或比较随便的聚会上,如果用了正规的书面英语,反而会闹出笑话来。因此在选择语体时要慎重。

其次回答第二个问题:中国人与西方人交谈时应用什么语体?显然,既然一个人用什么语体由所在的场合决定,那么这一点对中国人来说同样适用,而且在这个问题上,对任何国家的人来说都是一样的。然而,大多数非英语国家的人的英语水平不高,一般难以适应各种情况。英语水平很高又说得十分流畅的人,才能够运用几种语体,否则后果难以设想。如误用习语或俚语、省略不当、语体不合、口气不对等,都会闹笑话。有些人的英语水平不一定高,但为了显示自己,滥用不同语体的语气、词语,结果弄巧成拙。对中国人来说,在语言和文化方面都与英美人大不相同,这个问题困难就更多了。

应当指出,只知道不同语体还是不够的。还要熟悉使用每种语体时的习惯——在什么时候,在什么地方,以什么方式,使用什么语体。还要了解语体的变换规则。有时,在同一次谈话中,甚至同一个句子里,也可以变换语体,尽管这种情况不多。不过,这种变化一般仅限于相邻的两种语体,或"上"或"下"(如从随意体变为商议体或亲昵体),但不能相距过远。

最后回答第三个问题:教学英语的学生时,是否应教随意体和亲昵体的英语? 显而易见,既然使用英语的人想在思想上达到最大限度的沟通,既然正确运用不同变体又是进行有效交际的重要方面,有一些这一方面的知识至少是有益的。在学生实际需要运用各种语体之前,就应对此有所了解。因此最好把它作为语言训练的一部分来进行教学。

我们知道,目前在多数中学和大学中所教的英语是语言的"核心部分",即有各语体的共同特征的部分。这种语言"核心"几乎可用于一切场合,达到所有交际目的。换句话说,不论写一份申请书还是给朋友写一封信,不论同公司的高级职员交谈还是同好朋友闲聊,都或多或少可以使用同样的语言"核心"。既不会得罪人,自己也不会出洋相。这是一种稳妥可靠的语言——也许平谈无味,却不会引起麻烦。外国人用这种英语交谈,人们是会接受的,尽管无足称道,但交际的目的达到了。

所有的学生都必须学会"核心语言"。但要和别人进行更有效的交际,只会用"核心语言"还是不够的。人们在不同场合能使用相应的语体,根据不同环境说正式的或亲切的话,才能算是真正掌握了这种语言。

学习英语的学生和从事外事工作的人应及早接触英语的不同语体。如有可能,应在识别和理解各种语体方面进行训练和练习以培养语感,并为以后提高语言水平打好基础。

# 第十四章

## 身势语——非语言交际

一个中国男人和一个美国或加拿大妇女谈话时,看着对方是否失礼?

两个男青年或两个女青年同行时,其中一个搭着另一个肩膀或两个人手拉手向前走,西方人是否认为合适?

在有各种文化背景的民族中,点头是否都表示"是",摇头是否都表示"不"?

这不是语言问题,而是"身势语"(非语言交际,也称非话语交际或表情交际)问题。

我们同别人谈话时,交际的手段不限于词语,尽管我们没有意识到这一点。我们的表情、手势、身体其他部分的动作,都向周围的人传递信息。微微一笑伸出手来表示欢迎,皱眉表示不满,点头表示同意,挥手表示再见。听报告或讲演时,身子往椅背上一靠,打个呵欠表示厌烦、不感兴趣。人们公认这些动作表示上述意义,至少中国人和美国人都是这样的。这些动作是交际手段的一部分。"身势语"同语言一样,都是文化的一部分。

但在不同文化中,身势语的意义并不完全相同。各民族有不同的非话语交际方式。本章开头提的两个问题,答案都是否定的。甚至点头也可以表示不同的意义。尼泊尔人、斯里兰卡人和有些印地安人和爱斯基摩人用点头表示"不"。因此,要用外语进行有效的交际,在说某种语言时就得了解说话人的手势、动作、举止等所表示的意思。

我们可以观察一下阿拉伯人同英国人谈话。阿拉伯人按照自己的民族习惯认为站得近些表示友好。英国人按照英国的习惯会往后退,因为他认为保持适当的距离才合适。阿拉伯人往前挪,英国人往后退。谈话结束时,两个人离原来站的地方可能相当远!

在这个例子里,双方的距离是关键。不同的民族在谈话时,对双方保持多大距离才合适有不同的看法。根据研究,据说在美国进行社交或公务谈话时,有四种距离表示四种不同情况:关系亲密,私人交往,一般社交,公共场合。交谈双方关系亲密,那么身体的距离从直接接触到相距约45厘米之间,这种距离适于双方关系最为亲密的场合,比如说夫妻关系。朋友、熟人或亲戚之间个人交谈一般以相距45~80厘米为宜。在进行一般社交活动时,交谈双方相距1.30米至3米;在工作或办事时,在大型社交聚会上,交谈者一般保持1.30米至2米的距离。在公共场合,交谈者之间相距更远,如在公共场所演说,教师在堂上讲课,他们同听众距离很远。

多数讲英语的人不喜欢人们离得太近,当然,离得太远也有些别扭。离得太近使人感到不舒服,除非另有原因,如表示喜爱或鼓励对方与自己亲近等,但这是另一回事。记住这一点很重要。

谈话双方身体接触的次数多少因文化不同而各异。在这一方面,有一篇调查报告提供了一些有趣的数字。调查者在各地大学里或附近的商店中观察两人坐着单独说话时的情景,每次至少一小时,记下两人触摸对方的次数:英国首都伦敦(0);美国佛罗里达州盖恩斯维尔(2);法国首都巴黎(10);波多黎各首府圣胡安(180)。这些数字本身很说明问题。

在英语国家里,一般的朋友和熟人之间交谈时,避免身体任何部位与对方接触。即使仅仅触摸一下也可能引起不良的反应。如果一方无意触摸对方一下,他(她)一般会说 Sorry; Oh, I'm sorry; Excuse me 等表示"对不起"的道歉话。

在中国,常常听到西方妇女抱怨中国人抚弄了她们的婴儿和很小的孩子。不论是摸摸、拍拍、搂搂或是亲亲孩子,都使那些西方的母亲感到别扭。她们知道这种动作并无恶意,只是表示亲近和爱抚而已,所以也不好公开表示不满。但在她们自己的文化中,这种动作会被人认为是无礼的,也会引起对方强烈的反感和厌恶。所以,遇到这种情况,西方的母亲往往怀着复杂的感情站在一旁不说话,感到窘迫,即使抚弄孩子的是自己的中国朋友或熟人。

除轻轻触摸外,再谈一谈当众拥抱问题。在许多国家里,两个妇女见面拥抱亲亲是很普遍的现象。在多数工业发达的国家里,夫妻和近亲久别重逢也常常互相拥抱。两个男人应否互相拥抱,各国习惯不同。阿拉伯人、俄国人、法国人以及东欧和地中海沿岸的一些国家里,两个男人也热烈拥抱、亲吻双颊表示欢迎,有些拉丁美洲国家的人也是这样。不过,在东亚和英语国家,两个男人很少拥抱,一般只是握握手。若干年前,发生了这样一件事:当时日本首相福田纠夫到美国进行国事访问。他在白宫前下车,美国总统上前紧紧拥抱,表示欢迎。福田首相吃了一惊,日本代表国成员也愣住了。许多美国人感到奇怪——这种情况很少见,完全出乎人们意料。如果美国总统按日本人的习惯深鞠一躬,大家也不会那么惊讶。但在美国和日本都不用拥抱这种方式表示欢迎。

在英语国家,同性男女身体接触是个难以处理的问题。一过了童年时期,就不应两个人手拉手或一个人搭着另一个人的肩膀走路。这意味着同性恋,在这些国家里,同性恋一般遭到社会的强烈反对。

身势语的一个重要方面是目光接触。在这一方面可以有许多"规定":看不看对方,什么时候看,看多久,什么人可以看,什么人不可以看。这里引用朱利叶斯·法斯特的《身势语》一书中的两段,很有意思,可供参考:

> 两个素不相识的人面对面坐着,在火车餐车里他们可以自我介绍一下,吃饭的时候,说些无关紧要或者是无聊的话;也可以互不理睬,极力避免与对方的目光相遇。有个作家在一篇文章里描写过这种情况:"他

们翻来复去地看菜单,摆弄刀叉,看看指甲——好像头一回看见它们。免不了目光相遇时,立即转移视线,注视窗外沿途景色。"

该书作者指出对素不相识的人的态度是:

我们既应避免盯着看,也要避免显出不把他们放在眼里的样子……要看他们一会儿表示看见了,随后立刻把目光移开。

注视对方的不同情况决定于相遇的场所。如果在街上相遇,可以看着迎面走来的人。直到相距 8 英尺远时再移开视线走过去。但在到达此距离之前,双方都用眼睛暗示一下自己要往哪边走,打算往哪边走就往哪边看一眼。然后,双方侧身略变方向,即可错开,顺利通过。

同相识的人谈话时,根据美国习惯,说话的人和听话的人都应注视对方。任何一方不看对方,都可以表示某种意味。如:害怕对方,轻视对方,心神不定,感到内疚,漠不关心等。甚至在对公众讲话时也要时时目视听众,和许多人的目光接触。如果演说的人埋头看讲稿,照本宣科(许多中国人往往是这样的),而不抬头看看听众,对听众"说话",人们就会认为他对听从冷漠,不尊敬别人。

在谈话的时候,听的人一般要注视着说话的人的眼睛或脸,表示自己在听。如果对方说的话比较长,听的人要不时发出"嗯"、"啊"的声音,或者点头表示自己在注意地听着。如果同意所说的观点,可以点头或微笑。如果不同意或者有所保留,可以侧一下头、抬一下眉毛或露出疑问的神情。

在英语国家,盯着对方看或看得过久都是不合适的。即使用欣赏的目光看人——如对方长得漂亮——也会使人发怵。许多外国人到其他国去旅行,因当地人盯着他们看而恼火、很别扭,认为那里的人"无礼"而感到气愤,殊不知在该国是常事,看的人不过是好奇而已。许多在华的讲英语的外国人对此流露过不满情绪。作者的一位好朋友是个美国青年妇女,因为常常有人盯着她看而决定回国。她很喜欢在北京教书,对中国和中国人都有深厚的感情,但她实在忍受不了到处被围观的无礼场面。的确,她身材很高大,容易引起过路人的好奇心。但这并不能成为无礼围观的理由。她离开中国时恋恋不舍,但还是提前回国了。可见围观能引起多么强烈的反感。

"眉目传情"(或"目语")是青年或成年男女之间传递感情最常用的古老的方法之一——在美国尤其讲究。有人对此作过详细研究:人们对异性怎样表示感兴趣或不感兴趣,怎样表示鼓励或拒绝,怎样表示赞成或不满,怎样表示爱慕或厌恶。然而,在美国也有许多差别。男人用眼睛的方式就和妇女不一样。不同年龄、不同阶级、不同社会阶层、不同地域的人在这一方面都有差别。不同种族的人也有差别。

在一些国家里,人们认为能直视对方的眼睛是很重要的。在一部关于列宁的著名电影里有这样一幕:有一个肃反委员会的工作人员叛变了,肃反委员会主席捷尔任斯基得知情况询问他时,此人不敢正视对方的眼睛。根据这一点捷尔任斯基认为证实了他有罪。许多美国人也同样重视目光接触的作用,但并不是美国的所有民族都这样。

有过这样一件事:有个十来岁的波多黎各姑娘在纽约一所中学里读书。有一天,校长怀疑她和另外几个姑娘吸烟,就把她们叫去,尽管这个姑娘一向表现不错,也没有做错什么事的证据,但校长还是认为她作贼心虚,勒令停学。他在报告中写道:"她躲躲闪闪,很可疑。她不敢正视我的眼睛,她不愿看着我。"

校长查问时,她的确一直注视着地板,没有看校长的眼睛。而英美人有"不要相信不敢直视你的人"这样一句格言。

碰巧有一位出生于拉丁美洲家庭的教师,对波多黎各文化有所了解,他同这个姑娘的家长谈话后对校长解释说:就波多黎各的习惯而言,好姑娘"不看成人的眼睛"这种行为"是尊敬和听话的表现。"

幸而校长接受了这个解释,承认了错误,妥善处理了这件事。对这种目光视向不同的含义给他留下很深的印象,也使他记住各民族的文化是多种多样的。

目语的规定很多,也很复杂。从上面介绍的一些情况可见一斑,这里就不再细谈了。

在中国和讲英语的国家不论微笑还是大笑,通常表示友好、赞同、满意、高兴、愉快,但在某些场合,中国人的笑会引起西方人的反感。下面是一位美国朋友给作者的来信的摘录,谈到了某些行为在不同文化交际中间造成的误会:

……其中一个问题就是,中国的笑与美国的笑有不同的意思。比如,一个美国人存放自行车时,一不小心自行车倒了,他会因为自己动作不麻利而感到困窘。这时如果旁边的中国人笑起来,他会觉得受到耻笑,非常生气。我还看到在餐厅里发生过类似情况。一个外国人偶然摔了一个碟子,他本来就感到很窘,而在场的中国人发出笑声,使他更加觉得不是滋味,又生气,又反感。

当然,中国人的这种笑,不论是对本国人还是对外国人,并非是嘲笑当事人,也不是幸灾乐祸。这种笑有很多意思。可以表示:"别当一回事儿","一笑了之","没关系","我们也常干这种事"等。不过,对于不了解这些意思的人,这样一笑会使他们感到不愉快,而且会对发笑的人产生反感。

手势是个很难办的事。打手势时,动作稍有不同,就会与原来的意图有所区别;对某种手势理解错了,也会引起意外的反应。

在第二次世界大战中,领导英国进行战争的首相温斯顿·邱吉尔曾作了一个手势,当时引起了轰动。他出席一个场面盛大而又重要的集会,他一露面,群众对他鼓掌欢呼。邱吉尔做了一个表示victory(胜利)的 V 形手势——用食指和中指构成 V 形。做这个手势时,手心要对着观众。不知邱吉尔是不知道还是一时失误,把手背对着观众了。群众当中,有人鼓掌喝倒彩,有人发愣,有人忍不住哈哈大笑。这位首相所做的手势表示的是别的意思。那不是表示"胜利"的 V 形,而是一个下流的动作。

另一个例子同尼基塔·赫鲁晓夫有关。他是 50 年代后期到 60 年代初期的苏联领导人。在美国访问期间,他的言论和举止引起一些争议。引起争议的手势之一是,他紧握双手,举过头顶,在

256

空中摇晃。他的意思显然是表示问候,表示友谊。但是,在场的人和电视观众对此并不欣赏。美国人很熟悉这个动作——这是拳击手击败对手后表示胜利的姿势。在此之前,赫鲁晓夫曾说过要埋葬美国资本主义的话,许多美国人认为,这种手势表示他好像已经取得胜利,洋洋得意。难怪许多人感到不快。

中美身势语对比研究表明,两者有相似的地方。如男子相逢时不拥抱,一般见面时握手即可;挥手表示再见;皱眉表示不高兴;耸耸鼻子表示不喜欢、讨厌或不快;点头表示"是",摇头表示"不";噘嘴表示不痛快、情绪不佳、忿恨;拍拍男人或男孩子的背表示赞扬、夸奖、鼓励;咬牙表示生气、愤怒或下决心。

现将不同处举例列表如下:

## A
### 动作一样,意义不同

| 汉 语 意 义 | 身 势 语 | 英 语 意 义 |
| --- | --- | --- |
| 气愤,恼怒,灰心,悔恨 | 跺脚 | 不耐烦 |
| 谢谢,互相表示友好感情 | 观众和听众鼓掌,表演或讲话人也鼓掌(图1) | 为自己鼓掌;被认为是不谦虚。 |
| 好奇;有时是惊讶 | 目不转睛地看(图2) | 不礼貌;使人发窘;不自在 |
| 反对;责骂;轰赶 | 发"嘘"声(图3) | 要求安静 |
| (少见;一般见于成人对孩子)疼爱;(对成人或青年,会引起反感,是侮辱人的动作) | 拍别人的脑袋(图4) | 安慰;鼓励;钟爱 |

257

**B**

意义相同,动作有差异

| 意　　义 | 中国的身势语 | 美国的身势语 |
|---|---|---|
| "过来"(叫别人过来) | 把手伸向被叫人,手心向下,几个手指同时弯曲几次(图5) | 把手伸向被叫人,手心向上,握拳用食指前后摆动(中国人对此反感)(图5) |
| "丢人""没羞"(半开玩笑) | 伸出食指,用指尖在自己的脸上划几下,像搔痒,不过手指是直的(图6) | 伸出两只手的食指,手心向下,用一个食指擦另一个食指的背面(图6) |
| "我吃饱了"(吃饭后) | 一只手或两只手轻轻拍拍自己的肚子(图7) | 一只手放在自己的喉头,手指伸开,手心向下,(常同时说"到这儿了")(图7) |

**C**

只存在于一种文化中的动作

1

| 身　　势　　语 | 在　美　国　的　意　义 |
|---|---|
| 咂指甲(图)8 | 重大思想负担;担心,不知所措 |
| 用大拇指顶着鼻尖,其他四指弯着一起动(图9) | 挑战,蔑视 |

| 身　势　语 | 在　美　国　的　意　义 |
|---|---|
| 摇动食指(食指向上伸出,其他四指收拢)(图10) | 警告别人不要作某事,表示对方在做错事 |
| 把胳膊放在胸前,握紧拳头,拇指向下,向下摆动几次。(图11) | 反对某一建议、设想;反对某人;表示强烈反对 |
| 眨眼(很快地合上一只眼,微微一笑点点头)(图12) | 表示下列几种感情:会意,赞许,鼓励,传递信息,表示团结等 |

2

| 身　势　语 | 在　中　国　的　意　义 |
|---|---|
| 用食指点点或指指自己的鼻子(图13) | "是我","是我干的"(西方人认为这个手势有点可笑) |
| 说话时用一只张开的手捂着嘴(一般是老年人用)(图14) | 说秘密话(有时没有明显的意义) |
| 两只手递(即使可以用一只手拿起的)东西给客人或别人(图15) | 尊敬 |
| 别人为自己倒茶或斟酒时,张开一只手或两只手,放在杯子旁边(图16) | 表示感谢 |
| 伸出两个竖起的食指在身前慢慢接近(往往在戏曲中出现)(图17) | 男女相爱;匹配良缘 |

259

这几张表中所举的例子不全,但是可以说明身势语的差异,也说明了解另一种语言中的身势语的重要性。

对身势语的研究有助于对语言的研究。对前者的理解可以加深对后者的理解。有些权威人士认为两者相互依存。在多数情况下这是对的。在某些情况下,人体动作与所说的话不一致,口头说的话与身势语表达的意思不一样。这时要借助其他信息或从整个情景中猜测说话人的意思,从某种意义上说,一切身势语都要放在一定的情景下去理解;忽视了整个情景就会发生误解。

总之,希望读者注意:用一种语言交际时,一般也应该使用同那种语言相适应的身势语。根据观察,真正掌握两种语言的人在换用另一种语言说话时也换用另一种身势语。这种才能达到更好的交际效果。

# Bibliography

# 参 考 书 目

I . **Books in Chinese:**

陈原　《语言与社会生活》,生活、读书、新知三联书店,北京,1980.

罗常培　《语言与文化》,北京大学出版社,1950.

王佐良　《英语文体学论文集》,外语教学与研究出版社,北京,1980.
(Wang Zuoliang, *Essays on English Stylistics*, Foreign Language Teaching and Research Press, Beijing, 1980.)

II . **Books and Articles in English:**

Birdwhistell, Ray L. *Kinesics and Context*, University of Pennsylvania Press, Philadelphia, 1970.

Carroll, John B. ed. *Language, Thought, and Reality: Selected Writings of Benjamin Lee Whorf*, M.I.T., Technology Press, 1956.

Cherry, Colin *On Human Communication*, M.I.T. Press, Cambridge, Mass. 1978.

Chomsky, Noam *Language and Mind*, Harcourt, Brace & World, Inc., N.Y. 1968.

Dumont, Matthew P. "The Tavern Culture: The Sustenance of Homeless Men" in *Down to Earth Sociology*, 3rd ed.
　　by James M. Henslin, ed. Free Press, N.Y. 1980.

Eastman, Carol M. *Aspects of Language and Culture*, Chandler and Sharp Publishers, San Francisco, 1975.

Fast, Julius *Body Language*, Pocket Books, N.Y. 1971.

Giglioli, Pier Paolo *Language and Social Context*, Penguin Books, London, 1976.

Hall, Edward T. *The Silent Language*, Anchor Book Edition, Doubleday and

261

Company, N.Y. 1973.

Hudson, R. A. *Sociolinguistics*, Cambridge University Press, Cambridge, U.K. 1980.

Joos, Martin *The Five Clocks*. Harcourt, Brace, N.Y. 1967.

King, Martin Luther, Jr. "I Have a Dream" in *Values and Voices*, compiled by Betty Renshaw. Holt, Rinehart & Winston, 1975.

Lado, Robert *Linguistics Across Cultures*, University of Michigan Press, Ann Arbor, Michigan, 1957.

Light, Donald Jr. and Suzanne Keller *Sociology*, 4th ed. Alfred A. Knopf, N.Y. 1985.

O'Donnell, W.R. & Loreto Todd *Variety in Contemporary English*, George Allen & Unwin, London, 1980.,

Robertson, Ian *Sociology*, 2nd ed. Worth Publishers, N. Y. 1981.

Robinett, Betty W. *Teaching English to Speakers of Other Languages: Substance and Technique*, McGraw-Hill, N.Y. 1978.

Rubinstein, Annette T. "Teaching in a Changing China" in *Far Eastern Reportor*, June, 1984.

Sapir, Edward *Language: An Introduction to the Study of Speech*, Harcourt, Brace & World, 1921.

Stern, H. II. *Fundamental Concepts of language Teaching*, Oxford University Press, London, 1983.

Strevens, Peter D. "Varieties of English" in *English Studies*, Vol. 45, No.1

Terkel, Studs *Working*. Avon Books, N.Y. 1974.

Toffler, Alvin *Future Shock*. Random House, N.Y. 1970.

# III. Dictionaries:

*American Heritage Dictionary of the English Language*. Paperback edition. Dell Publishing Co., N.Y. 1976.

*Concise Oxford Dictionary of Current English*. 6th edition. Oxford University Press, London, 1976.

*Longman Dictionary of Contemporary English*. Longman. Eng. 1978.

*Longman Modern English Dictionary*, 1976 edition, Longman, London.

262

*Oxford Advanced Learner's Dictionary of Current English* 3rd edition, 1974.

*Oxford English Dictionary*, Compact edition, Oxford University Press, 1971.

*Webster's Collegiate Dictionary*, G. & C. Merriam, Springfield. Mass, 1981.

*Webster's Third New International Dictionary* G. & C. Merriam Co. Springfield, Mass., 1976.

《汉语成语词典》*A Chinese-English Dictionary of Idioms*, 商务印书馆 1982.

《汉英词典》*A Chinese-English Dictionary*, 北京外国语学院英语系《汉英词典》编写组, 商务印书馆, 1980.

《新英汉词典》, 上海译文出版社, 1978.

《英华大词典》, 修订第二版, 郑易里等, 商务印书馆, 北京, 1984.

《汉语成语大词典》, 湖北大学语言研究室, 河南人民出版社, 1985.

《中国常用成语典故名言故事源流辞书》, 若鹰等, 《新青年》杂志社, 哈尔滨, 1985.

《中外比喻词典》, 薛梦得, 中国物资出版社, 1986.

《英语成语与汉语成语》, 陈文伯, 外语教学与研究出版社, 1982.